Ronald Knox
and
English Catholicism

Ronald Knox seated on the fender in his room at The Old Palace, the Catholic university chaplaincy in Oxford, in 1938.
Photograph by Howard Coster © National Portrait Gallery, London.

Ronald Knox and English Catholicism

Terry Tastard

GRACEWING

First published in 2009

Gracewing
2 Southern Avenue, Leominster
Herefordshire HR6 0QF

UK ISBN 978 085244 250 0

Typeset by
Action Publishing Technology Ltd, Gloucester, GL1 5SR

Contents

Preface

My interest in Ronald Knox began when I became aware of the ubiquity of his literary output. Catholic libraries everywhere seemed to have his books on their shelves, and older Catholics told me how important his influence had been in their spiritual formation. In consequence it puzzled me that so little was known about him in our own day. It was all the more surprising given that Knox had been one of the most outstanding recruits to the Catholic Church of his generation. Even a hostile writer described him in the early 1920s as 'one of the wittiest men now living and one of the cleverest young men who ever came down from Oxford.'[1] Who was he, I wondered, and what had his life been like? After a period of research I began to write this book, and suddenly references to him began appearing around me. At a difficult session of the General Synod in February 2008 after his controversial *sharia* lecture, the Archbishop of Canterbury, Dr Rowan Williams, defused the tension by quoting Ronald Knox's wry description of a university debate: 'The prevailing attitude was one of heavy disagreement with a number of things which the speaker had not said.' A little later I discovered that Knox was depicted in a play about Harold Macmillan at the National Theatre in London. The play was a delight, but the cameo appearance of Knox did not ring true. The playwright seemed to have given Knox a histrionic personality. The real Knox was a man of spare emotions. There were other references to Knox in the national press and elsewhere, which led to me think that Knox, the quiet man, was gone but not forgotten.

The more I read, the more Knox fascinated me. First, there

was the sheer variety of the guises in which he appeared. He was a witty satirist, caring Oxford chaplain, popular preacher and broadcaster, writer of detective stories, Bible translator, *habitué* of English country houses and friend of Evelyn Waugh. Everyone referred to Knox's wit, yet sometimes there was also an air of melancholy about him. He was a warm and beloved friend to many. The more perceptive friends noticed that beneath the surface *bonhomie* he was a deeply private man, an inclination that increased with the passing of the years.

Another reason for my interest in Knox was a growing conviction that his story was, in part, the story of the Catholic Church in England at that time. By the end of the First World War Catholicism had quietly outgrown its ghetto status and was now once more reclaiming a place for itself in national life. For thirty years Ronald Knox was one of the best known personalities of English Catholicism. He defended and commended the Christian faith in general, and Catholicism in particular. His preaching was scripture based and yet irreproachably Catholic, a balance that appealed to those Catholics who wanted to explain their spirituality to Protestants. He was also utterly *English*, demonstrating, as Newman had before him, that an Englishman of his background could be at home in the Catholic Church. This may explain the BBC's eagerness to have him on the air. The rich *legato* of his well-modulated voice projected a reassuringly English and Oxford background. We have the witness of James Lees-Milne, who on Easter Sunday 1945 cycled over to Mass at Aldenham. He noted in his diary: 'Ronnie Knox said Mass in that unmistakable Oxford accent.'[2]

Knox's story was the story of his times in other ways. He was a small boy when his family fractured. His father could not cope and Knox and his siblings were sent to live with different relatives. Later, many of his friends died in the ferocious slaughter of the First World War. These ruptures left their mark on his soul. So, too, did the travails of the Church of England as it searched for its own identity. His father was a hard-working Anglican bishop, whose ministry epitomized much that was best about the Church of England. At the beginning of the twentieth century the Church of England had a deep sense of its responsibility for souls throughout the nation. It was to be found serving the people of every community, including the teeming slums. It also managed to keep its eye on the bigger national picture, and was a force in the land. Yet behind this confidence there was unease and uncertainty, as it tried to be all things to all people. It was increasingly torn between rival claimants who wanted it to be catholic, or evangelical, or liberal. There was also the difficulty of being a state church, with the expectation that it would be all things to all people. Knox was part of this tension, until he resolved it by becoming a Roman Catholic, one of a stream of distinguished converts received into the Catholic Church in the first half of the twentieth century.

Evelyn Waugh's biography of Knox appeared two years after Knox's death. Waugh's book on Knox is like Waugh himself: it is wonderfully insightful but also opinionated, irascible, vivid and a little dated. Rather surprisingly, Waugh says little about Knox as a writer. Fifty years later it is time for a new biography. The passage of the years will allow another perspective, in which we can situate Knox in the context of his times, and of ours.

Notes

1 Harold Begbie, *Painted Windows: A Study in Religious Personality* (London: Mills & Boon, 1922), p. 65.
2 James Lees-Milne, *Prophesying Peace* (London: Faber, 1977), p. 178.

Acknowledgements

My heartfelt thanks to the Asquith family for access to the Knox papers at Mells, and for their kindness and hospitality during my visits there.

Particular thanks are due to Viscount Asquith and Fr Nicholas Schofield, who read the whole typescript; also to the Hon. John Jolliffe and Mgr Walter Drumm, who read individual chapters.

I would also like to record my gratitude for that remarkable resource known as the London Library. For years I have read acknowledgements in which writers expressed their gratitude to the London Library and its staff. Now that I have joined the library I realize why it is so highly esteemed by writers. As a resource for writers it is without equal.

I would also like to thank the following:
Euan Cameron and Maggie Fergusson for early encouragement when I broached the idea of the book;
Robert Royston, psychoanalyst, for discussion of the effects of childhood bereavement;
Revd Dr Larry Kreitzer of Oxford University, for guiding me through some aspects of biblical interpretation;
Fr Paul Milanowski, who kindly drove me from Grand Rapids, Michigan, to Notre Dame University, South Bend, to consult the archives there.
Fr Nicholas Schofield of Westminster Diocesan Archives, and his assistant Miss Tamara Thornhill;

Dr William Kevin Cawley, of the Archives of the University of Notre Dame;
Mr Nicholas Scheetz of Georgetown University Library;
Mrs Joan Bond of the Catholic National Library, Farnborough, Hampshire;
Sean Gleason, professional photographer, for a brilliant result from an old negative;
Mr Jamie Fergusson for the use of books from his personal collection;
Sr Mary Joseph, OSB, for highly professional copy-editing.
I am also grateful for assistance from the staff of the Bodleian Library, Oxford; the BBC Written Archives Centre at Caversham Park; the British Library Manuscripts Division and the Newspaper Library at Colindale.

Grateful acknowledgment is made to:
A. P. Watt Ltd and the Earl of Oxford and Asquith for permission to print from the writings of Ronald Knox;
the Macmillan Trustees for permission to print from published and unpublished material by the late Harold Macmillan;
the Barbara Levy Agency for permission to quote from the writings of Siegfried Sassoon (copyright Siegfried Sassoon, by kind permission of the estate of George Sassoon);
the BBC for permission to print from material in their archives;
Br Lawrence Lew, OP, for the cover photograph of a present-day Corpus Christi liturgy at Blackfriars, Oxford.

1

Childhood Interrupted

In late 1891 the Reverend Edmund Knox moved to his new parish of Aston with some foreboding. The 44-year-old vicar was worried by the poor air quality of this part of greater Birmingham. He wondered what effect it might have on the health of his family, and especially of his frail wife Ellen. They were moving to the teeming city from a rural Leicestershire parish at Kibworth. Even there he had fretted about the air, fearing that the dank local clay harmed his wife's lungs. Now in Aston he worried about the soot spewing from chimneys. Trees in the adjacent Aston Park were slowly dying from the top downwards, poisoned by air-borne sulphur pollution. He worried, too, about the vicarage's unhealthy proximity to the churchyard, where new graves were still being dug among the smoke-blackened coarse grass.[1] But it was the smoke that disturbed him. Birmingham prided itself on being 'the workshop of the world' and Aston in particular had seen rapid industrial development during the period 1851–1881, utilizing the Fazeley canal which ran through Aston. There were many metal-finishing workshops. Also, nearly all the brewers in the Birmingham area were located at Aston, drawn by the quality of local well-water. A brewery dominated one side of the street where the vicarage was located. Surveying what he called 'a maze of small smoke-begrimed houses' Knox had nearly turned back during his first visit.[2]

Edmund and Ellen Knox brought with them their six children: Ethel (aged 12), Edmund junior, known as Eddie (10), Winifred (9), and Dillwyn (8). The two youngest were Wilfred (5) and Ronald (3). Ronald had been born on 17

February 1888. Winifred remembered their home in Aston as 'a gloomy vicarage in a walled grubby garden'. But there were compensations. In Leicestershire, the four elder children had been taught in a schoolroom in the vicarage by a resident governess. Their parents had decided to move to the city so that their children could receive a more formal education, and now the older children were able to attend proper day schools.

Not only was Aston physically unappealing, but the social challenges faced there by Edmund and Ellen Knox were also daunting. The pell-mell industrial growth of Birmingham in the nineteenth century had far outstripped the development of social and educational amenities. The parish contained long, rather monotonous streets of solidly built middle-class housing, but behind these streets there was a warren of slums. The population of Aston was poorer than that of adjacent Birmingham. Aston's poverty and local pride complicated its incorporation into the city of Birmingham, which took place only in 1911.[3] The atmosphere in the streets could be rough. A previous vicar's wife had once been pelted with stones on her way back from a Mothers Union meeting. There were 42,000 people in the parish, and only two churches – one Anglican, one Nonconformist. Looking back, Edmund Knox wrote that 'The bulk of the population was almost unaware of the existence of the Church.'[4] Things were not helped by the history of the parish. From 1824 to 1876 the living had been held by three generations of the Peake family, who had provided minimal services to the parish. Their main interest was pocketing the substantial income of the parish. Edmund Knox's summary of their tenure was scathing: 'The Vicar could enjoy himself, officiate occasionally, eat, drink and be merry, and congratulate himself on having one of the pleasantest and best paid benefices in the Church of England.'[5]

The 44-year-old Edmund Knox who moved to Aston in 1891 was from a very different cut of cloth. His strong faith enabled him to take on a daunting parish. He was an evangelical, and therefore he emphasized the mission of the Church, the truth of the scriptures and redemption wrought by Christ. A man of energy and practicality, he took up his work in

Aston with gusto. He recruited a staff of seventeen to help him, comprising seven curates and ten lay workers. He raised the money for their salaries himself. He divided the parish into seven districts, each with a mission room as a local focus for church activity. Each curate was assigned one of the districts, and at the Monday staff meeting would be given homes to visit within his district. Knox also organized a Bible study class for around 100 men and trained and supervised 200 Sunday school teachers. Ellen Knox entered into the work with enthusiasm and was soon in charge of a large group of girls who were too old for Sunday school but who were seeking Christian instruction. She quickly won the hearts of many in the parish.

Edmund Knox remembered Christmas 1891 as a particularly happy one. A few days later everything changed when Ellen Knox became seriously ill and began a long, slow decline. Her illness was attributed to the lingering after-effects of influenza she had contracted in 1889. That year a highly contagious viral infection swept the country, reappearing in successive years in waves after short intervals. One-third of the population of England and Wales was hit by the illness at some point, and around 125,000 people died. The influenza opened the way to other maladies, especially pneumonia, which left some victims with chronic lung conditions. Others were left with weak hearts. The 'Russian flu' epidemic also left a legacy, little understood at the time, of a subsequent tendency to encephalitis.[6] Exactly how Ellen Knox was affected cannot be established, but her husband's worry about the air leads us to suspect that she had been left with pulmonary difficulties. Her illness was implacable. For some months she was nursed at home among her increasingly anxious family, then she was taken to a nursing home in Birmingham. They tried a move to Llandudno on the north Wales coast, in the hope that the sea air might help her. After an operation in London she was moved yet again to Brighton. Edmund Knox's sister came to Aston to look after the six children, while he went to Brighton to be with his wife. Back at the vicarage the children waited and prayed, but the news, when it came, was what they dreaded. Their father wrote at the end of August 1892 to tell them that their mother had died.

A young mother who is dying will typically fight all the way, and it is a harrowing process for those who wait and watch. Possibly Ellen Knox's removal from the vicarage was to spare her children the sight of their dying mother. On the other hand, the eight months of decline that she endured, and her moves from one nursing home to another, also suggest an increasingly desperate fight to stay alive. Her youngest child, Ronald, was only four and a half when she died. His sister Winifred recalled years later: 'We were left in charge of a heart-broken father and a fragile and bewildered aunt.'[7]

Edmund Knox's grief was very real. Yet in his reminiscences he chose to say little about his loss. In his page-long account of his wife's terminal illness, he gave half the space to an incident when, taking a break on the promenade from her Brighton sickroom, he met and routed an open-air preacher of atheism. He either could not, or would not, bring himself to set down much on paper about his wife's decline and death. It seems to have been the same in his approach to his children. We gain the impression that there was little sharing of grief, which became in consequence a buried sadness. What brought about this reticence? Partly it would have been a natural desire to protect his children, not to expose them to the pain of his grief. By pretending to cope, he would help them to cope. Partly it was because, as an evangelical, he felt committed to making the experience of bereavement another opportunity to demonstrate faith. The historian Patricia Jelland has noted that Victorian evangelicals sometimes sought to deny the darker feelings of bereavement because, 'Normal responses in the grieving process, including, anger, bitterness, and depression, could be interpreted by the devout as rebellion against God's will and a failure to rejoice in the heavenly fate of the deceased.'[8] This seems to have been the case with Edmund Knox. Later he described the time around his wife's death in these words: 'No period in my life was more rich in experience of communion with God, and of the healing power of His Word; none more fruitful in the

great task of the winning of souls.'[9] A survey of Victorian
middle-class families in bereavement also shows that men
were more restrained in expressing their feelings of loss,
'especially towards the end of the century when they were
socially conditioned to believe that strong men controlled their
emotions.' This probably derived from the growing influence
of public schools and their cult of masculine reserve.[10]

Edmund Knox buried his grief by working harder than ever
in the grimy streets and poverty of Aston. This sense of loss
and yet of denial of loss meant that his children, too, could
not easily express their feelings. Eddie, twelve at the time,
never quite recovered from his mother's death. In the opinion
of his daughter, Penelope Fitzgerald, 'It gave him ... a
spartan endurance and a determination not to risk himself too
easily to life's blows, which might, at times, have been
mistaken for coldness.' Because his father would lose himself
in his work, Eddie spent long, miserable evenings by himself
upstairs.[11] Winifred had been ten when her mother died but
even in adulthood could only approach her feelings obliquely,
remarking that 'the tragedy of my mother's loss and the desolation of our home' had made school 'less interesting and
vivid'. At school there was a girl she could hardly bear to
watch because she reminded her of her mother.[12] We do not
know how Dillwyn reacted at the time. We do know that
during his student years at Cambridge it became clear that he
was an agnostic, and remained one for the rest of his life. It
is said that he criticized Christianity for inducing hope when
there was nothing to hope for.[13] Perhaps we hear in those
words the pain of a child who prayed that his mother would
recover – only to hear that she had died. Ronald Knox in his
early autobiography, the *Spiritual Aeneid*, simply mentioned
the fact of his mother's death and claimed to remember
nothing before the age of five, which, if correct, would mean
that he remembered nothing of her passing.[14] And yet, he
must have grown up with a sense of loss. His spiritual journey
would lead him to search for something of the warmth that
was missing from his life as a result of his mother's death. His
biographer, Evelyn Waugh, noted that while Knox himself

seemed oblivious to the fact, those who knew him well noticed that he loved to find the warmth of a vicarious family life in which he could compensate for what he had missed as a child. To Waugh this spoke of 'the uncertainty, loneliness, and persistent hunger of the heart which spring from a motherless childhood'.[15]

We may also wonder whether he was quite as unaware of the impact of his mother's death as he implies. In his spiritual autobiography he muses about a childhood habit of imagining that people around him were not objectively real. He thought of them as phantasmic creations of a divine agency that could also remove them at will. He would also, at moments of loneliness or silence, observe himself in the third person: 'Ronnie went into the garden.'[16] These tricks, as he called them, were evidence of dissociation, of someone who could disengage harmlessly from the reality around him for a while. It would be a child's way of distancing himself from a world where reality was sometimes too painful. The half-hidden sense of loss was there, and took its toll. Yet there is little evidence of self-pity in Ronald Knox, either in childhood or as an adult, perhaps because the Church anchored him, giving him a sense of belonging, a spiritual home. Sometimes, too, many years later, Ronald Knox would show an unobtrusive compassion of the kind that comes from one who has known suffering himself.

Initially Edmund Knox tried to hold the family together but he also had to keep on top of the exhausting demands made on him as vicar and team leader of his vast parish. The children did their best, devising new games to distract themselves. Sometimes the four older children would rush a cart containing Wilfred and Ronald around the garden. But eventually every member of the family grew ill.[17] Perhaps it was the smoggy air that Edmund Knox noticed on his initial visit, or perhaps it was the family's subterranean grief taking its toll. Even with domestic help, their father felt unable to care for them properly, and the only answer seemed to be to split up the family. Following their mother's death they had clung to each other more closely than ever. Now to the pain of their bereavement was added the distress of the parting of siblings. Ethel, Dillwyn and Winifred went to schools in Eastbourne where they boarded with an elderly great-aunt. The two youngest, Wilfred and Ronald, were sent to Creeton rectory near Grantham in Lincolnshire, where they lived with their father's brother, three unmarried sisters and mother. At first the lonely Eddie continued at Aston on his own, until sent to preparatory school a year later. The children went to their different destinations each school term and reunited for the holidays.

Creeton rectory was a quiet, rather serious household for two small boys. Their paternal grandmother Frances was a Quaker whose influence permeated the household, which in consequence was a place of seriousness, order and sobriety. Their uncle Lindsey took their education in hand, and taught them a good deal of Latin and Greek. This created the ground-work for Ronald's extraordinary abilities in classical languages. Perhaps it was also in his genes. His father had studied *Literae Humaniores*, or 'Greats', the wide-ranging classics course at Oxford which demanded proficiency in Greek and Latin. He had also been elected to the Boden Sanskrit scholarship. Ronald Knox's maternal grandfather, Thomas French, Bishop of Lahore, mastered several Indian languages and translated the Book of Common Prayer into Urdu. The tuition Ronald received from his uncle probably tapped into some innate ability. By the age of six Ronald was reading Virgil. But there was time for fun too. In a letter to his future stepmother the six-year-old Ronald wrote of making toy ships. 'They mostly consist of an oblong piece of wood, a thick piece of it for a funnel, a bit of it for a gun (they are men of war) and a bit of sheep's wool for smoke.' He kept his own patch of garden, learned fractions and kept a puppy.[18]

It was also at Creeton that Ronald's religious awareness began to develop. As the foster child of the rectory, he would of course have been taken regularly to church and have absorbed the rhythms and cadences of the Book of Common Prayer and the King James Bible. But it was above all the atmosphere of Protestant piety in the rectory itself that impressed itself upon his mind. Decades later he would not deride the faith of his upbringing, indeed he defended it, even in the very heat of his conversion to the Catholic Church. The Protestant spirituality of Creeton rectory was shown, he said, by 'a strong devotion to and belief in Scripture; a careful observance of Sunday; framed texts, family prayers, and something indefinably patriarchal about the ordering of the household.' He had never found 'anything repulsive or frightening in such a religious atmosphere.' Hell was mentioned but was not dwelt upon:

> Rather, the personal love which God devotes to us, the ever-surprising miracle of His Redemption, the permanent ease of access to the glorified Saviour – these are the central characteristics of Evangelical devotion, and these its formative influences.
>
> Was my childhood blighted? I was assured, indeed, that the heart of man was desperately wicked – was that quite untrue? At least, it was only the preface to the story of atoning grace . . .[19]

The answer to the rhetorical question of a blighted childhood is quite clear. His first awareness of God was not an association of fear. Yes, there was a sense of God's scrutinizing eye, as he went on to concede. But the context was always of a merciful God. God's will was that divine love should overcome the distance between himself and humankind.

In the contemporary era, we sometimes hear it said that any religious teaching amounts to indoctrination of children. The adult Knox, in recalling his childhood, was carefully rebutting those in his own day who would say that a religious upbringing was harmful. He named H. G. Wells and Edmund Gosse. The latter's bleak account of his upbringing (*Father and Son*) had been published a few years previously in 1907. Gosse's book has become a widely-cited account of how Victorian evangelical upbringing could terrorize a child. But Gosse came from a Plymouth Brethren family that was not typical of evangelicalism.[20] Of course, Knox was not typical either. It seems that the rectory was its own school, with Wilfred and Ronald taught by their uncle and not mixing much with other children. Children brought up largely with adults are often serious-minded beyond their years, and at times precocious. Ronald was both. People today might regard such an atmosphere as stifling for a child and it is interesting that he himself called the household 'patriarchal'. Yet clearly he had not been terrorized, and, on the contrary, we can see that his first Christian formation gave a sense of security. This would have helped him overcome the sadness of his mother's death. It would also have contributed to his confidence. He came to know a God of love who also set standards for his people. The children at Creeton were encouraged to grow into responsible adults.

And yet, Creeton was only one part of the evangelical influence on Ronald Knox. There was another, more dour side to evangelicalism which he would occasionally experience through his father. The family were reunited for the holidays, and on the first occasion Edmund Knox took his six children to Bridlington in Yorkshire. The children loved the broad sandy beach. They splashed in the water, took donkey rides and played with other children. One day the children were entranced by what in those days were called Nigger Minstrels, and joined rapturously in the robust comic songs of the era, such as 'Ta-ra-ra Boom de-Ay'. Their father was horrified when he discovered them and whisked them away. Thereafter he made sure that he supervised their amusements, and inaugurated family cricket and expeditions. The bathing hut they used was as far as possible from the beach entertainments.[21] His horror seems to speak of more than snobbery. He felt that such entertainment was so vulgar as to imperil his children's spiritual welfare. The high period of Victorian evangelicalism was already passing, but Edmund Knox was, despite his pastoral innovativeness, a rather old-fashioned man. He shared the evangelical stress on human nature as inherently wicked. Given that children could often be naughty or wayward, it meant that the evangelical parent could too easily associate simple childhood pleasures with occasions of sin.

Many evangelical parents in the Victorian age restricted and controlled their children in a rigorously puritanical regime. Their choice of friends was regulated and they were denied many of the normal pleasures and pastimes of childhood.[22] How to get out from under their father's shadow would be a question that Ronald and others had to answer for themselves as they grew up.

Meanwhile, their father's creative ministry and hard work had been noticed in the Church of England. In the autumn of 1894 he was offered three posts to be held simultaneously: Suffragan Bishop of Worcester, with the title Bishop of Coventry; Archdeacon of Birmingham; and, from 1895, Rector of St Philip's in the centre of Birmingham. The appointment of a man of such energy was a temporary solution to the pressing problem of Birmingham in the Church of England. It was the second city in England and the largest in the Midlands, yet it was not an Anglican see but part of the diocese of Worcester. To establish a new diocese would require money and an act of parliament. Moreover, Nonconformity was strong in Birmingham, whose MPs were marshalled in the House of Commons by Joseph Chamberlain, a Unitarian of great influence. In the early 1890s there were fears that Chamberlain's influence might be used to block a Birmingham diocese bill. More galling still was the fact that a Catholic diocese of Birmingham had been established when Pope Pius IX restored the Catholic hierarchy in 1850. As Bishop in residence in Birmingham, Edmund Knox would be expected to lay foundations for a future diocese, be a pastoral presence in England's second city and take his turn at confirmations and other episcopal duties in the enormous diocese of Worcester, whose diocesan bishop at that time was a keen gardener and happiest working in the attractive grounds of his official residence, Hartlebury Castle. Knox was consecrated in St Paul's Cathedral, London, on 28 December 1894 by the Archbishop of Canterbury, Edward Benson.

For Ronald Knox and his siblings, it meant that their father would be as busy as ever. But two improvements followed almost immediately. The first was that St Philip's rectory became their home. Even though it was in the busy centre of Birmingham, it was a vast improvement on the gloomy vicarage at Aston. The town hall, main hotels, clubs and shops were all nearby. Rail and tram connections were excellent. The family shared in the excitement of being at the centre of Birmingham with its strong sense of identity and civic pride, which had been enhanced by an ambitious programme of town planning. From the late 1870s onwards, Birmingham city centre had been reshaped under a plan promoted by Joseph Chamberlain. He had rebuilt much of the city centre, replacing grubby, narrow streets with broad, shop-lined thoroughfares, open squares and impressive civic buildings like the new art gallery.[23] Many poor people had been removed from the centre of the city to enable this rebuilding, and Edmund Knox was acute enough to notice that the Church of England had been largely blind to this effect of 'Joseph Chamberlain's great municipal reforms'. Birmingham clergy, he added, rarely looked outside the life of their own parish and felt 'a sense of utter helplessness in face of the vast influx of population'.[24] His role was to make sure that the Church of England was better represented in this bustling, self-confident and newly remade city where Nonconformists ran the municipal government.

To do this, though, he would need a wife. Here, too, things changed for the better for the Knox children. As a bishop he might now be considered a slightly more attractive catch. Edmund Knox was introduced to Ethel Mary Newton, eldest daughter of the Vicar of Redditch in Worcestershire. This man had inherited a vast fortune which enabled him to live in great style. Ethel was 27. Her future husband was 20 years older than herself and already tending towards corpulence. His six motherless children were emotionally starved and its evidence surfaced in many different ways. The usual sibling rivalries could become bitter feuds made worse by telling tales. Hair-pulling and hitting were quite common. Another sign of their hurt was the children's suspicion of the outside world. When they came together at Aston for the school holidays, they felt, said Winifred, like a clan facing a hostile world.[25]

The children were also lacking in some of the social graces because they had been left so much to their own devices. Regardless of all this, Ethel Newton married their father in 1895. Perhaps there was an element of *faute de mieux* given that she was an unmarried woman approaching thirty in the late Victorian period. Perhaps, too, there was a sense of duty, both to her own family and to that of Edmund Knox. Evelyn Waugh may have missed a clue when he quoted the entry from Ethel's diary for her wedding day: 'Finished the Antigone. Married Bip.'[26] Waugh saw it as evidence of her interest in classical literature. But perhaps it was significant that as the wedding approached she was reading the story of Antigone, who sacrificed her own life out of a sense of duty to her family.

The combination of the move to Birmingham and their father's remarriage transformed life for Ronald Knox and his brothers and sisters. Not only was a window thrown open, but the window gave a wide view of the world. Hitherto their life had been limited to smoggy Aston Vicarage, life with pitying relatives and private schools of low standards. It was as if everything changed. The gloom and unspoken sorrow of the Knox home was largely banished, partly through Ethel Knox's character, partly through her good taste, which ran to Liberty silks and William Morris prints. She undertook with aplomb the role of stepmother to six children between the ages of six and fourteen. She used her shorthand to help the bishop with his correspondence and represented him at meetings of the local education authority. She supervised the hospitality for an endless stream of guests and visitors at the rectory.

Her care and nurture of the children went some way to healing their sense of loss. The girls were particularly grateful to be rescued from ugly, shapeless clothes. Decades later Winifred still shuddered at the memory of 'horrid tight light-brown merino frocks and hats covered with buttercups in which we must have looked like two sausages lost in a lush meadow at a picnic.'[27] The smaller boys, Wilfred and Ronald, adored their stepmother. Ronald brought her small bouquets of wild flowers and wrote little poems for her. The older boys were more reserved, but she skilfully defused quarrels and arranged outings that helped the older boys to burn off some of their pent-up adolescent energy.

Having helped their poverty of affection she also tackled their poverty of ambition. Ethel Knox persuaded the bishop to review the schooling arrangements for the children, and to aim higher, much higher, in providing a good education for them. Eddie, the eldest, won a scholarship in 1896 to Rugby, where, despite the Victorian public school brutality, he would flourish. The two girls were sent to Wycombe Abbey School, which prided itself on giving its girls an education as good as that given to boys in the best public schools. It aimed to turn out young women who were intelligent, independent-minded and public-spirited. Wilfred would in due course follow Eddie to Rugby. It was decided that Dillwyn and Ronald should go to one of the leading preparatory schools in England, Summer Fields at Oxford, which had an unequalled record in getting its pupils into Eton. This was ambition indeed. But there was a problem. In 1896 Dillwyn was aged 11 and the school had a rule that no boy would be accepted over the age of ten. Informed of this Bishop Knox rose to leave, turning, observing as he did so that it was a pity, as Dillwyn would have been accompanied by Ronald who had been reading Virgil since he was six. This titbit of information about his youngest son had the anticipated effect. The school did not want to pass up such a precocious child, and both Dillwyn and Ronald were accepted for Summer Fields in 1896. Ronald was eight. Winifred was sure it was her stepmother who had thought up the winning stratagem that convinced Summer Fields to take the two boys.[28]

Summer Fields sat in seventy splendid acres of its own, in the Summer Town area just north of the centre of Oxford, although it was then on the edge of open country. The main building with its three-storey double-bay front and verandah looked reassuringly like a vicarage. The Cherwell River flowed alongside part of the grounds. The school began in the early 1860s as a venture of Archibald and Gertrude Maclaren. He was a pioneer in physical training, she was a classical scholar. The school motto was, not surprisingly, *Mens sana in corpore sano* – A sound mind in a healthy body, a phrase much used by public schools at the time. The Maclarens had two daughters: Mabel, who married the Revd Charles Williams, DD ('The Doctor') and Margaret, who married the Revd Hugh Alington. When Ronald Knox went to the school in 1896 Gertrude Maclaren was still in charge, but she died the following year and Charles Williams became headmaster. There was thus a strong sense of family continuity within the school, which was reflected in its tight-knit ethos. Moreover, there was a tendency for the masters to stay for many years. The school encouraged genius in its pupils and to this end tolerated eccentricity in some of its more brilliant teachers. As one headmaster put it, the masters somehow managed not to get too much on each other's nerves: 'There could hardly be, or have been, a more individual and varied – not to say eccentric – group of men. And this again has been a source of strength. For it would be hard for any boy not to find some master who could understand him.'[29] It was, therefore an ideal place to send the eight-year-old Ronald Knox, with his well-developed intellect and underdeveloped social skills. It gave him a chance to make the transition from the isolation of his uncle's cramming at Creeton to a more socialized scene, while taking further his already remarkable intellectual capacity.

Summer Fields has been described as a school of 'intense conservatism, sound classical teaching and *esprit de corps*'.[30] The *esprit de corps* derived from the fact that there were only 125 pupils and all were boarders. There was also the influence of the family ownership and the continuity of teachers already described. This strong sense of community helped Ronald Knox find his place, and socially, his four years there were a great success. Three friends in particular came to mean a great deal to him: Edward Horner, and the brothers Julian and Billy Grenfell. In his last year Ronald Knox was made head of school and a prefect. Although not good at sports he was agile and enjoyed the swimming sessions in the Cherwell which were compulsory in summer. The neighbouring Dragon School usually beat Summer Fields at most games, but the

Summer Fields boys comforted themselves with the reflection that the Dragon Boys, having practised on Sundays, would certainly go to hell.[31]

Although the school gave a good all-round education it was not strong in mathematics or history. It was strongest in classics, which meant that the school was very effective in winning Eton scholarships. Summer Fields was geared towards winning places and scholarships at the major public schools, Eton above all. Between 1864 and 1960, of the 2,800 boys who had entered the school, 951 had gone to Eton, 343 with scholarships. Large numbers were also sent to Winchester, Harrow and Wellington. In the Fifth Form, the boys had to work harder than ever for their public school exams, and could be caned if they did not work hard enough. One near contemporary of Knox's recalled: 'If one was going in for a scholarship, one was trained like a racehorse.' 'The Doctor' gave extra tuition to the boys he thought good Eton material. When they sat their Eton exams he would accompany them to Windsor where he would give them some last-minute tuition. Ronald recalled how, when it was his turn for this experience, 'the Doctor' seemed intuitively to know the examiners' minds.[32] Knox, with his already extraordinary ability in Latin and Greek further enhanced, would always have been a natural for Eton. 'The Doctor' later spoke of him as one of the cleverest boys that he had taught and, after he had left, Knox was held up as an example to others.[33] In the event, he was placed first in the list of those who won Eton scholarships. It would take him into the very heart of the English establishment, with its privileges and its sense of duty.

His stepmother's steadying influence on the family, and her ambitions for her stepchildren, had brought them far, socially speaking, in a very short time. Did his achievements at Summer Fields go to Ronald Knox's head? He recorded that during this time he was 'a rather horrid little boy'. But this was the adult speaking, and anyway, as he admitted, pre-teen boys were typically self-absorbed and without the finer feelings.[34] Perhaps the real question was not whether he was a prig, but whether he would come to terms with his intelli-

gence, so creative and so mesmerizing for him. By the age of
eight he was writing a long Latin play in instalments. By the
age of twelve he was composing verses in Latin and Greek,
and in letters home enthused about his progress in these
languages.[35] In part, this was nothing more than juvenilia,
typical of any prep-school educated boy of his period. In many
respects he was very ordinary, at one point being beaten for
keeping an untidy locker. He wrote home boasting about
scoring two goals in football ('the only goals which my side
got'). Other letters tell of snowball fights and chilblains, of
measles epidemics and whooping-cough. There is no sign of
the homesickness that children sometimes show at boarding-
school, evidence, perhaps, of a growing inner resilience.[36] At
home he delighted in trips with his brothers to cheer on Aston
Villa at its football ground. Yet we may also wonder whether
his intellect was a means of consolation, of reassuring himself
in a world where he had known some hard blows and separa-
tions. He seems to have compensated for his emotional loss by
building up his intellect.

Religiously there was nothing remarkable about him as he
prepared for the move to Eton. He worried about being inat-
tentive in chapel, but he had little sense of catholicity and he
thought in retrospect that Summer Fields taught a doctrinally
thin broad Christianity. In this he remembered correctly.
Summer Fields at that time taught nothing about the sacramental side of Christianity for fear of offending some of the
boys' parents who were Presbyterian.[37] As a child of the
vicarage he would also have believed that the Church of
England was the soul of the English nation. He had before him
the example of his hard-working father, who had ministered
to rich and poor alike. He took for granted the Church of
England's privileges and duties and would have assumed that,
generally speaking, to be English was to be Anglican. By the
age of twelve he had also experienced his family's evangelicalism, not only its dourness but also more positively its
sincerity and earnestness of purpose, all of which had rubbed
off on him more than he realized. Eton would bring him to a
very different perspective.

Notes

1 These and other details are taken from Edmund Knox's *Reminiscences of an Octogenarian 1847–1934* (London: Hutchinson, 1935). See especially chapter 8.

2 On Aston industry, see Asa Briggs, *History of Birmingham* Vol 2, *Borough and City 1865–1938* (London: OUP, 1952), pp. 28, 145–6 and 298. On the vicarage, Knox, *Reminiscences*, p. 131.

3 Briggs, *History of Birmingham*, p. 146.

4 Edmund Knox, *Reminiscences*, p. 138.

5 Edmund Knox, *Reminiscences*, p. 135.

6 This influenza epidemic was popularly believed to have originated in Russia and was often known as Russian Flu. For a recent survey of its history and effects, see F. B. Smith, 'The Russian Influenza in the United Kingdom, 1889–1894', *Social History of Medicine* 8.1 (1995) pp. 55–73. For a contemporary account of after-effects, see E. S. Thompson, *Influenza, or Epidemic Catarrhal Fever: A Historical Survey of Past Epidemics in Great Britain from 1519 to 1890* (London: Percival and Co, 1890) pp. 405–6. For the encephalitis, see Niall Johnson, *Britain and the 1918–19 Influenza Epidemic: A Dark Epilogue* (London: Routledge), pp. 5–6 and 76–7. This influenza epidemic prefigured the devastating 'Spanish Influenza' of 1918.

7 Winifred Peck, *A Little Learning, or A Victorian Childhood* (London: Faber, 1952), p. 35.

8 Pat Jelland, *Death in the Victorian Family* (Oxford: OUP, 1996), p. 279.

9 Knox, *Reminiscences*, p. 153.

10 Jelland, *Death in the Victorian Family*, p. 252. See also p. 5.

11 Penelope Fitzgerald, *The Knox Brothers* (London: Macmillan, 1977), p. 37.

12 Peck, *A Little Learning*, pp. 45 and 91.

13 Fitzgerald, *The Knox Brothers*, pp. 72 and 256–7.

14 Ronald Knox, *A Spiritual Aeneid* (London: Burns and Oates, 1950 revised edition of 1918), p. 5. Cited hereafter as *SA*.

15 Evelyn Waugh, *The Life of Ronald Knox* (London: Chapman and Hall, 1959), pp. 38–9. Cited hereafter as EW, *RK*.

16 *SA*, pp. 9–10.

17 Peck, *A Little Learning*, p. 35; Knox, *Reminiscences*, p. 153.

18 Ronald Knox to Ethel Newton, 11th July 1894, Knox Papers, Mells Manor, Somerset.

19 *SA*, pp. 5–6.

20 See here Owen Chadwick, *The Victorian Church* Part 1 (London: Adam and Charles Black, 3rd edn, 1971), pp. 445–6.

21 Winifred Peck, *Home for the Holidays* (London: Faber, 1955), pp. 44–5. She dates this as 1891 but it could have been later.

22 Ian Bradley, *The Call to Seriousness: The Evangelical Impact on the Victorians* (London: Cape, 1976); Peck, *Home for the Holidays* (London: Faber, 1955), p. 182.

23 See the description of Birmingham in the Chamberlain era in Tristam Hunt, *Building Jerusalem: The Rise and Fall of the Victorian City* (London: Weidenfeld and Nicolson, 2004), pp. 258–266.

24 Knox, *Reminiscences*, p. 163.

25 Peck, *A Little Learning*, pp. 96 and 99.

26 Waugh, *RK*, p. 43.

27 Peck, *A Little Learning*, p. 97.

28 Peck, *A Little Learning*, pp. 99–100.

29 Richard Usborne, (editor), *A Century of Summer Fields* (London: Methuen, 1964), p. 6.

30 L. W. Barnard, *C. B. Moss: Defender of the Faith* (London: Mowbray, 1967), p. 14. Moss was there at the same time as Knox.

31 Christopher Hollis, *Along the Road to Frome* (London: Harrap, 1958), p. 50.

32 On the public school statistics, *A Century of Summer Fields*, p. 33; on intense training, and Windsor sessions, p. 54; and EW, *RK*, p. 49.

33 Usborne (ed.), *A Century of Summer Fields*, p. 122, as reported by Williams's daughter. See also p. 54.

34 *SA*, p. 10.

35 Usborne (ed.), *A Century of Summer Fields*, pp. 41–2.

36 Ronald Knox to Ethel Knox, 30th January 1894, Knox Papers, Mells Manor, Somerset.

37 Barnard, *C. B. Moss*, p. 14.

2

Floreat Etona

Ronald Knox went to Eton in the autumn of 1900. New boys arrived at Eton with a sense of expectation arising from Eton's history and prestige. Eton was founded by royal charter in 1440 and now stood at the apex of the English public school system.[1] The school was valued not only for its education but also for the connections a pupil made there. Old Etonians could be found playing prominent roles in parliament, the Church of England, the law, the armed services, Oxford and Cambridge universities, and in the administration of the Empire. Eton was also well represented in the banks and business life of the City. The school inculcated in its pupils the expectation and the obligation of preparing for leadership. For centuries it had been educating the sons of the landed aristocracy, and now it was educating many of the sons of the upper middle class as well. By the late nineteenth century the social mix of the school had broadened a little to include boys from other backgrounds. Some came from families that had moved upwards in late Victorian England, made wealthy from commerce or industry. There was a small number of Jews. A few sons of rich Indian princes were admitted. Annual scholarships did allow entry to boys from families of modest means, but the social mix remained limited because, even to enter the scholarship exam, a boy had to know Latin and Greek.

The geography of Eton underlined its social importance. To the south could be seen Windsor Castle, the royal standard fluttering over the Round Tower when the sovereign was in residence. Queen Victoria on an afternoon's drive would sometimes stop her carriage to watch games on the school playing-fields. Eton's architecture also spoke eloquently. The oldest part of Eton was School Yard which the new pupil entered by an archway off Long Walk. He would have been struck by the fifteenth-century chapel soaring away to his right, an imposing edifice of pinnacles, massive buttresses and stained-glass windows in stone tracery. Straight ahead on the far side of the quadrangle he saw the red brick of Lupton's Tower. Built in 1520, its clock face and huge oriel window made the tower almost as imposing as the chapel. In the centre of the quad a bronze statue of the founder, King Henry VI, brooded over the pupils and masters as they scurried past.

When Ronald Knox went to Eton in 1900, it had just over 1,000 boys who lived in twenty-seven houses, scattered across the small town, but close to the school itself. They were known as Oppidans. Knox, however, joined a group of seventy Collegers or King's Scholars. College comprised those who had won a scholarship; they lived a little apart from the Oppidans, and formed a distinct group within Eton. From the day of his arrival until the day he left the letters 'K. S.' were attached to Knox's name, indicating a King's Scholar. His name would appear on clothes, books, results lists, school magazines and elsewhere, as 'Knox, K.S.'. Collegers were colloquially known as Tugs, probably from the Latin, *Togati*, wearers of gowns or togas. He had a gown that he would wear for all formal occasions, and as a Colleger also wore a surplice in chapel on Sundays and Saints days.

In a Colleger's first year, his life centred on Chamber, the upper floor of a building dating from 1443, on the north side of School Yard opposite the chapel. Like others, Knox was assigned one of fifteen cubicles in Chamber. It contained a fold-up bed, a 'burry' or kind of desk, and a chair. The partition walls of every cubicle bore the carved names of former occupants. In the corridor leading off from Chamber there were separate rooms for the Six Formers. Half-way down Chamber was an open space. Here stood an ancient round table with newspapers and magazines. There was a large fireplace and bootlockers that doubled as benches. This area was the centre of Chamber life, especially in winter. As they progressed through the school, Collegers moved from the Chamber to rooms of their own in the adjacent New Buildings, but they often missed the easy conviviality of Chamber. Chamber also saw one of the more notorious features of public school life. A boy being punished could be ordered by the Captain of Chamber to bend over the table for 'siphoning', seven strokes with a rubber tube called a siphon, otherwise used for drawing water into baths. Here, too, the first year boys would have to 'fag' for the senior boys, doing chores like making tea or running errands.[2] Adjusting to Eton could be a painful experience. There were arcane rules to be learned and punishment if you infringed them. Incremental privileges were earned with growing seniority in the school. If a boy was to survive, then he had to be mentally and emotionally robust. The constant emphasis on games as a way of promoting the prestige of one's house or of the school itself meant that physical fitness was also important.

Ronald Knox not only adjusted well to the school, but thrived in its environment. Knox arrived at Eton just in time to take advantage of the classical tradition in English public school life, which was already on the wane. The study of Latin and Greek language and literature had long dominated public school education. The classics were esteemed for their ability in developing an analytical mind and precision in the use of words. Greek and Latin were also valued for the insight they gave into the ideals of classical civilisation. But by the middle of the Victorian era, the narrow focus of public school education attracted increasing criticism. This concern among the governing classes about the state of public schools had led to the Public Schools Act of 1868, in which the seven leading public schools were required to broaden their curriculum. At Eton this process coincided with the long headmastership of Edmond Warre (1884–1905) who increased the time given to mathematics and French. Later, he allowed the more able older boys to move away from the classics and to specialize in other subjects that attracted them. Boys began winning scholarships to Oxford and Cambridge in subjects other than classics.[3] Even so, around 1900 Eton was still a school whose main strength was in the classics. As late at 1907, Eton realized that it still did not meet the requirements of the 1868 Act for the teaching of science.[4] Ronald Knox was able, therefore, to continue to build on his strengths in the classics just before they were dethroned in public school education. In later years, it sometimes gave his writing a slightly dated feel, as he unconsciously assumed a widespread knowledge of classical references.

Knox won prizes and a further scholarship through his achievements at Eton. In 1904, however, he was disappointed in his bid to win the most glittering prize of all, the Newcastle Prize. Aspirants for this had to sit through eight gruelling papers in divinity and classics. Ronald Knox was widely expected to win, but it was snatched by the relatively unknown Patrick Shaw-Stewart who had been quietly and feverishly working for that day. It was, as Knox ruefully acknowledged, a chastening experience for him. He was not knocked back for long. The following year, he won a scholarship to Balliol College, Oxford, sitting the scholarship exam a year earlier than necessary. In his early years he had written exuberantly, '*Floreat Etona*'. Eton had flourished, and so had he.

As a child Knox had believed that Catholic influence in history was 'very real and very abominable'. Looking back he believed that English children were powerfully influenced by Charles Kingsley's historical novel *Westward Ho!*[5] Kingsley presented Catholics as unmanly, deceitful and priest-ridden, the antithesis of rugged English patriots. Knox's own Catholic antipathy was first dented on Christmas Day 1903 when he read R. H. Benson's *The Light Invisible*. Benson's collection of stories portrays a priest who, from time to time, is able to see into the supernatural realm permeating the ordinary world. Benson was the son of an archbishop of Canterbury, and became a Catholic shortly after writing *The Light Invisible*. Perhaps its mixture of fact and fantasy made it just the kind of book to appeal to an impressionable 15-year-old as he pored over its descriptions of the Virgin Mary, the sacrament of confession, and the Holy Sacrifice of the altar. The book was written when Benson was still an Anglo-Catholic. In one story a pre-Reformation convent has once again become a place of intercession, this time with enclosed Anglican sisters; another story centres around a confessional restored to use in the Anglican parish church. As he read, Catholic spirituality began to make sense for Knox. He wrote later: 'All that Catholic system which I had hitherto known only distantly, felt as something wicked and felt attracted to only because it seemed wicked, now for the first time entered my horizon.'[6] It was, he said, a turning-point.

There was, however, one story in the book which must have tugged at his heart-strings, and opened his emotions. In the chapter 'Consolatrix Afflictorum', the priest at the centre of *The Light Invisible* told of receiving a letter from someone of advanced years whose mother had died when he was aged only seven. The letter-writer remembered how, after her death, he would cry himself to sleep night after night, heartbroken and longing for his mother's presence. One evening, to his astonishment, his mother appeared in the bedroom which was lit only by the gleam from the fireplace:

She lifted me gently in her arms, but said no word. I too said nothing, but she raised the cloak a little and wrapped it round me, and I lay there in bliss, my head on her shoulder, and my arm round her neck. She walked smoothly and noiselessly to a rocking-chair that stood beside the fire and sat down, and then began to rock gently to and fro . . . those arms held me firmly, and I was soon at peace; still she spoke no word, and I did not see her face.

The visits became regular and during one of them, as the child rested on her shoulder he became aware of

A strange sound, like the noise of the sea in a shell, but more melodious . . . it was like the murmuring of a far-off crowd, overlaid with musical pulsations . . . there were words, but I could not distinguish them . . . The voices cried out in every sort of tone – passion, content, despair, monotony.

We are to understand that the boy was hearing from afar the prayers of those asking the intercession of Mary. Eventually the boy realized in a moment of shock that this was not his own mother. Instead, 'another great Mother had taken her place.' It was the Virgin Mary who had come to comfort him.[7] What effect, we might wonder, did those words have on Knox? He must have recalled how he and his siblings had lost their own mother, and the sense of desolation that remained in the family circle. Benson's book is uneven and often over-wrought, but through this memory of a mother lost and found, its message of Catholicism as the door to spiritual reality must have penetrated deeply into Knox's soul.

Knox's nascent Anglican catholicity was shortly reinforced by a book he read for the Newcastle Prize, Henry Wakeman's *Introduction to the History of the Church of England.* Wakeman's account was strongly influenced by Tractarian sympathies and presented the Oxford Movement as the rein-statement of catholic tradition to its rightful place in Angli-can life and thought. Knox was sixteen when he read the book, and found himself captivated, not least by the atmos-phere of controversy and struggle which surrounded Angli-can catholicity:

> I read, and was carried off my feet; I lived through the early struggles, followed breathlessly the story of *Tracts for the Times*, trembled for Newman, mourned for him as lost to the Church, and rose with the knowledge that some-where, beyond the circles I moved in, there was a Cause for which clergymen had been sent to prison, a Bishop censured, noble lives spent; a Cause which could be mine.[8]

The ironic tone in which the adult Knox looks back at his adolescent self almost makes light of the change. Yet it was the start of a re-orientation of his whole outlook. Indeed, he thought of it as a conversion. The cause he referred to was that of the Catholic party in the Church of England, and he made it his own. One effect of this was that he began to look at Eton itself with a fresh eye and saw that Eton still bore traces of what it had been at its foundation, namely a Catholic institution. Henry VI had established Eton as the College of Our Lady of Eton. He intended it to be a pilgrimage centre in honour of the Blessed Virgin Mary, as well as a school. Knox, now aged sixteen, developed a reverence for Mary in the place where her name was once venerated: 'Her name was part of our title; her lilies figured on our coat of arms; the blue of her robe you could see daily on the blazers of the Eight and the caps of the Eleven.'[9] This sense of an unnoticed Catholic history would come back to him again at other points in his life. It was a signal that he would become increasingly aware of something buried in the English psyche, namely the repressed memory of a Catholic identity that needed to be recovered for the sake of national integrity.

Was the shift to a kind of Anglo-Catholicism in his life really the fruit of reading fiction and Wakeman's account of English church history? There were other, deeper, currents at work. First of all we may notice that it came at a time of heightened religious emotion for him. A few months before he read Benson, Ronald Knox was confirmed by his father, having been prepared at Eton by his classical tutor. In the Anglican tradition, confirmation usually admits to communion, and Knox prepared carefully for his communions. Second, he was becoming aware of Anglican doctrinal vagueness: 'The nature of God, the position and destiny of man, the meaning of terms such as "soul" and "spirit" ... are subjects on which expert Anglicans would pronounce variously, and non-expert Anglicans, if they could help it, would not pronounce at all.'[10] A bright teenager like Ronald Knox noted the difficulty of giving any definitive account of Christian doctrine in the Anglican tradition. He also saw how the incommensurability of the various claims led many Anglican clergy to a studied vagueness. In later years this tension within Anglicanism would increasingly preoccupy him. Third, like most teenagers, Knox was struggling to come to terms with his burgeoning sexuality. An added complication here was the homoeroticism which featured so prominently in public school life.[11] The relatively self-contained life of Collegers made for a more intense atmosphere among them. Not surprisingly boys developed crushes on one another. More seriously, younger boys could find themselves cultivated by older ones. One Colleger contemporaneous with Knox wrote that he could think of 'more than one weak effeminate little fool, who has been absolutely ruined, very likely for life, by being taken up by an older boy . . .'[12] Knox must have seen and known about these things, indeed he said that an ordinary boy in public school would hear 'obscene conversation and much scandalous gossip'. His confirmation had included moral exhortation on the subject of purity. He was becoming aware of his need for 'close and intimate friendships . . . for human sympathy and support'.

One evening, aged seventeen, Knox knelt on the staircase in College and bound himself by a vow of celibacy. Neither then nor later did he have any idea where this ascetic impulse came from, but even then he saw it as a self-offering to God.[13] The detail about kneeling (presumably unseen) on the stairs is a telling one. It speaks of a teenage boy, churning with emotion as he walks from one part of the building to another, with that ever-present sense of sexuality which many boys experience in late adolescence. Suddenly he is overwhelmed by his feelings and seeks resolution and peace through an early avowal of chastity. It was an affirmation of his faith in God, but it also locked away dangerous feelings. They could have been dangerous in the sense that Eton, with its crushes and hothouse passions, could destabilize those who were swept away by their sexuality. Dangerous, too, in so far as the emotions often inter-link, and deep within him was the hidden pain arising from the loss of his mother. Catholicism beckoned, though he could hardly have realized it at the time, because of its affectivity. Its ceremonies and symbols communicated through the senses, as they were intended to do. This allowed a safe outlet for the emotions that he struggled to discipline. Of course, this was not all. Catholicism appealed to him precisely because it made sense. It gave answers and spoke to the questions that he was beginning to ask about the bigger picture and the nature of truth. But it also spoke to him at a subterranean level, allowing emotion a safe expression. It gave him a rationale for containing his emotions within a context where they could be acknowledged but not explored.

We may also wonder whether Catholicism allured precisely because it challenged him to go beyond what was regarded as sufficient, spiritually speaking, for an Englishman of his class. Catholicism of the High Church, Anglican kind would allow him to carve out a mental space in which he could breathe, away from the muscular Christianity that characterized so much of public school life. Public school religion had been greatly influenced by Charles Kingsley, Anglican priest and writer, and indeed the phrase 'muscular Christianity' seems to have been invented by him. David Newsome says that if we put together the ideals promoted by Kingsley and others like him, then it adds up to

> The duty of patriotism; the moral and physical beauty of athleticism; the salutary effects of Spartan habits and discipline; the cultivation of all that is masculine and the expulsion of all that is effeminate, un-English and excessively intellectual. [By the end of the 19th century] the same ideals or something very like them might be taken to be the creed of the typical housemaster of the typical public school.[14]

Eton provided richer spiritual fare than that, and yet to an important degree this *was* the religion of the school, and it gave little nourishment to an intelligent seeker like Ronald Knox. To grow spiritually required him to look further afield, and even, therefore, to be prepared to cut across the prescribed spirituality of his place and time. More than that, in the quiet of his heart he had to resist Eton's spirituality even as he flourished within it. Consider, for example, what one near-contemporary wrote of the tone set by Edmond Warre's headmastership:

If we were all of us what Warre in his highest flight of aspiration would make us, we should be magnificent, but not heavenly at all – not for a moment. We should all be the best baronets ever seen, loyal, true and kind, the salt of the earth; we should all be honest secretaries of state, open-handed village squires, broad-minded bishops; it would be a good day for the land of our fathers.[15]

It was this common sense, but limiting religion that did not appeal to Knox. He wanted exactly what Warre's bloodless Christianity could not supply: poetry, vision, and a challenging spirituality. The official religion of public school Anglicanism was too sensible and self-limiting. The priest in *The Light Invisible*, that book which so powerfully influenced Knox, at one point ruminates about his own childhood religion:

It was the religion of most well-taught boys. In the foreground, if I may put it so, was morality: I must not do certain things; I must do certain other things . . . Here about me lay the tangible enjoyable world – this was reality; there in a misty picture lay religion, claiming, as I knew, my homage, but not my heart.[16]

This respectable religion, with God at a safe distance, now seemed inadequate to Knox. And whether he realized it consciously or not, the priest in the book could have been describing the religion of the public school system.

Warre would have been baffled by Knox's growing conviction about the importance of Catholic truth. It has been said of Warre that 'Christianity was to him almost entirely a matter of ethics. The disputes of schools or of churchmanship . . . had no meaning for him and their presence among boys he would have condemned as unhealthy.'[17] But Knox, in embracing an Anglican Catholicism, was becoming precisely what Warre would have discouraged, a party man, one who believed that the true nature of the Church of England was to be found in its membership of the historic and ancient Catholic Church, which it shared with the Roman Catholic and Eastern Orthodox churches. No wonder that the Master in College, Cyril Alington, wrote that Ronald Knox in his last years at Eton had 'an excess of faith.'[18] In Eton terms, Knox did have a surfeit of faith, and it was necessary for his growth because it gave him inner space and freedom, precisely because it transcended Etonian reserve in matters of religion. What launched him into seeking a Catholic spirituality as an Anglican might have been a chance encounter with a book, but his quest was entirely serious and would have equally serious consequences for him.

For the next two years Knox's new-found Catholic sympathies were largely implicit. He was encouraged by a College matron who had served as a missionary with the Universities Mission to Central Africa, which was a vigorous Anglo-Catholic missionary organisation. Through her, he lunched with Bishop Frank Weston, a stormy petrel of ecclesiastical politics whose cathedral in Zanzibar was built on the site of the old slave market. Weston was a vigorous promoter of Catholic practices and theology in the Church of England. Knox read the *Church Times*. He discovered gothic architecture and developed a liking for pre-Raphaelite art, both of them signs of devotion to the worship of the pre-Reformation era. Mostly, however, it was in the privacy of his conscience that he began to pray and think like a Catholic. The question arises of the extent to which all this was the outcome of typical adolescent interior pressures, and the extent to which it was part of his relationship with God. The one does not exclude the other. If God's presence does permeate the world, rather as Knox had grasped when reading Benson, then the trivial events and sustained pressures of everyday life can be synapses along which the divine electricity can flicker. When Augustine of Hippo heard a child chanting 'Tolle lege', on one level it was no more than the piping voice of a neighbour's child engaged in learning, or in a game. But Augustine's response was to take up the New Testament, and picking a passage at random found that his doubts disappeared and a new way of living opened up before him. The sacred and the secular are sometimes not easily separated.

Knox's inner wonderings and tensions did not prevent him from becoming a well-liked member of College. He could also be the butt of good humour. Once in a history class the master was reading Thomas Carlyle's account of the incident in St Giles Cathedral, Edinburgh in 1637, when a protest against the introduction of Anglican liturgy led to riots in the city. When, unthinkingly, the master read Carlyle's comment 'None but a cast-iron bishop from Birmingham could stand such an attack' everyone suddenly remembered that Knox's father was a bishop and had served in Birmingham. The class collapsed in laughter.[19] Knox late wrote that

> This was just the time at which I was blossoming out into a sympathetic friend and a tolerable companion. I knew everybody around me, I wasted endless hours in talking . . . I was only exceptional as regards literary ability . . . I was supremely happy, and accepted everywhere at my own valuation as a very normal Etonian.[20]

We have no need to doubt his word. He was elected to the exclusive Eton society known as 'Pop', a self-selecting society of twenty-eight senior boys who wielded enormous influence on the life of the school. He also belonged to a high-spirited group of friends many of whom went to Oxford together, and to the same college, Balliol. Some of them co-operated on a short-lived magazine *The Outsider* which gently tweaked the tail of Eton authority. This editorial group included Charles Lister, Julian Grenfell, Patrick Shaw-Stewart and Edward Horner, all of them close friends of Ronald Knox. It said much for his personality that he was popular in a culture where, in the words of one historian, 'Games undeniably counted for too much.' Even in College with its reputation for academic achievement far outstripping that of the Oppidans, the College book, which recorded prize-winners and scholars, around 1900 was mostly concerned with College's sporting record.[21] Knox's achievements were ones of intellectual rather than sporting prowess, but he seems always to have felt at home in College, which was like a surrogate family for him. His achievements were recognized by the school and his peers. In his last year, as the most scholastic member of the Sixth Form, he became Captain of the School – a misleading title, since it referred to his authority over College, Oppidans having their own Captain. Here again we find a hint of Knox's quiet distancing of himself from the prevailing culture. Public schools, following the initiatives of Dr Arnold at Rugby, put enormous amounts of responsibility into the hands of the boys. Much of the discipline was enforced by the boys themselves, as well as some of the organisation of school life. This was the case at Eton, where every member of the Sixth Form had the power to beat junior boys who were judged to be malefactors. Knox never did so, and in fact left the room when the punishment was inflicted by others. As Captain it was his duty to punish for certain offences, but he delegated this to his deputy.[22] Knox might be a son of Eton, but he was not a subscriber to everything Etonian.

Notes

1 In the English context, a public school is of course a private school. Eton is technically Eton College. However, within Eton College there is a small distinct group called the Collegers. To avoid confusion I have called Eton (the whole) a school and when referring to College I mean the body of scholarship holders who lived separately from the rest.

2 These details are taken from C.H.M. [Charles H. Malden], *Recollections of an Eton Colleger* (Eton: Spottiswoode, 1905) chapter 1; and from Philip Brownrigg, 'College', a separate chapter within Bernard Fergusson, *Eton Portrait* (London: John Miles, 1938).

3 Tim Card, *Eton Renewed: A History from 1860 to the Present Day* (London: John Murray, 1994), pp. 88–91 and 100–1. From the mid-nineteenth century there was concern that Britain was falling behind its rival, Germany, because of its failure to give modern subjects a proper place in the curriculum: see Edward Mack, *Public Schools and British Opinion 1780–1860* (London: Methuen, 1938), pp. 393–8; also Mack, *Public Schools and British Opinion Since 1860* (New York: Columbia University Press, 1941), pp. 218–19.

4 L. S. R. Byrne, *Changing Eton* (London: Cape, 1937), pp. 87–8. Notwithstanding the limitations on science teaching, Eton was still able at this time to turn out future scientists of note such as J. B. S. Haldane and Julian Huxley.

5   *SA*, pp. 7–8. Ian Ousby came to the same opinion in *The Cambridge Guide to Literature in English* (Cambridge: CUP, 1993): 'Jesuits plot the ruin of England, the Inquisition tortures prisoners and roasts them alive; Englishmen fight fair ... Its heady mix of patriotism, sentiment and romance set the attitudes of English children for several generations' (entry on *Westward Ho!* ad loc.).

6   *SA*, p. 32.

7   Robert Hugh Benson, *The Light Invisible* (London: Burns, Oates, & Washbourne, n.d. but 1903), pp. 93–9, quoting from 93, 96 and 99.

8   *SA*, p. 33.

9   *SA*, p. 41.

10 *SA*, p. 23.

11 See, for example, Mack, *Public Schools and British Opinion Since 1860*, pp. 126–7 and 409–10; David Newsome, *Godliness and Good Learning: Four Studies on a Victorian Ideal* (London: John Murray, 1961), pp. 85–8; Card, *Eton Renewed*, pp. 62–8.

12 C.H.M. [Charles H. Malden], *Recollections of an Eton Colleger*, p. 238.

13 *SA*, pp. 43–4.

14 Newsome, *Godliness and Good Learning*, p. 216.

15 Percy Lubbock, *Shades of Eton* (London: Cape, 1929), pp. 17–18. Lubbock left Eton in 1898, two years before Knox arrived.

16 Benson, *The Light Invisible*, p. 22.

17 Christopher Hollis, *Eton: A History* (London: Hollis and Carter, 1960), p. 288.

18 EW, *RK*, p. 57.

19 Ronald Knox to Edmund Knox, 13th February 1905, KPM.

20 *SA*, p. 44.

21 Card, *Eton Renewed*, pp. 101 and 103.

22 EW, *RK*, p. 74. For the powers of the Captain, see C.H.M. [Charles H. Malden], *Recollections of an Eton Colleger*, pp. 29–32.

3
Oxford Student

On 22 January 1901, Queen Victoria died at Osborne on the Isle of Wight. On 2 February her body was taken by train from London to St George's Chapel, Windsor. Cadets from Eton, the Eton Volunteer Rifles, formed a guard along the route of the cortège from Windsor station to the castle. Ronald Knox joined the rest of the school who stood behind the cadets in absolute silence. As the coffin of the queen and empress passed them, the Eton Volunteer Rifles presented arms then stood 'arms reversed', muzzles of the rifles on their boots, hands on the butts of the rifles and heads drooped on their breast in the military stance of mourning.[1] The national sense of loss was very real, but soon there was a sense of something having been lifted, a Victorian dourness, perhaps, and an ostensible concern with propriety. By 1906 when Knox went up to Balliol College, Oxford, to read for a Classics degree, the Edwardian era was in full swing. Edward VII's reign was marked by a mood of self-confidence. Britain was enjoying the fruits of prosperity and the prestige of being at the centre of a global empire.

The privilege and the promise of Eton were manifest in the group that went with Knox to Balliol in October 1906. Of the fifty-two new men who came up to the college that year, nineteen were Etonians. By comparison, only ten of the new Balliol students came from the grammar schools of the industrial cities of the Midlands and North.[2] Close friends from Eton who came with Knox to Balliol included Julian Grenfell, Edward Horner, Charles Lister and Patrick Shaw-Stewart. The phalanx of Etonians was a dominating force in the life of

Balliol. They were a rumbustious element. Another Balliol Etonian, the future biologist Julian Huxley, remembered Knox and Lister as belonging 'to the smart and rather rowdy set.'[3] The Etonians took control of one of the Oxford dining clubs, the Annandale, and after drunken dinners would send cascades of smashed crockery down the staircase. The Fellow and Classical Tutor A. D. Lindsay was appalled when Julian Grenfell chased Philip Sassoon out of the quad cracking a bullwhip at him.[4] Grenfell was a boxing champion and athlete who trained hard; this incident was probably part of the ongoing war at Oxford between hearties and aesthetes. These Etonians were, says Waugh, 'arrogant, rowdy and exclusive'. Waugh excused their high spirits, pointing to their athleticism, their academic prizes, their talent for poetry and their sometimes surprising faith in God.[5] In reality they were often tiresome, or worse. A. D. Lindsay later wrote of them: 'They were brilliant and personally charming and I was very fond of most of them; but they were most of them insolent, and only condescendingly aware that there were other sets in the College besides their own.'[6] Knox does not seem to have shared in the more exuberant escapades of the Etonian group. He was not athletically inclined, and he did not have their deep pockets to pay for wining, dining and damage. But he seems, initially at least, to have been influenced by the insouciance of his fellow Etonians. At the end of five terms he had to sit fourteen papers for Mods, the first examination for Greats (the Classics degree course). He was nonchalant in his preparation, assuming that he was a natural for a first, but found in the examination hall that more was expected of him than he had realized. In some papers he was relying on his formidable memory, having read the set texts when at Eton. In his hubris he even walked out of several exams early. He was awarded a second class pass. As he himself admitted, it was a salutary shock.

Throughout his time at Balliol and beyond there was a quietly stabilizing influence in the background: Francis 'Sligger' Urquhart, at that point the Junior Dean and Fellow in Modern History and the first Catholic tutorial fellow of an

Oxford College since the Reformation. He lived in Balliol for nearly forty years, from 1896 until his death in 1934. He befriended many of the students from each year. Undergraduates could be found in his rooms overlooking St Giles night after night, and he would drop a back gate key from the window to those who were locked out. James Lees-Milne says that 'Sligger talked to these unfledged undergraduates on absolutely equal terms, without the slightest patronage or censure. Yet he managed to humanize their arrogance, and render their superiority less vulgar.'[7] Urquhart never fished for converts, yet all who knew him were aware that his unostentatious Catholic faith was central to his life. Knox formed an enduring friendship with Sligger Urquhart, and increasingly turned to him in later years as his own Catholic yearnings grew stronger.

Although the influence of the crowd around him might have played its part, Ronald Knox's busy social life was probably more to blame for his disappointing Mods result. He joined clubs and debating societies of every hue. 'My evenings were a riot of discussion,' he recorded, 'my mantelpiece smothered in fixture-cards.' He was marked down as a speaker who could be depended upon to support any view in debate, and enliven the proceedings while doing so. Once, owing to a shortage of speakers, he opened and opposed the same motion.[8] He shone at the Oxford Union, the venerable debating society where speakers and audiences alike relished debates about controversial topics. The debating hall itself was furnished like the House of Commons. A Free Church student of the period remembered Knox many years later and wrote: 'The most witty and famous speaker of my time was Ronald Knox of Balliol. One speech that he delivered consisted exclusively of limericks. It was supposed that he could speak with equal fervour and gusto upon any aspect of any given subject.'[9] The esteem of his peers is seen in his swift rise through the elected offices of the Union: Secretary, Junior Librarian and finally President in the Hilary term of 1908. A historian of the Oxford Union concluded that Knox was the intellectual driving force that kept the Union going in the

years immediately before the First World War.[10] This depiction of a man who could argue equally fluently for incommensurable points of view raises the question of where Ronald
Knox himself was in all this. What did he really believe? He
found himself coming to terms with socialism on the one
hand, and Anglo-Catholicism on the other. To socialism he
gave a mild, temporary assent through his friendship with
Charles Lister. To Anglo-Catholicism he gave his heart.

Despite the elitism of most of Knox's Eton confrères, social
concern was in the air at Balliol. The elderly Master of the
college, Edward Caird, was a strong advocate of education for
women and of working-class men. Moreover, two of the
fellows at Balliol were active in the Workers' Educational
Association, through which they sought to bring some of the
educational resources of Oxford to working people. Under this
scheme a summer school for working-class people was held at
Balliol in 1910.[11] Although this concern to help the poorer
sections in society was in the air around him, more potent, and
more challenging for Knox was the influence of Charles
Lister. Lister first began to move to the left when he was at
Eton. It seems that just as Knox found breathing space in
Anglo-Catholicism, Lister found it in socialism and in particular membership of the Independent Labour Party. He and
Knox had both been members of Pop at Eton, and both had
helped run the short-lived independent Eton magazine called,
significantly, *The Outsider*. Knox remembered Lister as
someone who was a champion of the oppressed, with a 'width
of mind reacting on an intense passion for justice'.[12] Lister
became a socialist, and he tried to take Ronald Knox with him.

Lister was prominent in making socialism a practical force
among undergraduates at Oxford. Knox was swept up in this
fervour. He wrote of Lister: 'You would find yourself enter-
taining a Labour Member [of Parliament] for the evening, or
helping to organize an exhibition, or bicycling out with him
on a winter's night to Banbury and back to address a nascent
trades union.'[13] Lister, like others at Balliol, was interested in
adult education for workers and organized and paid for some
courses. He started two trades unions in the town and orga-

nized an exhibition about 'sweated labour'. With his drive behind it, the university Fabian Society membership expanded from 20 to 100. On Sunday he would go with Knox to the 11 a.m. Mass at the Cowley chapel of the men's Anglican religious order, the Society of St John the Evangelist. But just as Lister's religion depended upon Knox's commitment, so Knox's support for socialism derived from its fiery commendation by Lister: 'I supported Charles Lister in numberless progressive activities, and was prevailed upon by him to join the Fabian Society ... Lister allowed me to drag him to church, and I allowed him to drag me to meetings.'[14] In the Balliol years if Knox seemed to hesitate in social commitment, Lister would bombard him with scriptural quotations that called for practical love of neighbour. In December 1907, Knox moved a motion at the Oxford Union 'That this House would welcome the advent of a Labour Government.'[15] But as noted above, he was capable of turning his oratorical skills to argue for any cause. Ronald Knox was never to be pigeon-holed politically, and even during this period many at the Union supposed him to be a Conservative. Neither at Oxford nor later was he ever captivated by a political creed. In so far as he espoused an ideology, it was the Catholic faith, with its vision of the material world transformed by the spiritual world. To this faith, too, he devoted his rhetorical skills, defending and commending it wherever necessary. And yet, in later years an incident of injustice, oppression or social need would occasionally seize his attention, and at such times we may trace an echo of Charles Lister, who first made him aware of a suffering world beyond the easy assumptions of the Balliol Etonians.

What socialism had been to Lister, belief in the catholicity of the Church of England was to Knox. This was what fired his imagination and stirred his energies. From his undergraduate years onwards he became an untiring advocate of Anglo-Catholicism, which held that the Church of England was truly a branch of the Catholic Church. Anglo-Catholics strove to reshape Anglican liturgy and spirituality to reflect Catholic principles. They believed that the Church of England was most truly itself when it drew on its Catholic origins for its present-day life and witness. A century or so after this Anglo-Catholic heyday it is hard to grasp the fervour it aroused and the commitment it inspired. In part the movement was driven by a broader cultural stream, particularly Romanticism, which held that symbols could reach into the psyche, to touch the deepest human feelings. This cultivation of feeling also rebelled against the drabness and dehumanisation of the industrial revolution. But Anglo-Catholics were impelled by genuine theological conviction, above all by a high esteem for the sacraments. Throughout the latter half of the nineteenth century Anglo-Catholicism gathered strength as a force within the Church of England.

Much of Anglo-Catholicism's strength came from the desire of its adherents for the spiritual renewal of the Church of England. The eucharist was to be celebrated more frequently and with a new solemnity and seriousness. This in turn called for churches and sanctuaries designed to highlight the centrality of the Mass in Christian life and worship. People went to confession. For the first time religious orders were founded in the Church of England and vocations to them flourished. Anglo-Catholicism was changing the Church of England, outwardly in liturgy and architecture, inwardly in the hearts of those who responded to the new spirituality. And therein lay the problem. On the one hand the movement built up momentum because of the power of conviction behind it. On the other hand, Anglo-Catholicism was controversial because of its innovations, which created resistance. This new spirituality needed its own forms of worship and prayer, and these developments were not uniformly welcomed. At first the movement had focused on recovering the fullness of the Book of Common Prayer, which turned out to have more catholic elements than previously suspected. But soon this moderate, Tractarian approach was replaced by two other schools of thought. Some looked back to the pre-Reformation Church of England for inspiration. Others looked to the Roman Catholic Church. This Romeward turn brought resentment among Anglicans in the pews who loved the forms of traditional, undemonstrative Anglican piety that had served them and their ancestors so well. There was fear, too, that Romanizing influences were undoing the work of the Reformation and irrevocably changing the character of the Church of England. Inevitably, there was a backlash, with the bishops increasingly under pressure to rein in or even roll back the catholicizing innovators. The struggle spilled over into the courts, with Anglo-Catholic clergy prosecuted for breaches of Church law and discipline. It reached even into parliament, for ultimately parliament was responsible for the discipline of the Church of England. Movements and societies were formed to promote Anglo-Catholicism; others were formed to resist its claims. This struggle focused on what often seemed externals: candles on altars, vestments, prayers for the dead and, above all, reservation of the Blessed Sacrament. When Edward King, Bishop of Lincoln, was prosecuted in 1888 for Romish practices the charge sheet included using a mixed chalice, i.e. a chalice with a little water added to the wine, in the Catholic tradition. Because sometimes there was a loss of proportion, it is important to remember that beneath it all lay what Adrian Hastings called Anglo-Catholicism's 'intense desire to recover the deep sense of sacrament, ritual and symbolism, the concern with prayer, mysticism and monastic asceticism, [and] a theology of the Church.'[16] Ronald Knox threw himself into this struggle on the Anglo-Catholic side because of this desire for a greater, transcendent truth that could be reflected in the externals of church life.

During his time at Oxford, his Anglo-Catholic convictions grew deeper and were reflected in his discipline and piety. He worshipped at Balliol College chapel, Pusey House and the Cowley Fathers' chapel (the chapel of the Society of St John the Evangelist). Knox went to Balliol college chapel, but found it as uncongenial as the public school religion of Eton. What he wrote damningly of Balliol chapel he could equally have written of Eton: 'The tone of the ordinary services was marked by a tradition of "superior" music, indefinite dogma and a manly sentiment.'[17] By contrast he loved Pusey House around the corner from Balliol and only a five-minute walk away in St Giles. This was a private foundation with a staff of five Anglo-Catholic priests. It was established to welcome students, with the intention that the Anglican priests on the staff should 'feed Catholic insights and practice into the life of the University' through teaching, lecturing, preaching and friendship.[18] Knox went to the Anglican eucharist there at least twice on weekdays. His account of it is revealing, because it shows how much this strongly intellectual man was led by his feelings when it came to religious faith. Just as the mystical atmosphere of a novel had influenced him at Eton, so, too, the atmosphere of Pusey House and especially its chapel led him into something approaching excitement. He recalled dashing out of the mists in the early morning and hurrying upstairs into the chapel where a handful were kneeling: 'It conveyed a feeling, to me most gratifying, of catacombs, oubliettes, Jesuitry and all the atmosphere of mystery that fascinated me so long.'[19] His faith engaged his mind completely, but it was his feelings nourished by his senses that led his mind to catholicity.

His continuing spiritual development meant that he began to make his confession regularly at Cowley, where he also went to Mass on Sundays with whatever friends he could persuade to accompany him: 'To Cowley I would take friends, of every and no denomination, in the hope of entrapping them into my own religion.'[20] He was known as a party man – a staunch Anglo-Catholic – and felt that he had to live up to the role. Yet the fires of ultramontane spirituality were not yet burning within him. In 1907, at the age of nineteen, he visited Rome for the first time with two of his brothers but was unimpressed. He was faithful to the Church of England. From Julian Huxley we catch a glimpse of Knox on a Sunday afternoon walk with fellow students in the Oxford countryside. At Cumnor they heard the church bell ring for evensong and Knox piously ushered his fellow students into the service: 'The parson and handful of villagers, unaware of Ronnie's devoutness, were visibly surprised at this irruption of undergraduates in blazers and white flannels. Indeed we surprised ourselves.'[21] It points to an undergraduate mind that, for all its innate powers, was in a state of flux. He loved mystery in religion, its sense of connection with past ages, the power of its symbols to reach deep within the psyche. There was even an element of the sensual at work here as he soaked in the details of the atmosphere that he loved. Yet this was also someone steeped in Anglican tradition. This was the case not just that evensong at Cumnor, but also helping his bishop father with a beach mission at Blackpool and taking part in a Church of England mission to the city of Leeds, both in 1908. It would take time, but he could not endure for ever this tension between his growing catholicity and his instinctive Anglicanism. Gradually the catholicity won, and once again it was the senses that moved his mind.

The key was a visit he made in 1909 to the Anglican Benedictine community at Caldey Island off Tenby in Wales. After an itinerant period, this Anglican community had settled on Caldey in October 1906. It was headed by Abbot Aelred Carlyle who has been described as possessing 'dynamic energy, vivid imagination and irrepressible optimism'. Carlyle wanted nothing less than a fully-fledged Benedictine community whose atmosphere and practices reflected the strictest interpretation of the Rule of St Benedict. Consequently, 'the Abbot's charismatic and hypnotic personality attracted many who nostalgically longed for the glories of a medieval and united Christendom.'[22] Knox was, as we have seen, strongly attracted by atmosphere, and with this in mind it is worth quoting at length part of Peter Anson's description of Caldey at this time:

No other monastery in Britain could boast of such a magnificent refectory as Caldey's, with its oak-panelled walls, open timber roof, and long massive tables of solid mahogany. The abbot's house was planned on the scale of those found in medieval and Renaissance monasteries; a fitting background for the only mitred abbot in the Anglican Communion. He received his guests and interviewed members of the Community in an immense, oak-panelled, parquet-floored reception room. In winter logs blazed in the great open fireplace. His private chapel was paved with highly polished black and white marble. The Renaissance altar was fashioned of pink alabaster from the island quarries. The sanctuary lamp hung from a silver galleon in full sail. A four-sided cloister surrounded the turfed garth.[23]

In the abbey church, canopied oak stalls in fifteenth-century gothic style faced each other across the choir. The high altar was built of stones collected from pre-Reformation monasteries. In Anglican religious life there was nothing like this exotic plant. All services were conducted in Latin, including the chanted offices, and the abbot celebrated Mass in vestments styled after those of a medieval prelate. Despite its exoticism in the Church of England, the Caldey community attracted vocations. By March 1912, there were thirty-five monks.[24] On his first visit in 1909, Knox was smitten, and thereafter he visited frequently, especially at pivotal times in his life. Caldey gave him a vision of a revived pre-Reformation church, and thereafter he tended to measure Anglican churches against the ideal of Caldey.[25]

What sense can we make of this passion for the medieval that seized Knox so strongly? It would be a mistake to see it as just liturgical antiquarianism. What mattered here for Knox and his fellow Anglo-Catholics was not just the immediate abbey setting but all that it represented. They were drawn by the vision of the faith as a whole, one unbroken history. Thirty years later, Knox was embarrassed by his earlier enthusiasm about Caldey. He wrote that 'There was a faint air of make-believe about the old Caldey ... you were projected, not into some revival of a Gothic past, but into a world of the imagination, in which there was neither Roman nor Anglican ... It was a dream-world.'[26] It was the more severe, intellectual Roman Catholic Knox who wrote those words. Yet even in this recension of the past, Knox gave away more than he realized. The very language of a dream-like timelessness captured neatly how Caldey gave him a vision of a transcendent truth accessible here and now, drawing him into its mystery. Perhaps there was an element of mummery about the

place, and certainly he was an impressionable young undergraduate. But for someone whose emotions were buried
deeply, who distrusted feelings, and who had made an early
vow of celibacy, it is remarkable how his conversion
depended so much upon the senses. He could let his feelings
rise to the surface safely in a religious context – and it was
here in his depths that he could be open to God.

Conversion often takes place on a plane of mixed emotions.
Surprising elements sometimes mix together to create a new
spiritual opportunity. One of those elements in Knox seemed
to be, as at Eton, a sense of establishing his own identity. This
was to be expected in a student. Knox was a person of strong
Christian faith, but he was also the son of a bishop who was
himself, of course, a person of strong Christian faith, and a
leader of the evangelical party to boot. His father was also a
strong personality. How could Knox be his own person in the
shadow of his father? Certainly not by being an evangelical,
which would make him a clone of his father. The Catholic
faith beckoned independently of this, but we may surmise that
it beckoned all the more strongly because it offered Ronald
Knox a chance of discovering and deepening his own identity.
The clearest evidence is where Ronald Knox reports the
constant chatter about 'the bishops' in the guest house at
Caldey. The bishops were being discussed in negative terms
because it was felt that they were obstructing the progress of
the Anglo-Catholic revival in the Church of England. Knox
quoted a friend who visited with him as saying afterwards that
an eavesdropping stranger with little knowledge of the Church
might have thought that 'the bishops' were a band of criminals.[27] Ronald Knox seemed not to notice that this hostile
gossip implicitly included his own father. Back home he asked
his father's permission before going to confession for the first
time. We may wonder whether he was defiantly telling his
father rather than asking him. Even in the Edwardian age, life
was not so patriarchal as to require every Catholic-minded son
to ask his father's permission for this. When staying in
Manchester on university vacations, on Sundays Knox went to
Anglo-Catholic parishes where his father, as diocesan bishop,

was trying to rein in the ritual. It begins to resemble a spirit of rebellion, and it was to be found also in at least two of his closest friends at Balliol, Charles Lister and Julian Grenfell.

Charles Lister was the son of Lord Ribblesdale who had married Charlotte 'Charty' Tennant. Lister's parents were members of the loosely-knit group of aristocratic and intelligent young people known as the Souls who coalesced in the 1880s. The Souls had been bright, articulate and questioning. They had questioned some of the social conventions of their day. Some of the Souls such as Arthur Balfour and George Curzon had risen to great eminence in the life of the nation. But by the time their children were at Oxford, the Souls had become a rather brittle, sterile group, their incipient radicalism smoothed away. As one writer puts it,

> Their politics were seen to revolve primarily around the maintenance of their own life of aristocratic wealth and privilege. Even in the first years of the century, it was already clear that deep currents of social change and technological progress were rushing through the broad river of English government ... The Souls did not discern these movements. They behaved as though nothing would change, or ever could; and they pursued an increasingly hollow round of pleasure.[28]

It was this world view and its cosy assumptions that Charles Lister rejected. He had a strong sense of the social disparities that underlay Britain's prosperity. His father was keen to play down his son's socialism, which of necessity faded when Lister joined the diplomatic corps. But Ronald Knox was clear that even after abandoning politics for the Foreign Office, Lister was determined to set his own course in life independent of inherited prestige: 'He could not tolerate the idea of a political path made easy by the possession of an income and a horizon bounded by the prospect of a seat in the House of Lords.'[29] Lister, like Knox, was determined to find his own distinctive path through life.

As for Julian Grenfell, his parents Lord and Lady Desborough were also known as members of the Souls. Grenfell chafed against the social restrictions of life and the easy assumptions of society around him. At the age of twenty-one he wrote in an essay that

> Conventionality's terrible power consists perhaps chiefly in its grip on the cradles of our race. Its talons fasten relentlessly on the newborn infant; and at just the time when the future man is utterly at the mercy of any influence ... then conventionality reaps its easy victory ... anything believed sinks ineradicably into the soul, conventionality envelopes him like a pall, thrown over him by his parents and his relations.[30]

In one sense there is nothing surprising about these sentiments. Every generation feels the obligation to assert itself against its parents. What is striking however is the language of suffocation, entrapment and death. Grenfell, too, wanted to find some way of living that did not involve taking what was handed down to him. He joined the army after Balliol, and was glad to be away from England with what he considered to be its hypocrisies and animosities.[31] Knox had been a frequent guest at Taplow Court in Buckinghamshire, the home of the Desboroughs, not far from Oxford. Grenfell, Lister and Knox spent a great deal of time together in earnest discussion. Each, in his own way, chose to resist convention and to follow a path distinct from that of his parents, and each bolstered the other in this quest.

Knox's rapture with things Roman grew steadily. He began to use the rosary, to invoke the saints, to pray to Christ present in the tabernacle, to rejoice when Roman Catholic accretions were added to the Anglican liturgy. Knox formed a circle of fellow students around him who were moving towards an Anglican version of Romanism. He wrote: 'Unconsciously the Papacy came to take a place, wholly undefined and calling urgently for consideration, in the horizon of my mind. I suppose I allowed it to be assumed that I was a Papalist without troubling to scrutinize my own theory of the

Church; this process came later.'[32] Meanwhile he visited Oberammergau for the Passion Play and on the way back with friends visited several places in Belgium. The devotion of the people greatly moved him, especially in Bruges, where he was edified by the constant stream of visitors to the shrine of the Precious Blood. Nothing Roman Catholic, it seemed, was beyond his approving purview.

A moment of farce irrupted into his increasingly earnest Anglo-Catholicism. He obtained a First in his finals for Greats in 1910. He was offered a fellowship at Trinity College next door to Balliol, but was to have a term's leave first. He was to spend the autumn as private tutor to the youthful Harold Macmillan at the family home, Birch Grove, near Haywards Heath in Sussex. The future Prime Minister was preparing to try for an Oxford scholarship. Knox was twenty-two, Macmillan was seventeen, and they immediately established a great rapport. More than sixty years later Macmillan recalled of Knox, 'He was sweet and he influenced me because he was a saint . . . and if you live with a saint, it's quite an experience, especially a humorous saint . . . and he did have a marvellous sense of humour.'[33] Knox by this stage was a proselytizer for Anglo-Catholicism, and soon explained his faith to Macmillan, whom he felt needed spiritual counsel. Harold was immediately drawn to Knox's exposition of Anglo-Catholicism and asked to be taken to a Mass. Harold's mother Nellie found out and was appalled, possibly because she had strong traditional Protestant sympathies. She said that Knox could stay only if he promised never to discuss religion in private with her son. Knox described it as a 'heart-rending and nerve-wracking dispute'. He consulted his spiritual director who encouraged him to stand firm.[34] Knox wrote to Mrs Macmillan, informing her that he would find it very difficult having 'no one with whom to discuss my most vital views at a time when they are particularly effervescent.'[35] Effervescent? The word leaps out at us. Was there an element of self-parody here? Unlikely, but it demonstrates the strength with which Knox held his views and the way his faith would bubble up within him. He had to speak, or burst. The letter had the brash confidence of a

22-year-old Etonian, but it was clearly an unsuitable way for a tutor to be writing to his employer. On 3 November, Nellie told him to leave on the next train, a departure so swift that he had to write afterwards asking for his bicycle and his laundry to be forwarded.

In a recent biography of Harold Macmillan, Charles Williams has concluded that Knox was homosexual and that this was an element in his friendships with Macmillan and others. The evidence cited is mainly an opaque passage by Waugh about schoolboy crushes at Eton. Williams also cites Knox's letter to his sister Winifred about the Macmillan debacle. Knox wrote that he had become extremely fond of Macmillan, and Macmillan fond of him, and that their parting was a wrench.[36] Lord Williams may be right in his conclusions, but the truth is that we simply do not know. He seems to infer a great deal from the ecology of English public school life, and from a single letter. We also need to bear in mind that in the Edwardian era, close male friendships were perfectly common. A single woman of the upper classes could not even go into a restaurant for a meal with a male friend unless a brother, or cousin, was there to chaperone her. Premarital sex between young people of that class was almost impossible because of strong social controls.[37] Male friendships became correspondingly more intense. In any event, Williams believes that Knox was restrained by his adoption of chastity, and that although Knox and Macmillan might have been on the verge of falling in love,

> it was homosexual, but it was not homoerotic ... On the other hand, there is no doubt that Ronnie Knox, whatever the nature of the attachment, was the greatest male figure of influence in Macmillan's early life – certainly very much greater than his father. Through him, Macmillan learnt the Christianity which was to stay with him for the rest of his life.[38]

His expulsion from the Macmillan household had wounded Knox, but if he had lost a pupil, he had gained a friend.

Notes

1   C.H.M. [Charles H. Malden], *Recollections of an Eton Colleger,* pp. 243–4.

2   Drusilla Scott, *A. D. Lindsay: A Biography* (Oxford: Blackwell, 1971), p. 47. Waugh, *RK*, p. 82, says that seventeen of the intake were Etonians, which is the figure given by Knox himself in his contribution to the memorial book for Charles Lister.

3   Julian Huxley, *Memories* (London: Allen and Unwin, 1970), p. 64.

4   Peter Stansky, *Sassoon: The Worlds of Philip and Sybil* (New Haven: Yale University Press, 2003), p. 26. Stansky reports the incident as taking place in Tom Quad, Christchurch, but other sources place the incident in Balliol. Stansky also reports the incident as an example of Grenfell's xenophobia, but given that Sassoon was Jewish, it might equally have contained an element of antisemitism. Both Grenfell and Sassoon had been at Eton.

5   Waugh, *RK*, p. 83.

6   Quoted in Scott, *Lindsay*, p. 47.

7   James Lees-Milne, *Harold Nicolson: A Biography* Vol 1: *1886–1929* (London: Chatto & Windus, 1980), p. 22.

8   *SA*, pp. 48 and 50.

9   Nathaniel Micklem, *The Box and the Puppets 1888–1953* (London: Bles, 1957), p. 34.

10   Christopher Hollis, *The Oxford Union* (London: Evans Brothers, 1965), p. 148.

11   On Caird, see James Lees-Milne, *Harold Nicolson*, p. 20; on WEA/tutorial classes, see Scott, *Lindsay*, pp. 68–9.

12   Chapter by Ronald Knox on '[Lister at] Eton and Balliol, 1905–6' in Lord Ribblesdale, *Charles Lister: Letters and Recollections, with a memoir by his father* (London: Fisher Unwin, 1917), p. 238.

13   Knox, in Ribblesdale, *Lister*, p. 240.

14   *SA*, pp. 48–9.

15   Hollis, *The Oxford Union*, p. 149.

16   Adrian Hastings, *A History of English Christianity 1920–1985* (London: Collins, 1987), p. 81.

17   *SA*, p. 56. See also L. E. (Lawrence) Jones, *An Edwardian Youth* (London: Macmillan, 1956), p. 31.

18   William Davage and Barry Orford, (eds), *Piety and Learning: The Principals of Pusey House 1884–1902* (Oxford: Pusey House, 2002), p. 3.

19   *SA*, p. 58.

20   *SA*, p. 59.

21   Huxley, *Memories*, p. 65.

22   Peter Anson, *The Call of the Cloister: Religious Communities and Kindred Bodies in the Anglican Communion* (London: SPCK, 1964, revised edition), p. 169; Rene Kollar, 'Anglo-Catholicism in the Church

of England, 1895–1913: Abbot Aelred Carlyle and the Monks of Caldey Island', *Harvard Theological Review* 72.2 (1983), p. 205.

23 Anson, *Call of the Cloister*, p. 171.

24 Kollar, 'Anglo-Catholicism in the Church of England', pp. 213–14.

25 *SA*, p. 71.

26 Quoted in Anson, *Call of the Cloister*, pp. 170–1.

27 *SA*, p. 70.

28 Angela Lambert, *Unquiet Souls: The Indian Summer of the British Aristocracy, 1880–1918* (London: Macmillan, 1984), p. 129.

29 Knox on Lister in Ribblesdale, *Charles Lister*, p. 243.

30 Quoted in Nicholas Mosley, *Julian Grenfell: His Life and the Times of his Death 1888–1915* (London: Weidenfeld and Nicolson, 1976), p. 150.

31 Mosley, *Grenfell*, p. 217.

32 *SA*, p. 72–3.

33 Alistair Horne, *Macmillan* Vol 1 *1894–1956* (London: Macmillan, 1988), p. 18, from an interview with Macmillan taped by Horne.

34 See letters to his sister Winifred 29th October and 4th November 1910, KPM.

35 Quoted in Horne, *Macmillan*, p. 19.

36 Ronald Knox to his sister Winifred, 4th November 1910.

37 For the frustrations suffered by Julian Grenfell, see Angela Lambert, *Unquiet Souls*, p. 157.

38 Charles Williams, *Harold Macmillan* (London: Weidenfield and Nicolson, 2009), pp. 22–31, quoting from page 31.

4

Defender of the Faith

Four years of academic studies brought Knox glittering prizes. In 1907 he gained the Hertford scholarship, in 1908 the Craven Scholarship, the Gaisford Prize for Greek verse and the prestigious Ireland prize, awarded by competition among Classics students. In 1910 he won the Chancellor's Prize for Latin verse and topped it all by taking a widely-expected first in his finals. Well before then he had caught the eye of Oxford dons who were keen for him to join their ranks. Knox could have remained at Balliol to teach as a Classics tutor. Instead he accepted an offer from Trinity College, next door, to be Chaplain and Fellow, which opened the way to ordination in the Church of England. We get very little sense of the development of Ronald Knox's vocation to priesthood in the Church of England. Instead it is implicit in his personal discipline, his life of prayer and his visits to Caldey. For example, he spent seven weeks at Caldey in the summer of 1911 before his ordination to the Anglican diaconate and of this time he wrote lyrically:

I passed at Caldey seven weeks of extraordinary happiness and peace. Thinning out carrots in the gardens with a fierce sun beating on my cassock, bathing with the community in recreation on those interminable days of sunshine, standing in a blaze of light at Vespers, or in almost complete darkness at Compline, while the slow cadences of the Divine Office rolled over my head, hurrying out to Matins before the break of dawn along a razor's edge path past the quarry garden – I do not think that ... a theological college could have provided me with more of religious inspiration for my coming ministry. [1]

Knox himself was in no doubt about becoming a priest: 'I wanted, with all my soul, to enter the Anglican ministry.'[2] Yet it was also a vocation within a vocation. He preceded the passage just quoted with these words: 'I had a message ... to return to the old paths and renew the waste places.' By this he meant that he would be a voice in the Church of England, calling for it to live a fuller Catholicism modelled on the Roman Catholic Church.

The Bishop of Oxford agreed that there was no need for him to attend a theological college, nor to pass a year as a deacon in parish work. Instead he was to pursue his own programme of study guided by his own mentors. After being evicted from the Macmillan household, Knox lived for the last few months of 1910 at Pusey House, preparing for ordination. Early in 1911, he moved to Trinity College and continued the preparation there. Knox was due to be ordained deacon at Michaelmas 1911, so until October of that year he had few formal duties in Trinity and was able to devote himself to his ordination studies. His preparation for ordination required him to read widely in theology, a process that he continued during his year as a deacon. Knox did not like what he discovered. From the mid-nineteenth century onwards English biblical studies had been greatly influenced by German scholars, who regarded the Bible as literature, to be analyzed dispassionately and critically like any other book. This move away from a reverential approach had yielded many new insights, but at the price of scepticism regarding any supernatural content.

When Knox joined a group of youngish dons who met regularly for Friday lunch and discussion of theological issues, he found that German scholarship had strongly influenced them. They tended towards a progressive interpretation of theology. He also heard that seven of the group were collaborating on a volume of essays giving a contemporary restatement of Christian belief. Of the seven, five would become bishops; one of them, William Temple, was a future Archbishop of

Canterbury.[3] The book would be published in November 1912 as *Foundations* with the subtitle *A Statement of Christian Belief in Terms of Modern Thought.*[4] In 1912 Knox went again to the monastery at Caldey for most of the summer, like the preceding year. As he prayed and read he found himself brooding about the forthcoming *Foundations*. Gradually he worked out a counter-blast: *Absolute and Abitofhell*, a long pasquinade or lampoon poem written in the manner of Dryden. Knox began by sketching the modernizing tendency in the Church of England:

> So, Freedom reign'd; so Priests, dismayed by naught,
> Thought what they pleas'd and mention'd what they thought . . .
> Till men began for some Account to call,
> What we believ'd, or why believ'd at all?
> The thing was canvass'd, and it seem'd past doubt
> Much we adher'd to we could do without . . .

The poem then moved on to satirize each of the contributors plus two other theologians with liberal tendencies, each person's name being hidden under biblical or classical aliases. William Temple had been known at Rugby as 'the Bull' and so Knox named him Og, after the King of Bashan, an area famous for its bulls. The bustling, well-known Temple was described thus:

> A man so broad, to some he seem'd to be
> Not one, but all Mankind in Effigy:
> Who, brisk in Term, a whirlwind in the Long,
> Did everything by turns, and nothing wrong,
> Bill'd at each Lecture-hall from Thames to Tyne
> As Thinker, Usher, Statesman or Divine.

Knox poked fun at their theological positions, despite the fact that he had not seen the book which was not yet published. He made some shrewd guesses at the positions they would take. B. H. Streeter, for example, wanted a less dogmatic approach to religious belief. He was portrayed by Knox as one who, showing

... suave Politeness, temp'ring bigot Zeal
Corrected 'I believe' to 'One does feel'.[5]

Initially Knox intended to circulate his poem privately, but the
Oxford Magazine persuaded him to allow them to publish it.
That issue of the magazine promptly sold out and had to be
reprinted. The evening of its appearance Knox was astounded
when the President of Trinity, H. E. D. Blakiston, congratulated him at high table in hall. The *Oxford Magazine* was
widely read among the dons. Whether they were believers
themselves or not, they appreciated that the poem not only
questioned the elasticity of liberal theology, but did so in a
witty and elegant way.

After the success of *Absolute and Abitofhell* Knox found
himself hailed as a champion of orthodoxy. Soon the suggestion was made that he should write a book rebutting *Foundations*. After some initial reluctance, Knox concurred and
following a bout of furious writing produced *Some Loose
Stones*, the very title of which was a tilt at *Foundations*. A
book published as a reply to another usually lacks some of the
sparkle of the work it opposes, and despite its occasional
shafts of humour *Some Loose Stones* is no exception.
However, the underlying passion with which Knox wrote still
comes across clearly. He took exception to the way the
various contributors to *Foundations* tended to see faith as
subjectively true rather than objectively true. The component
parts of Christian doctrine were reinterpreted in the light of
the questions, doubts and hesitations of the modern era. It was
assumed that something could be true only if it fitted within
each writer's prior understanding of what a Christian of the
modern period could believe. The test was not whether these
doctrines had been held by the whole Church and elucidated
through the centuries. Here the influence of German theologians on *Foundations* was quite marked, especially the influence of Adolf Harnack (1851–1930). Paul Tillich summed up
Harnack as wanting the Christian message 'free from its
dogmatic captivity' which meant that Harnack distinguished
sharply between 'the gospel of Jesus and the gospel about

Jesus.'[6] To arrive at what he believed to be the real Jesus, Harnack wanted to pare away any doctrinal speculation about him, including Pauline and Johannine interpretations. This minimalizing approach was often discernible in the essays in *Foundations*. Richard Brook on the Bible, for example, saw scripture as the record of how men had found God rather than as the account of God's self-revelation. Indeed, about the latter he sounded rather begrudging: 'Granted even the possibility of the existence of God, there is nothing intrinsically unreasonable in the supposition that He may have revealed Himself.'[7] Brook went on to argue that what mattered was each person's recourse to their own religious experience. The latter could then be tested against the record of scripture and the tradition of the Church. But, replied, Knox, this testing of experience depended upon a Church that taught with authority – which was exactly what Anglicanism lacked.[8] In their essay on Christ, A. E. Rawlinson and Richard Parsons had suggested that eucharistic theology had developed because Christian communities, having experienced Christ's presence through the eucharist, sought to explain their experience. No, replied Knox, eucharistic theology derived from the Church's attempt to understand the words of Christ, 'This is my body, this is my blood.'[9] Of all the essays, however, it was B. H. Streeter on the historic Christ which proved the most controversial. He appended to his essay a lengthy disquisition on the resurrection, carefully making clear that its views were to be attributed to him alone. The emptiness of the tomb was not what mattered, he said, and anyway *if* the tomb was empty a naturalistic explanation could still be adduced. What mattered was that Jesus was an example of resurrection life, possibly having survived the cross in some kind of spiritual state, and able to communicate with his disciples. God might have brought this about by working within the usual forces of nature. The physical body of Jesus might have remained in the tomb.[10] Knox pointed out that this left unexplained the New Testament reports of the empty tomb; overall, the traditional account of the resurrection was the more economical explanation.[11] Knox's riposte caused quite a stir. His own book sold well and generated shoals of correspondence. Streeter criticized him from the pulpit of St Mary the Virgin, the University church.[12]

In the course of *Some Loose Stones* Knox made two broader points which are still relevant in debate on theological issues today. First, he questioned whether the contributors were truly motivated to seek the truth. What mattered to many theological liberals, he said, was not the truth, but what would be considered acceptable to the modern mind. Modern theology, he wrote,

> shows, at times, such a cynical indifference to abstract truth. For we are not concerned, now, to find how we can represent truth most adequately, but how we can represent it most palatably. We ask of a doctrine, not, 'Is it sound?', but, 'Couldn't we possibly manage to do without it?'; not, 'Is it true?', but, 'Can I induce Jones to see it in that light?'[13]

Doctrine was trimmed and diluted, rather than illustrated and explained. Each modern reformulation of doctrine was like money being changed every time you crossed a frontier: a process of devaluation set in, which meant that you got less in return every time.[14] Knox doubted anyway that such reformulations impressed those for whom they were intended. He pleaded that theology 'must still be a complete system or body of dogma ... not a series of attractive propositions, attuned to the outlook and temper of a particular age.'[15] If God offered humankind salvation, then the truth could not be fragmentary. Always, Knox was drawn to truth as an interlocking whole. Here the mind could dwell and explore, within a body of truth that would always be far greater than the greatest mind seeking to understand it. Against the modern attempt to make the truth attractive, he placed the inherent attractiveness of the truth.

Knox's criticism of the minimalist tendency of modern theology was both accurate and not quite fair. Accurate, because he had articulated the often unspoken assumption which haunted liberal theology both then and now: namely, that Christian doctrine should be attuned to the modern mind, not the modern mind attuned to Christian doctrine. As one theologian of our own times has put it, Knox's critique 'has nagged liberal thinkers ever since'.[16] And yet Knox's critique was not quite fair, because theological trimming itself was not what motivated the essayists. They had wanted to find fresh ways to articulate the faith that would make sense to their generation, and, for that matter, to themselves. William Temple pointed out in a long private letter to Knox that he was not asking what an average man would be prepared to swallow. He himself *was* an average man of his day, asking what there was to nourish him.[17]

Knox also protested in *Some Loose Stones* about the omission of the supernatural element from consideration of religious truth.[18] This meant that there was little attempt to understand, for example, what God was doing in and through Christ. It might be possible to seek an account of Jesus that would, following Harnack and others, strip away supposed theological accretions to give a fresh and more human picture. But how would this figure have given hope to humankind? To put the same question differently, how would this Jesus have motivated and inspired his disciples the way he did? Knox understood well that if you excluded any attempt to understand how God was acting in the world, then you impoverished the account you gave of Christ. As the biblical scholar Stephen Neill puts it, 'When Jesus had died, apparently discredited and disillusioned, what was it that made the disciples so sure, in face of all the facts, that he had been right, and that in his death the kingdom of God had actually come?'[19] Jesus could only have inspired and given hope because the first Christians believed that he fulfilled the promises of God. Right from the earliest understanding of Jesus there had been 'theology'. Who Jesus was understood to be was inseparable from the struggle to understand Christ as the revelation of God. And here, said Knox, the guidance of the divinely commissioned Church was essential, as over centuries it sifted out the true and the false.

As an Anglican of Catholic mien, Knox was not bound by

Roman Catholicism's discipline, but many aspects of *Some Loose Stones* seem to reflect ultramontane loyalties. He wrote that 'there are limits defined by authority, within which theorizing is unnecessary and speculation forbidden.'[20] At the time he wrote, the Catholic Church was in the middle of the Modernist controversy. Pope Pius X was seeking to eradicate from the Catholic Church precisely the kind of theology found in *Foundations*. The anti-modernist decree *Lamentabili* of 1907 condemned a long list of modernist opinions, and was soon followed by the encyclical *Pascendi* which argued against modernism and, more ominously, called for vigilance within the Church against such deviations. The resulting anti-modernist oath specifically rejected the idea that dogma should be tailored according to what was suitable for each age and culture. This protected the Catholic Church from theological liberalism's tendency to erode faith by going for ever more radical interpretations; but a heavy price was paid, as scholarship froze in the atmosphere of suspicion. This was conceded at the time by one of those affected. Cuthbert Butler, the impeccably orthodox Abbot of Downside in 1922 wrote to Baron Friedrich von Hügel to explain why he turned away from scholarship:

> Years ago I recognized that these things – Christian origins, New Testament, History of Dogma etc – have been made impossible for a priest, except on the most narrow apologetic lines ... The only freedom in Biblical things and the rest is that of a tram, to go ahead as fast as you like on rails, but if you try to arrive at any station not on the line, you are derailed ... When the Biblical Commission got under way, and the *Lamentabili* and *Pascendi* were issued, I deliberately turned away from all this work – my being made Abbot made it not apparent.[21]

The impact of the modernist crisis on Catholic intellectual life was, says Eamon Duffy, catastrophic.[22] As a very High Church Anglican, Knox was free to be guided by Catholic teaching and to regard the Catholic Church as the interpreter and validator of theology. But Knox was also free to criticize his own tradition, and to reject the leadership of his church where he found it wanting. (We remember, for example, that that 'the bishops' were spoken of at Caldey as if they were a gang of criminals.) Knox never seemed to see this paradox, that he claimed Catholic discipline on the one hand, while on the other he engaged in unbridled criticism of the Church of England. It was, surely, inconsistent to appeal to Roman Catholic-style authority while continuing to live within Anglican-style freedom.

Knox was ordained priest at St Giles, Reading, on 22 September 1912, by the Bishop of Oxford, Charles Gore. His first Mass as an Anglican was at St Mary's, Graham Street (now Bourne Street). This church near Sloane Square was a parish of unalloyed Anglo-Catholic ritual. Its main Sunday service was High Mass. Its décor was firmly Catholic. Even the feast day was significant, for Knox chose the Feast of Our Lady of Ransom, a Roman Catholic devotion. He was laying down a marker that he would be a priest of the most extreme Anglo-Catholic hue. Even within the accommodating framework of the Church of England, Knox sometimes had to search to find a church where he could celebrate Mass. He was lucky in that Oxford itself had many Anglican sisterhoods whose chapels made him welcome. In his own Trinity College chapel he had to be more restrained in ceremonial. But during the university vacations he was free to travel on invitation to parishes, and with his growing renown as the author of *Absolute and Abitofhell* and later of *Some Loose Stones*, Knox received many invitations and became well known in Anglo-Catholic circles. He was particularly sought after as the preacher for special occasions, and within a few years had preached by his own estimation in over fifty to sixty parishes in different parts of England.

One of the chief influences on him at this time was another Anglican priest, Maurice Child. Not everyone warmed to Child. Some found him perfectly charming, others thought him sinister.[23] He was an Anglican priest of strong Catholic conviction. He seemed to have private means and kept a flat

in a fashionable part of London. Child held several curacies
in succession, but these seemed to allow him plenty of time
for other activities, chiefly plotting how to advance the cause
of the Catholic movement in the Church of England. Knox
met Maurice Child through a well-connected mutual friend,
Samuel Gurney. Gurney came from a banking family and the
Norfolk squirearchy; his father had died when he was very
young and his mother had subsequently married Lord Talbot
de Malahide. Gurney had known Knox at Eton and Oxford
and had also become an Anglo-Catholic. In February 1911
Child, Gurney and Knox set up the Society of Saints Peter and
Paul which, through church furnishing, liturgical artefacts and
publishing was intended to align Anglican spirituality with that
of the Roman Catholic Church. According to Eric Kemp, the
three founders

> looked ... to the practice of the Church of Rome in their
> own day. They noticed the pastoral efficiency of the Roman
> methods, the piety inspired among the multitudes by Bene-
> diction, the Rosary, and other such devotions, and they
> argued that since the Church of England was but a branch
> of Western Catholicism any ceremonial innovations should
> be based on the use of the present-day Church of Rome ...
> Their purpose was missionary – the evangelization of
> England by confronting people with the splendour and
> power of Catholic worship.[24]

The Society had Gurney's money behind it, Child's aggressive
marketing ability and the theological acumen of Knox. The
Society caused quite a stir, much of it intentional. It published
liturgical books of all kinds, such as a Missal showing how
the 1662 Communion Service could be made to appear like a
Roman Mass by adding the externals of the Tridentine liturgy.
It sold objects of piety, candlesticks, lamps and crucifixes, as
well as votive candle stands named after Ridley and Latimer,
Anglican bishops who had been burned at the stake at the time
of Queen Mary. Many of their publications advocating
Catholic prayer or liturgical practices were designed to be

provocative, as were their advertisements in the *Church Times*. To goad the bishops, the Society began putting 'Publishers to the Church of England' on its literature.[25]

As an ideological principle, the Society of Saints Peter and Paul adopted the baroque style rather than the gothic style favoured by so many High Church clergy. Gothic implied that the Church of England was reclaiming its pre-Reformation spirituality. Baroque said in effect that even pre-Reformation English spirituality on its own was inadequate, and looked instead to the Counter Reformation for inspiration. N. P. Williams, writing pseudonymously as 'Philoxenus', said in a pamphlet published by the Society in 1917 that the Catholic movement in the Church of England should regard itself

> *not* as a return to the past, but as a *resumption of arrested development*. It is not an attempt to get back to what we were before the Reformation; *it is an attempt to get forward to what we should have been if the Reformation (in its more destructive aspects) had not happened.*[26]

The Society's approach therefore struck at the Church of England's image of itself as a church both Catholic and Reformed, by rejecting the value of the latter. But it also resisted the more moderate mainstream Anglo-Catholicism, particularly those who urged a catholicity consonant with the Book of Common Prayer, or those who sought to resurrect pre-Reformation English liturgical practice.[27] Some of the Anglican papalists were actually dismissive of the more moderate Anglo-Catholics.[28] By his association with this movement Ronald Knox was becoming well-known in Anglo-Catholic circles as an extreme Catholic. It was assumed that he would be a Romanizing presence within Anglo-Catholicism in the ensuing decades.

At Trinity College, he took his work as chaplain and tutor seriously and applied himself assiduously. In addition to being chaplain he shared in the tutorial work for Greats, teaching students in Logic, Homer and Virgil. He also had to help students pass the Divinity Examination, which until 1931 was required of all undergraduates. 'Divvers' followed a very limited and largely unvarying curriculum. It had become an ossified gesture towards making sure that, in addition to their own speciality, students had some Christian understanding. They regarded this requirement as a bore. To encourage them in memorizing the appropriate information, Knox devised mnemonics and a version of the missionary journeys of St Paul, modelled on Snakes and Ladders. In chapel he tried to restrain his preaching so that he did not add too much Roman Catholic doctrine to the mixture. He did not always succeed and was occasionally aware of a frisson of disapproval from college authorities. At the altar he used the words of the Prayer Book Communion service; inaudibly, he added the words of the Latin Missal. Oxford, though, was a very tolerant place. It appreciated interesting people and understood that sometimes an element of notoriety was inseparable from what made a person interesting.

Any chaplain had to be able to socialize with the students, so that he could win their trust and be regarded by them as a source of counsel in times of need. Accordingly Knox could be found bathing and picnicking with students on the Cherwell, or punting with them down the same river. Every Wednesday evening he would be 'at home' dispensing port and bananas to any who dropped in. Knox was also sought out by students from other colleges, by visiting clergy and by theological students. Ecclesiastical gossip was relished, especially at Friday afternoon tea. Waugh says that, 'Ronald usually stood in his soutane leaning on the chimney-piece, pipe in hand, with a lock of hair drooping over his forehead while the party listened to the latest squib and to the gossip from [St Mary's] Graham Street and the Society of SS. Peter and Paul.'[29] Some of the students became his friends and companions. Among them was Harold Macmillan, who had come up to Oxford in 1912, free at last from his mother's supervision. Another was Guy Lawrence, who came from Winchester School where he had achieved eminence despite battling serious illness. At Oxford Lawrence played soccer for the university and was president of the Oxford University

Dramatic Society. For these students and a handful of others, Knox organized vacation reading parties. To them all, Knox conveyed his conviction that only the Catholic movement in the Church of England was capable of bringing the nation to spiritual health. Some of the students served his Mass and came to him for confession.

Early in August 1913 Knox, Sam Gurney, Guy Lawrence and another student from Trinity drove in Gurney's huge Talbot car down to Plymouth, where Maurice Child was curate in charge of St James's Church. They stayed nearby on the edge of Dartmoor. The days were spent bathing and exploring the countryside, the cool evenings were rich in conversation. Over three weekends Knox preached at Evensong each Sunday at St James's. At the back of his mind was criticism, some of it friendly, some of it not, which had been challenging him to clarify his understanding of the Church of England vis-à-vis the Roman Catholic Church. The three sermons he gave were an attempt to do this. It is a measure of a bygone age that, in the middle of the summer holiday, there would be a congregation of 800 people each evening to hear him preach. Knox argued that the Reformation had taken away church administrative power from the papacy and put it in the hands of parliament. Spiritually the Church of England retained its essentials but now power had been abandoned by parliament and accrued to the bishops, who were trying to make all religion fit into a prescribed mould by opposing Anglo-Catholicism. They had no right to do this, and were ignoring the creeping spirit of modernism which was infiltrating the Church. The only move that would protect the Church of England and lead it into the fullness of faith would be corporate reunion with the Roman Catholic Church. In purple prose Knox described the prospect of Anglicans united once more with Rome as like wilful, lost and frightened children stumbling back to their mother. Until such corporate union took place, individual submissions were out of the question.[30] His account of history was tendentious, and again, there was the strange tension in his approach to ecclesial authority. He was encouraging revolt against the bishops of the Church of

England, while simultaneously admiring the authority shown by bishops in the Roman Catholic Church. He also wanted Anglican bishops to allow Anglo-Catholic innovations but to resist those of the liberal modernists. His ecclesiology was quite simply incoherent, and subconsciously, at least, he may have realized this. That August, each Sunday morning he would walk four miles across the moor to celebrate Mass in a little church at Mary Tavy, and as he walked he found, he wrote later, that 'a hideous feeling that none of it was worthwhile sometimes oppressed me.'[31]

The three sermons were a convoluted mixture of trying to reconcile catholicity, state control of the Church, and Petrine ministry. How could Knox's penetrating mind have believed that these incompatible elements amounted to a Church which he could believe in himself and commend to others? The different parts of his argument might have been incommensurable, but overall Knox was articulating a problem increasingly felt by Anglo-Catholics. The older High Church generation had built up a catholic sensibility within the Church of England by appealing to its undivided pre-Reformation past. In art and architecture, in hymnody and in liturgy, and in many other ways, they had created a prayerfulness and a dignity which renewed the Church of England and brought a fresh understanding of the call to holiness.[32] But the more the High Church movement succeeded, the more they faced an implicit question: what was the justification for what they were doing? If they appealed to the Catholic past, this raised the question of why they were not part of the Roman Catholic Church now. If they argued the necessity of the Reformation, this called into question the pre-Reformation Catholicity which they were using as a template. Twenty-five years later Knox, writing as a Catholic, put these and related questions into the mouth of a fictional Oxford don who opposed High Church Anglicans. The don addresses them thus:

> You and your friends are pursuing, as it seems to me, the phantom or ideal of a Church, which has no substance in reality ... You will admire all the errors of Rome, and then

call the Romans schismatics because they will have nothing to do with you. You will despise the Dissenters because they have no bishops, and then you will raise a cry against our bishops, that they have betrayed the Church.[33]

There was a further tension in all this, between local culture and universal catholicity. Within fifty years of Keble's Assize sermon, Anglo-Catholicism had rooted itself in English life. After much opposition it was at last beginning to seem part of the cultural landscape. But to be Catholic was to be part of a universal faith. If Anglo-Catholicism was (as its name implied) inseparable from England and English culture, then its catholicity was compromised.[34] Anglo-Catholicism was facing the questions thrown up by its own success, and it was these that Knox was trying to resolve by arguing for an Anglican catholicity that was real, but impaired. Impaired, because it would be unfulfilled until corporate reunion with Rome. He believed that without that reunion, the Church of England could not truly speak with authority. In all this it was increasingly obvious to others that Knox's spiritual home lay in the Roman Catholic Church. He could not see it himself. Part of the problem here was the sheer suasive power of his own mind. Knox later came to acknowledge that his verbal dexterity and his ability to pick holes in any argument probably made it more difficult for him to accept Catholicism. He recognized that rhetorical gymnastics had left him with an 'extraordinary distaste for the obvious.'[35]

The Society of Saints Peter and Paul wanted Anglican priests and parishes to be as Roman as they wished in faith and practice. But its campaign style contained a strong note of ridicule, even burlesque, about the Church of England. They set out to tweak the tails of the leaders of the Church of England and frequently succeeded. One wonders where Knox's heart was in all this. Sometimes his own father, Bishop Edmund Knox, was proscribing in the diocese of Manchester the very practices that the Society was promoting. Only a few years previously Ronald Knox had written to his father telling him that he was 'thoroughly horrified' at the diversity of extreme Anglo-Catholics. In this letter Ronald commended Percy Dearmer, who was trying to recover the pre-Reformation ritual of the Church in England.[36] This was the very school of thought that he and the others were now depreciating. He seemed to lack perspective on how his thought had developed.

It was not only evangelicals like Bishop Knox who were alarmed at the innovations. Many Anglo-Catholic leaders were also uneasy. Even though papalists like Knox, Child and Gurney were only one element in a highly-variegated Church of England, they were influencing the larger Anglo-Catholic movement. Roman Catholicism still faced an undertow of suspicion in England, where memories of the Spanish Armada and Bloody Mary ran deep and Roman Catholicism was seen as alien to the English way of life. Roger Lloyd recorded how from the diaries of Queen Victoria to the cartoons of *Punch*, Anglo-Catholics were regarded with suspicion: 'Of all the terms of abuse which were flung at them, un-English was the commonest. The taunt was hurled again and again.'[37] Viscount Halifax, the doyen of Anglo-Catholicism, while not exactly a papalist was convinced of the need for reunion with the Roman Catholic Church and threw his weight behind exploratory talks with Roman Catholic leaders, and although these came to nothing, his support gave some respectability to the Romanizing tendency.[38] Knox was concerned only to press forward with the cause of bringing Catholic praxis into the Church of England. Not even the defection of the Caldey community to Rome in 1913 deflected him. Knox and his friends believed that they were the shock troops of a movement that would eventually re-attach the Church of England to the Roman Catholic Church, and that they were already therefore able to live the fullness of Catholic life in anticipation of its consummation, regardless of how other Anglicans felt. This was the campaign which Knox shared with those students who followed his flag. But there was also an element of unreality about this creation of a parallel ecclesiastical universe. One person who noticed this was the 19-year-old Harold Macmillan. Through being part of Knox's circle Macmillan was strongly attracted not only to Anglo-Catholicism but also to the Roman Catholic Church. But he was perceptive enough to notice the contradictions of the stance taken by Knox and those who shared his convictions. On Christmas Day 1913 Macmillan wrote to Sligger Urquhart, himself of course a Catholic, a letter sharing his secret thoughts about the whole imbroglio:

> Guy [Lawrence] is coming to the view which I've long secretly been inclined to, that we are living, in our little Oxford group, in rather an unreal, in some ways rather unhealthy, dreamland ... inclination, convictions of Faith, and other reasons, would urge us to join the Roman Church. But the (humanly speaking) impossibility of helping England from the outside make us feel our duty to stick to the Anglican Church ... I'm in great distress and feel rather lonely here, without sympathy. The family would be awful if it comes to the point ... Pray for us, dear friend, that God may give us strength to choose without fear, or shrinking from suffering the course which our consciences would have us follow.[39]

To be a Roman Catholic and in the national mainstream was still inconceivable and too high a price for Macmillan to contemplate. But the contradictions of papalist Anglicanism hardly seemed to Macmillan to offer a permanent spiritual home.

One of the reasons for Knox's Romanizing was his conviction that the Church needed a source of authority to preserve it from error and to guarantee the authenticity of its message. He believed that the Church had received this kind of authority in its commissioning by God to preach the gospel to the end of the earth, and in the institution of Petrine ministry. This was why Knox always reacted strongly against any blurring of boundaries. Against this he deployed his deadliest weapon, satire. It was soon deployed again. In *Spiritual Aeneid* Knox gives us a wonderful glimpse of how his creative mind was fertilized and worked. Late in the Lent of 1914, he was at Cranborne for a reading party. While waiting for a game of billiards to finish, he perused the library shelves there and renewed his acquaintance with the satire of Jonathan Swift. It struck Knox that here was a wonderful vehicle for conveying an ecclesiastical message, namely a work of literature which, by advancing a spoof argument, would highlight the folly of what it was ostensibly proposing. The idea slept in his subconscious until the end of the Three Hours address which he gave later at St James's Plymouth on Good Friday. Seized with inspiration he sat and typed furiously and by Easter Tuesday *Reunion All Round* was finished. It was published as a pamphlet by the Society of Saints Peter and Paul, with great care taken to reproduce the type and spelling of Swift's day. Even the paper was a brownish cream, to give the impression of antiquity.[40] *Reunion All Round* is written in faux Swiftian prose and purports to demonstrate how religious doctrine could be accommodated in the interests of unity, merging all religions in one undifferentiated soup. Sometimes by *reductio ad absurdum* it sends up those who would bring about pan-religious unity. Sometimes it gently punctures the pretensions of religion itself. And sometimes it mocks English sensibilities. With regard to union with the Roman Catholic Church, for example, the pamphlet declares:

> We have much to look for from the gradual softening Influence of Time, from the Progress of civiliz'd ideas, and the wider Diffusion of Knowledge. And I (for one) am so persuaded of the Mission of Our Church to unite all the Religions of the World under its own Auspices, that I do not hesitate to assert what may seem at first a very distasteful Possibility, namely, that at some time it will be our Duty to consider on what terms we shall accept the Submission even of the *Church of Rome*.

The Catholic Church (it argued) with its ideals of celibacy and martyrdom would surely decrease. Any apparent increase was not due to conversions, for 'the whole cause of Increase is the Immigration of Irishmen.'[41] Once the Catholic Church had been absorbed into the Church of England, the cardinals could be dispersed among the common rooms of Oxford and Cambridge, where they could exercise their talent for intrigue without any effect on the nation. And so on, until at last atheists too were united in the one religion, for that would allow the recognition of 'the Divine Governor of the Universe who exists, yet does not exist, causes Sin yet hates it, hates it yet does not punish it, and promises us in Heaven a Happiness, which we shall not have any Consciousness to enjoy.'[42] Once this had happened the Church of England would have fulfilled its vocation to contain within its ranks all shades of opinion in one instrument of unity. The booklet was well-received, even though in some quarters its humorous proposals were for a moment taken seriously. The *Spectator* pronounced that 'The turn of Swift's sentences is admirably caught'. The Prime Minister, Asquith, had it read aloud to him while he sunbathed on the banks of the Thames at Sutton Courtenay.

In an article in the *Daily Telegraph* in our own times, Christopher Howse has pointed out how Knox's satire has been overtaken by events. Some of the things mentioned by Knox as spoof have come about quite naturally. For example, Knox mused that for Islam to be absorbed it would be necessary to edit the early morning announcement from the minaret that God is Great, for it was shocking to Western minds that muezzins 'should give a pronouncement so public to so controversial a statement.' There was, at the time Howse wrote, controversy in Oxford over an application to broadcast amplified calls to prayer from a mosque. Howse gave some other examples of Knox's satire-turned-reality and concluded: 'As so often with satire, the comic inventions of the author are overtaken by the absurdity of reality.'[43] Howse could have gone further. Knox's spoof rationale for a Church in which atheists could also feel at home reads eerily like the language and argumentation used now by postmodernists. Postmodernism insists that language is an ever-shifting field of references dependent upon the power relations of the culture in question. There are no essences, no fixed definitions or distinctions; such things are inherently impossible, given the fluidity of meaning within language. This approach would say that there is no God outside human inventions of him; however, because the idea of God is so powerful, and because the divine is associated with the ultimate good, religion is still significant and to be analyzed for its effects. So at one and the same time God both does, and does not, exist. As Knox might have said, such an approach assumes that meaning has no meaning. He would probably not have been surprised by such a development. He saw that a Church without an understanding of its own authority to define and explain would dissolve into many interpretations of the truth and lose all sense of identity.

Soon, as Europe drifted haplessly into a terrible war, questions of authority and identity would press hard on Knox and his circle of friends.

Notes

1   *SA*, p. 89.
2   *SA*, p. 86.
3   The other future bishops were Richard Parsons of Hereford, Neville Talbot of Pretoria, Alfred Rawlinson of Derby and Richard Brook of St Edmundsbury and Ipswich. The other two contributors were (Sir) Walter Moberly, active Anglican layman and future Vice-Chancellor of Manchester University; and B. H. Streeter, first Dean then Provost of Queens College, Oxford.
4   B. H. Streeter (ed.), *Foundations: A Statement of Christian Belief in Terms of Modern Thought* (London: Macmillan, 1912). By May 1913 it had been reprinted four times.
5   The poem is reprinted in R. A. Knox, *Essays in Satire* (London: Sheed and Ward, 1928), pp. 81–8, in which Knox identifies each of the seven in footnotes. The book went through three impressions in six months. For Knox's own account of it, see *SA*, pp. 98–102.
6   Paul Tillich, *A History of Christian Thought: From its Judaic and Hellenistic Origins to Existentialism* edited by Carl E. Braaten (New York: Simon and Schuster, 1968), pp. 518–19. William Temple's chapter on The Divinity of Christ also showed German influence, in this case Hegel. See F. A. Iremonger, *William Temple, Archbishop of Canterbury: His Life and Letters* (London: OUP, 1949), p. 162. The last chapter in the book by Moberly on 'God and the Absolute' was also strongly Hegelian.

7   Brook, 'The Bible' in Streeter (ed.), *Foundations*, p. 59.

8   Knox, *Some Loose Stones: Being a Consideration of . . . 'Foundations'* (London: Longmans, 1914), pp. 191–2.

9   Rawlinson and Parsons, 'The Interpretation of the Christ in the New Testament' in Streeter (ed.), *Foundations*, pp. 162–3; Knox, *Some Loose Stones*, pp. 179–80.

10 Streeter, 'The Historic Christ' in Streeter (ed.), *Foundations*, pp. 136–140.

11 Knox, *Some Loose Stones*, pp. 72–82.

12 Ronald Knox to Ellen Knox, 7th March 1914, KPM.

13 Knox, *Some Loose Stones*, p. 9.

14 Knox, *Some Loose Stones*, p. 15.

15 Knox, *Some Loose Stones*, p. 19.

16 Keith Clements, *Lovers of Discord: Twentieth-Century Theological Controversies in England* (London: SCM, 1988), p. 59.

17 Iremonger, *William Temple*, p. 162.

18 Knox, *Some Loose Stones*, Chapter 7 'The Great Omission' and Chapter 8 'Restatement in the Balances: The Incarnation', *passim*. Knox drew attention, for example, to how the book's depiction of Jesus omitted any consideration of his conception and birth. It is not clear whether he knew that some of the contributors doubted the Virgin Birth and the group had agreed to omit all consideration of it. See Iremonger, *Temple*, pp. 156–7.

19 Stephen Neill, *The Interpretation of the New Testament 1861–1986* (second edition, revised by N. T. Wright) (Oxford: OUP, 1988), p. 214. Neill here is offering a critique of the work of Albert Schweitzer, but the point applies to Harnack too.

20 Knox, *Some Loose Stones*, p. x.

21 Quoted in Hastings, *English Christianity*, pp. 152–3.

22 Eamon Duffy, *Saints and Sinners: A History of the Popes* (London: Yale, 2006), p. 357, Folio Society edition.

23 Evelyn Waugh distrusted Child. See Mark Amory, ed., *The Letters of Evelyn Waugh* (London: Weidenfeld and Nicolson, 1981), p. 544. For a favourable depiction of Child, see Desmond Morse-Boycott, *They Shine Like Stars* (London: Skeffington, 1947), pp. 261–2.

24 Eric Kemp, *N. P. Williams* (London: SPCK, 1954), p. 33.

25 A good account of the Society of SS. Peter and Paul can be found in Rodney Warrener and Michael Yelton, *Martin Travers 1886–1948: An Appreciation* (London: Unicorn Press, 2003), pp. 31–44.

26 Quoted in Kemp, *N. P. Williams*, p. 39. Italics in quotation as given. Williams later moved away from some of his more extreme Anglo-Catholic positions.

27 Peter Anson, *Fashions in Church Furnishings*, pp. 316–18.

28 Judith Pinnington, 'Rubric and Spirit: A Diagnostic Reading of Tractarian Worship' in Kenneth Leech and Rowan Williams, eds., *Essays*

Catholic and Radical (London: Bowerdean Press, 1983), pp. 109–12.

29　Waugh, *RK*, p. 124.

30　Ronald Knox, *Naboth's Vineyard* (London: Society of SS. Peter and Paul, 1913), p. 24.

31　*SA*, p. 131.

32　One of the most remarkable examples of this was the revival of the religious life, i.e. life lived under vows in community, either monastic or apostolic. The best overall account is still Peter Anson, *The Call of the Cloister*. More generally, see Geoffrey Rowell, *The Vision Glorious: Themes and Personalities of the Catholic Revival in Anglicanism* (Oxford: Clarendon Press, new edition, 1991).

33　Ronald Knox, *Let Dons Delight* (London: Sheed & Ward, 1958), p. 183.

34　There is a critical survey of these tensions from a Roman Catholic perspective: George Tavard, *The Quest for Catholicity: A Study in Anglicanism* (London: Burns & Oates, 1963), chapter 8, *passim*.

35　*SA*, p. 50.

36　Ronald Knox to Edmund Knox, 6th May 1907, KPM.

37　Roger Lloyd, *The Church of England 1900–1965* (London: SCM, 1966), pp. 125–31, quoting from page 126.

38　Michael Yelton, *Anglican Papalism: A History: 1900–1960* (Norwich: Canterbury Press, in association with The Society of the Faith, 2005), chapter 2.

39　Macmillan to Urquhart, 25 December 1913, Macmillan Papers, Bodleian Library, Box 452 folios 28–31.

40　*SA*, pp. 145–6.

41　*Reunion All Round* is reprinted in *Essays in Satire*, quoting here from pp. 70 and 72. I have modernized the spellings.

42　*Essays in Satire*, p. 76.

43　Christopher Howse, 'When Islam and the C of E Unite' *Daily Telegraph*, 16 February 2008, p. 27.

5

The Turning Point

In 1914 England luxuriated in a golden summer. As the Trinity term ended and the university went down, Ronald Knox was looking forward to a reading party in August with several undergraduates. It was to be held at More Hall near Stroud in Gloucestershire, the home of a small Anglican religious community called the Brothers of the Common Life. He anticipated three weeks of reading, companionship, laughter and celebrating a daily Mass. Instead, rising tension in Europe saw a British ultimatum to Germany expire on 4 August. The nations were at war. His companions began to enlist in Kitchener's army. There was to be no reading party. Instead Knox found himself on solitary retreat at More Hall, brooding on the war, taking long lonely walks over the Cotswold hills. Later, as he read the first casualty lists he had some inkling of the slaughter that lay ahead. The numbers of dead were still small, but these were for him 'days of overpowering depression and nightmare anticipation'.[1] In September he wrote to Sligger Urquhart that he wanted to weep because so many beloved friends and students were enlisting in the New Army in preparation for warfare. He feared for their safety and well-being.[2] At that time the army was still composed of recruits rather than conscripts, but patriotism, and the social pressure to step forward meant that many of the young people in his circle did not hesitate.

In September 1914 he went back to Trinity College to take up his duties as Chaplain and Fellow. Reminders of the war were all around. Student numbers were severely depleted as undergraduates and the younger dons volunteered to join the army. Trinity College itself had only one-third of its normal complement of students and staff. Disconsolate at the sudden quietness of Oxford, Knox tried to keep himself busy. Between September 1914 and May 1915 he made at least eleven visits to friends and students in military camps in southern England. He was still in demand as the preacher for a special occasion, but his many engagements also hint at a desire to keep despondency at bay by burying himself in busyness. For example, on 28 September he preached in York. The following day he preached again 220 miles away in Southampton. In Holy Week 1915 he gave a course of sermons at two of London's most fashionable Anglo-Catholic churches, All Saints, Margaret Street and St Mary's, Graham Street, speeding from one to the other by taxi.

By the spring of 1915 the carnage was increasing. The Allied and German forces faced each other across the Western front in Belgium and northern France, their respective lines almost impenetrable. Any attempt to move forward brought terrible casualties. On 22 April at the second battle of Ypres the Germans tried to break through the British lines by using chlorine gas for the first time on the Western front. In this battle alone the British suffered over 59,000 casualties.[3] By then Knox was feeling utterly disconsolate in an Oxford echoing with emptiness. Trinity College had only forty students, and several of those were expecting commissions at any moment. He wrote to his father saying that 'a cloud of depression' was hanging over Oxford.[4]

He obtained leave of absence from Trinity College, so that he might teach classics at Shrewsbury School in Shropshire. This allowed one of their junior masters to sign up for the forces. It took Knox away from the melancholy reminders around him in Oxford, and gave him a proxy contribution to the war effort. He brought to the teaching all his usual inventiveness, creating games and puzzles to encourage the boys to learn. Inwardly he found his soul slowly detaching itself from its Anglican moorings. He attended the early morning Sunday communion, but rarely celebrated the eucharist himself. He also went to the main services in the school chapel along with the rest of the school. He recognized much that was good in the worship there. But Church of England public school worship now revealed to him his growing alienation from the church of his birth:

> [T]he feeling which the services chiefly inspired in me was one of profound melancholy; I was a mere spectator, cut off from the religion around me by some mysterious self-imprisonment of the conscience, I could not pray in chapel, I could only watch people pray and rejoice that they were doing it.[5]

Knox's interior desolation matched the darkening of the public mood in Britain as the country increasingly mobilized towards the war effort. By the end of 1915, 2,466,000 men had enlisted in the army; even so, more were required, and in January 1916 conscription replaced enlistment. Civilians were increasingly drawn into the war effort, particularly for the production of munitions. In May 1915, Lloyd George was put at the head of a newly-created Ministry of Munitions. Within the next twelve months, annual production of artillery guns rose from 90 to 3,200.[6] At the same time, civilians began to feel that they too were targets, as Zeppelins bombed British cities and U-boats sank merchant shipping. Samuel Hynes has pinpointed mid-1915 as the time Britain began to realize that the world would be changed irrevocably by the war: 'A mood, not quite of disillusionment, but of loss begins here ... Loss is the great theme of this war, not victory, not defeat but simply *loss*.'[7]

The war burrowed deeply into Knox's consciousness. He was horrified to hear of the death of Fr Basil Maturin who drowned when the liner *Lusitania* was torpedoed by a U-boat off the coast of Ireland on 7 May 1915. Maturin was Catholic chaplain at Oxford University. He had been received into the Catholic Church after having been a member of an Anglican religious community, the Society of St John the Evangelist at Cowley, where Knox had gone for confession during his time as an undergraduate. Maturin remained calm as the ship sank, giving absolution to several passengers and handing a child into a lifeboat with the words, 'Find its mother'. When his body was washed ashore in Ballycotton Bay, County Cork, it was found without a lifebelt, leading to speculation that he had refused one as there were not enough to go around.[8] Knox repeatedly found himself visualizing Maturin 'as he moved fearlessly to and fro in those last moments on the Lusitania'.[9]

A week or so after Maturin's death, Guy Lawrence came to consult Knox at Shrewsbury. Lawrence belonged to the circle of students who gravitated around Knox at Oxford and was especially dear to him. As a Trinity student, Lawrence was exposed to Knox's Anglican style of Catholicism – and also exposed to Knox's doubts about the spiritual vitality of the Church of England. Lawrence had enlisted as soon as war broke out, and was now a 22-year-old lieutenant in the South Staffs Regiment. He knew that he would soon see active combat in a bloody war in which he might be killed. He came to seek Knox's counsel. Should he, or should he not, abandon the Church of England and become a Roman Catholic? Knox himself was facing growing doubts about Anglicanism. As Knox and Lawrence sat in front of the fireplace in his room at Shrewsbury, the sputtering fire gave them little warmth. It seemed to symbolize how little comfort he and Lawrence could draw from their ancestral faith at this crucial time. Knox admitted to Lawrence his uncertainty about the Church of England. The most positive thing he could find to say about their church was that it might set its house in order after the war. Lawrence, however, wanted to know what spiritual consolation the Church of England could give him, considering that he might soon be killed in action. Should he join the Catholic Church instead? Knox, already uncertain about his own position, prevaricated: 'I told him I could not advise him, except (of course) to follow his own conscience.' Knox also suggested that Lawrence consult Harold Macmillan, another of their circle, who was asking the same questions.[10]

By the end of that month, Knox's spiritual vacuum had become inner turmoil. In his own phrase, he had seen a ghost. His brother Wilfred was ordained to the Anglican priesthood and on 26 May 1915 said his first Mass. It should have been an occasion of unalloyed joy for Ronald. He was particularly close to Wilfred – they had shared the exile of their uncle's home when the family was split up after their mother's death. They had gone to the same preparatory school. Moreover, Wilfred's first Mass was at Ronald's favourite London church St Mary's, Graham Street. Ronald Knox had preached there several times on special occasions and indeed it was here that he himself had said his first Mass as an Anglican priest in 1912. But now, as he watched Wilfred, Ronald suddenly felt the ground fall away beneath his feet. He doubted whether the Church of England was really part of the wider Catholic Church. Worse, the very external elements that had been proof to him of Anglican catholicity seemed to mock him and increase his doubts. He found himself thinking that if Anglican claims were false,

> then neither he nor I was a priest, nor was this the mass, nor was the host the Saving Host; the accessories of the service – the bright vestments, the fresh flowers, the mysterious candle-light, were all settings to a sham jewel; we had been trapped, deceived, betrayed into thinking it all worthwhile ...[11]

As the service ended, far from being in a holy frame of mind, he found himself silently cursing Henry VIII, the progenitor of the English reformation.

At first glance, Knox's agonizing may seem curiously detached from the ferocious combat and terrible suffering of the First World War. The trigger to his doubts was a pioneering event in ecumenism. In 1913 some sixty missionaries working in East Africa met at Kikuyu in Kenya to explore how they could work more cooperatively. They represented the Anglican dioceses of Mombasa and Uganda, the Church of Scotland, the Methodist Church, and the interdenominational Africa Inland Mission. They drafted a scheme for greater cooperation in missionary activity through a loose confederation. At the end of the conference the Bishop of Mombasa celebrated a united communion service in the Presbyterian church at Kikuyu.[12] This episcopally sanctioned act of inter-communion infuriated Anglo-Catholics. Their position was the same as that of the Roman Catholic Church: eucharistic communion should reflect a united faith. Communion together expressed the unity of those who were already in agreement. Intercommunion was an oxymoron. If the eucharist signified unity in faith, how could those who were disunited share communion?

After the Kikuyu conference, Catholic-minded Anglicans protested to the Archbishop of Canterbury about the united communion service. The Archbishop of Canterbury, Randall Davidson, referred the matter to a committee of bishops whose report was released at Easter 1915. The committee, while ostensibly not passing judgement on the united commu-nion, concluded that it should not be regarded as a precedent. Knox was scornful of what he regarded as theological prevar-ication. He lampooned the committee's adjudication. The committee had concluded, he said, that 'the service at Kikuyu was eminently pleasing to God, and must on no account be repeated.'[13] He wrote that the report came out in a 'hole-and-corner way, in war time ... behind the barrage of a world's artillery.'[14] In retrospect it is clear that Knox and his party were exaggerating the significance of what was essentially a small affair. Roger Lloyd concluded sometimes that Anglo-Catholics seemed happiest if there *was* a challenge to their faith and practice from the Church of England authorities: 'If no true crisis existed at any particular moment they adroitly magnified and publicized some trivial incident, and then dealt with it at the tops of their voices until it had the artificial life of the rushing, raving crisis in which their souls delighted.'[15] But the fact is that the war had sharpened Knox's spiritual dilemma. Could doctrinal truth be present in a state church which seemed concerned more with dampening controversy than affirming the ancient faith?

Although it burst out now, the doubt had been growing in his mind for months. Knox found himself advising soldiers like Guy Lawrence who were facing the possibility of death or serious injury. These were men of Anglo-Catholic conviction, but in the armed services they found little Catholic sensibility among the chaplains. These men from Knox's circle wanted to prepare themselves spiritually. They sought a sacramental strengthening: confession, communion, and in the event of grave injury, anointing. In the army they encountered chaplains who came from other streams of Anglican tradition. Many of the chaplains did not believe in sacramental absolution or anointing. Some of the chaplains would have preferred a parade service to a celebration of the eucharist. Matters were not helped by restrictions which prevented Church of England chaplains from going to the front line. Roman Catholic chaplains by contrast were frequently seen sharing the rigours of troops under fire. In general there was considerable criticism from serving soldiers of the Anglican chaplains' inability to communicate.[16]

Two days after Knox was seized with doubt at his brother's first eucharist, Lawrence was seized with equal certainty about Catholicism. He went to the Jesuit Church at Mayfair in London. Within an hour he was conditionally baptized, received into the Catholic Church and made his first confession. The speed of the reception suggests that the priest understood that Lawrence might die in the war. It also suggests an acceptance that Lawrence was already well formed in the faith. Lawrence wrote to Knox:

> I know I'm happy and I only long for you to be happy with me too. Come and be happy. Harold [Macmillan] will, I think, follow very soon ... You've been and still are my best friend, Ron: there is no shadow between you and me.[17]

Lawrence went to see Harold Macmillan that afternoon. His faith in Macmillan's conversion was misplaced. Macmillan was strongly attracted to the Catholic Church, but decided to remain Anglican. Prompted no doubt by Lawrence's conversion, Macmillan wrote afterwards to Knox: 'I'm not going to "Pope" until after the war (if I'm alive).' He cited the objections of his family, and the turbulent state of his mind.[18]

Despite the clear implication that he would become Catholic, the future prime minister stayed an Anglican. In his heart of hearts he knew that to take the step of becoming a Catholic would doom his hopes for a glittering political career. At that time for a Catholic – or a Jew – there were limited possibilities of political advancement. There were doors in society and politics that would be closed to him as a Catholic. One historian considers that in England around 1900 'Catholics were still treated with suspicion and reserve; and their whole ethos and lifestyle was considered as un-English.'[19] Although this prejudice diminished after the war, even in the 1930s a loyal address from the Catholic Bishops of England and Wales was not accepted by Buckingham Palace.[20] The social divisions of English Catholicism in the first few decades of the twentieth century would also have been an obstacle for a budding Conservative politician. The English Catholic upper class was small and for historic reasons it tended to prize unobtrusiveness. In the cities there were substantial segments of working-class Catholics, but before the First World War these tended to vote Liberal and after the war, for Labour.

This marginalization of Catholics was one of the things that Knox would have to face if he left the Church of England and became a Catholic himself. Shaken by his experience of doubt that May, he returned to Shrewsbury to try to discern which way his future should lie. He found it increasingly hard to minister as an Anglican priest. It felt hollow to him. For the rest of 1915 Knox fulfilled engagements to which he had committed himself. He celebrated the eucharist and led a retreat at Oxford, although he found hearing confessions 'extraordinarily difficult' because he had begun to doubt the reality of the sacramental absolution that he bestowed. However, he persevered for a time, arguing to himself that feelings were a notoriously unsafe guide to religious truth.[21]

In this spirit, during the long vacation, he paid a visit to Viscount Halifax at Hickleton in Yorkshire. The 76-year-old Halifax was one of the moving and guiding forces behind the Anglo-Catholic movement in England. He listened gravely and a little sadly to Knox and counselled careful reflection.

Surely he could serve Anglican-Catholic unity more effectively if he stayed in the Church of England? More significant for Knox was a chance encounter with a fellow guest, Fr Cyril Martindale. Martindale was a Jesuit priest and writer. Knox poured out his doubts about the Church of England to Martindale and asked about the possibility of being received. Martindale, to Knox's shock, replied that Knox could not possibly be received in that negative frame of mind. He needed to be positive about the Catholic Church rather than negative about the Church of England.[22] Knox reduced his activities as a priest to a minimum. In September 1915 he preached as an Anglican for the last time. He ceased to hear confessions. He also told his father about his now deep and abiding attraction to Rome. Edmund Knox had been Bishop of Manchester since 1903. He was as much a convinced Evangelical as his son was a convinced Catholic. The news distressed his father, who clung to the hope that Ronald could still be dissuaded, and recommended a number of books to him that were critical of the Catholic position. Ronald dutifully read them but was unconvinced.

In response to pleas from Shrewsbury, Ronald Knox continued to teach there until the end of 1916, but it was a lonely year. He found that because he was trapped in a spiritual vacuum, the wells of inspiration had dried up. He who had often written or preached about the faith with great confidence now had nothing to say. He had foresworn preaching. His friends and students in the army were posted overseas, so he could not even visit them in their regimental camps. Like Newman at Littlemore, this was a time when he could move neither forward nor back. It was also a time of spiritual aridity. In the summer of 1916 he left Shrewsbury and joined the staff of the War Office where he was assigned a role in studying the newspapers of neutral countries in order to trace the influence of enemy propaganda. The Christmas of 1916 with his father and stepmother at Bishopscourt in Manchester was a sombre one. Ronald and his father could not avoid the subject of Roman Catholicism, and their argument was so painful that it was pursued at times through notes left on the hall table. Waugh says that 'Ronald explained his position to his father, and they parted in despair of reconciliation.'[23]

Edmund Knox felt that he could not let his son go without a struggle, and wrote to him several times in early 1917 attempting to dissuade him. Ronald told him that he was drawn by the Catholic Church's faith in its divine commissioning. His father replied that if the Catholic Church was what his son believed it to be, how was it that many honest and devout people for the last four centuries had escaped its attraction? Protestantism, he added, was able to accommodate an inquiring mind while still teaching authoritatively, because it drew on 'the tested spiritual experience of the Church of God.'[24] Bishop Knox conceded that his son would object to Protestantism's 'variety of interpretation, the want of definitions, the uncertainty'. But truth was 'not what we are required by authority to believe, but what a full knowledge of the facts compels us to believe or ... inclines our will to believe. Authority may compel assent, but it never does in fact produce conviction.'[25]

There was an emotional argument here as well as a rational one. Edmund Knox feared that if his son became a Catholic, his career would be over and his talents would be wasted. Thus in the first letter Edmund warned Ronald that submission to Rome would mean 'The burying of your talent. That talent has been conspicuously the gift of exercising religious influence on young men of education ... As you are now, that force is arrested.' He pointed out that Ronald 'by sheer force of character and brains' had held his own in a circle of some of the most brilliant young men of his era, 'without their advantages of birth and position'. He added a little later: 'Honestly I look upon the Roman priesthood as the grave of that talent which is specially yours'.[26] The second letter ended with him expressing his fear that Ronald would one day wake 'out of a hypnotic trance' to find that his career, with all its potential, had been wrecked by following a phantasm.[27] In March he ended yet another letter asking bluntly: 'To my mind the question is this: Are you making the right use of your life?'[28] He occasionally resorted to anti-Catholic stereotypes, writing for example, that a Catholic priest 'ceases to voice his own convictions, he is simply the mouthpiece of a creed'. True Englishmen preferred liberty to Roman oppression, and anyway, it was chiefly the uneducated who were Catholic: 'Romanism will never be the faith of more than a coterie in the educated circles. Among the uneducated it never has got or will get far beyond the Irish.'[29]

In one respect, Bishop Knox was right. It was precisely Protestantism's inability to speak with an authoritative voice that had increasingly troubled his son. Hitherto Ronald Knox had believed that Anglicanism had its place within the broader Catholic tradition, and would eventually be re-absorbed back into the Catholic Church. From mid-1915 onwards he came to see that this was a chimera. If he was to accept this, he had to acknowledge also that he could no longer serve in a national church, with all the privileges and opportunities available to a minister of the Church of England. These advantages would cease. When he drew up a list of reasons for and against becoming a Catholic, the list contained little doctrine but much about how his place in society would change. Evelyn Waugh wrote defensively that the list was intended 'to dispose of the selfish and frivolous elements that might affect a decision.' This rather missed the point that these changes would greatly influence Knox's day-to-day life and would flow ineluctably from a change in what he believed.[30]

Knox could no longer believe what he once believed about the Church of England and its place in the nation. The war challenged some of his most deeply-held beliefs through making him ask what, in all honesty, he could say to men who were going to the front. In this he shared the general soul-searching which left the nation profoundly changed. Knox could not be immune to this shaking of the foundations as more and more of those he loved were killed. He wrote that during this time: 'I could hardly read a paper or open a post without a fresh stab that threatened to shake my whole faith to its roots.'[31] Even for someone of strong faith like himself, the evil of warfare and its slaughter left him wondering whether God was a reality or an illusion. Many others around him were asking the same question. This armageddon took some deeper into faith while for others the sights, sounds and smells of slaughter destroyed any belief they had in God. One of the latter was Arthur Graeme West, who was probably known to Knox. West was a member of Knox's old college, Balliol, next door to Trinity where Knox was now chaplain. West's *Diary of a Dead Officer* charted his growing doubts about the war, patriotism and religion itself. In August 1916 he wrote: 'I now find myself disbelieving utterly in Christianity as a religion, or even in Christ as an actual figure. I seem to have become harder, more ferocious in nature ... I loathe and scorn all emotionalism and religious feeling.'[32] Siegfried Sassoon, who was making a name for himself as a poet, also found himself disillusioned on the Western front. In December 1915 he wrote a poem 'Prince of Wounds' which ended:

> Have we the strength to strive alone
> Who can no longer worship Christ?
> Is He a God of wood and stone,
> While those who served him writhe and moan,
> On warfare's altar sacrificed?

He omitted the poem from published collections of his verse, perhaps fearing that its implied agnosticism would ignite a furious reaction. In April 1916 he again used a Christian theme in a way guaranteed to shock many readers. His poem 'Stand-to: Good Friday Morning' depicts a bone-weary soldier coming off duty and musing:

> O Jesus, send me a wound today,
> And I'll believe in Your bread and wine,
> And get my bloody old sins washed white!

Sassoon sets up an ironic contrast between the implied picture of Christ, wounded on the cross, and the solder wanting a 'Blighty wound' that will take him back to safety and rest in England. The irreverence, and the message that this is not a holy war, emerges even more clearly in a poem written in October 1916, entitled 'They'. This poem portrays a bishop telling soldiers that they are serving in a just war against the anti-Christ. The soldiers reply that the war has indeed changed them, but it is not a conversion of which they speak: they are now maimed, blinded, syphilitic. As the war went on Sassoon's mood darkened. In February 1917 he described God as 'a cruel buffoon, who skulks around somewhere at the Base with tipsy priests to serve him.'[33] In July that year Sassoon risked court-martial by refusing to rejoin his battalion as an act of protest against the war. Thirty years later Sassoon would cross paths with Knox. Their friendship would help him come to a very different perspective about God and Christian faith.

Just as the war brought some to atheism, it brought others back to their Christian inheritance. The poet Wilfred Owen's relationship with Christian faith was hardly unquestioning. But of his work as an officer in July 1918 he wrote in a letter to Osbert Sitwell that

> For fourteen hours yesterday I was at work – teaching Christ to lift his cross by numbers, and how to adjust his crown, and not to imagine he thirst until the last halt. I attended his supper to see that there were no complaints; and inspected his feet that they should be worthy of the nails. I see to it that he is dumb and stands at attention before his accusers. With a piece of silver I buy him every day, and with maps I make him familiar with the topography of Golgotha.[34]

Owen found in the story of Christ the words and images in which he could express the pain and powerlessness of men, including himself, caught up in vast forces against which they could do nothing and were hurried to destruction.

In a more pointed way this was the response of Knox and his circle when they turned to Christ and Catholic Christianity. Here they could find spiritual nourishment in a dark time, because the Catholic Church offered clear teaching and its own corporate certainty of belief. Sometimes that corporate

Catholicity was visibly displayed, as on 8 May 1915 at Aubers Ridge when 550 men of the 2nd Battalion of the Royal Munster Fusiliers formed up in companies in front of their chaplain, Fr Francis Gleeson, who was on horseback. He gave them general absolution. The following day more than half of them were dead. This kind of Catholicism was not a faith that was tied to a narrow nationalism – indeed, many in the enemy trenches would have been Catholic as well. Rather, in their turn to Catholicism the soldier friends of Knox and others like them demonstrated a belief that even in a terrible war, the individual soul still mattered. In this war there was often no time even to bury the dead. Those advancing to the front sometimes found themselves slithering over a mixture of mud and bodies. In the face of this degradation, incarnational religion was a quiet act of defiance. To believe that God in Christ came in and through a human body was at least subconsciously to resist the dehumanizing force of the war. To seek sacramental consolation gave hope, but it also asserted that each person still mattered, and that one's choices and dispositions still found significance in and through Christ.

Knox clung to this as more and more of those near and dear to him went to their death. His Eton and Balliol contemporary Julian Grenfell was wounded at the battle of Ypres in 1915. Knox had often visited the Grenfell family home at Taplow Court in Buckinghamshire. Julian died of his wounds in a military hospital at Boulogne. A few days before his death he and his parents Lord and Lady Desborough received communion together at his bedside from a visiting Anglican chaplain, a sign, perhaps, of Knox's influence on Julian. Julian's brother Billy went back to the trenches after the funeral and his family never saw him again. Two months later he was killed leading a charge near where Julian had been wounded. Billy's body was never found.[35] There were many others whose deaths followed: Edward Horner, Guy Lawrence, Charles Lister, Patrick Shaw-Stewart among them. The social class which provided most officers was precisely the class which suffered the heaviest casualties. Overall one in eight of the men who served in Britain's armed forces was killed. The death rate among those who had been at Oxford or Cambridge was double that at one in four, reflecting the greater danger to which officers were exposed. The historian whose research provided these figures commented that the mortality rate among the elite 'helps to explain why contemporaries wrote repeatedly that a whole generation of the young fell in France and Flanders.'[36]

The bloodbath of the war and the sheer irrationality of it ended the widespread belief of the era that history was now a story of progress, in which a basically rational humankind would increasingly harness its innate abilities. In this sense the war was a *caesura*. The challenge of the war left a heritage of cultural dislocation in which the dominant notes were alienation, loss, uncertainty or even cynicism. According to Samuel Hynes all the leading figures in English literature 'entered the post-war world with the same sense of radical disconnection from a dead, dishonest past'.[37] Knox and his circle were shaken too, but for them the response was to move not into doubt but deeper into faith, through seeking the security of community. They were drawn to the Catholic Church through its unbroken history and its teaching authority. Knox was not immune to the questioning brought by the war, but he was less vulnerable to its corroding doubts because he had never subscribed to the liberal view of history. He was always sceptical about the claims made for the unfettered human mind. As we saw in *Some Lost Stones,* Knox believed that human reason was best exercised within a tradition and a community. These would guide inquiry and offer a process of discernment which would help sift the true from the false, the transient from the eternal. Even so, Knox had to change too. As Evelyn Waugh put it many years later, the war jolted Knox into realizing that 'verbal card-castles so delicately built in the Trinity common-room did not provide spiritual defence in the battle-fields where his friends were falling daily.'[38]

We get a glimpse of the process in Knox's mind from the pamphlet *The Essentials of Spiritual Unity* (1918). He began this pamphlet as an Anglican in 1915 and finished it in

September 1917, just before he was received into the Catholic Church. It is a rather dry work, advancing by logical syllogisms. Knox argues in Thomist style that neither scripture nor the councils of the Church are enough to guarantee fidelity to the truth. This requires a divinely ordained Church with a centralized leadership on which God bestows a special grace, ensuring that when it comes to the essentials of the faith the Church will never be led astray.[39]

Knox followed the logic of his own argument. In June 1917 he replied to an inquiry from Trinity College, Oxford, where he was still a fellow, to say that he would not be seeking re-election to his fellowship. He dreaded telling his father that his mind was made up, and before visiting him in August wrote: 'I'm afraid you must look forward to seeing me with something like pain, considering the direction my mind is now set in; but you will believe too, that if I could help it – well, there isn't any way to finish the sentence.'[40]

On 8 September he took time off from his War Office work to go on retreat with the Benedictines at Farnborough Abbey in Hampshire. The big, well-established Benedictine abbeys at Downside and Ampleforth were soberly designed bastions of English gentility. Farnborough, by contrast, was built in 1888 through the initiative of the Empress Eugénie who wanted a mausoleum to enshrine the tombs of her husband, Napoleon III, her son the Prince Imperial, and ultimately, herself. The abbey belonged to the Solesmes congregation and indeed most of the monks were French. By 1917 only the older monks were in residence, because those of military service age had been called up under French law.[41] Knox was advised to go to Farnborough precisely because as a community with strong French links it was above English religious polemics. Knox already acknowledged to himself 'that what I contemplated would cut me off from the past – the official religion of England . . . the world of school and university, of the worship that hallows national, civic, and municipal life.'[42] To the losses he knew through the war, he added the loss of a way of life in which his faith could meld easily and unthinkingly with his national identity.

There was no special course of instruction for him at Farnborough. The monks and Knox himself seem to have assumed
that he was well formed in the Catholic faith. He read and
prayed, and asked some questions of the guestmaster to make
sure that he understood correctly certain aspects of Catholic
teaching. On 22 September, Abbot Fernand Cabrol of Farnborough received him into the Catholic Church. Letters and
telegrams of congratulation arrived, and his arrival was
reported in the Catholic press. His father wrote, briefly and
poignantly expressing his pain but wishing his son well. Knox
returned to London, to the War Office, and to take up for a
short time the life of a Catholic layman.

Knox sought sure ground, and he found it. Nearly a century
later many will find his quest for authority rather baffling.
Even the Catholic perspective has shifted. The Second Vatican
Council ushered in an era where the self-images of the Church
changed. The Catholic Church in Knox's era was strong on
images of itself as teacher and judge. It was also the high point
of a monarchical style of papacy. Today the Catholic Church
is more governed by images of itself as evangeliser, servant,
pilgrim people, sacrament, prophet. Yet the Church still sets
great store by its ability to speak authoritatively. The *Catechism of the Catholic Church* says that

> The mission of the Magisterium is linked to the definitive
> nature of the covenant established by God with his people
> in Christ. It is this Magisterium's task to preserve God's
> people from deviations and defections and to guarantee
> them the objective possibility of professing the true faith
> without error.[43]

This confidence in the teaching office of the Catholic Church
was part of its attraction to Knox. Today there is considerable
suspicion of authority in Western culture, with authority
almost automatically assumed to be oppressive. But as the
travails of the Anglican Communion have shown, without
authority a Church can fall apart. Authority can be an instru-

ment of service, through enabling and protecting communion. This brings the local church into a shared identity with the universal Church, creating a sense of community which allows believers to recognize one another all over the world. It also helps balance the Church's response to the needs of the present moment with its fidelity to tradition. Too little authority means that things fall apart. Too much means that creativity is stifled. We ought to note, too, that later in life Knox had a realist understanding of the role of the papacy. To an inquirer he once wrote:

> It is not as if [the papacy] receives a kind of inspiration, like the prophets; it enjoys the negative privilege of not going wrong . . .
>
> And because we are accustomed to living in a commonwealth, [God] has given us a kind of sacramental commonwealth; fallible men are the outward and visible sign of it, but he makes use of them for his own supernatural purposes. In matters of policy or discipline these fallible men will often go wrong; at least, they will fall short of the ideal. But because the message of salvation is indispensable . . . God will not allow the fallibility of his human agents to take effect where a solemn definition of Christian truth is concerned.[44]

In what sense was Knox's reception into the Catholic Church a conversion? In recent decades there has been caution about using the word 'convert' to describe new Catholics received from other churches. Conversion properly refers to movement from one faith to another. Knox was always christocentric, and so strictly speaking this was hardly a conversion. Yet it was a *metanoia*, a turning-point in which Knox met Christ afresh and renewed his self-offering. For all his high moral seriousness, until September 1917 there had been a frivolous side to Knox. He and others like him in Anglican Papalism delighted in shocking their fellow Anglicans by adopting the most ultramontane stance that they could. The church furniture they provided, the style of vestments they adopted, the liturgy they practised, were all as ultramontane as they could make them.[45] Sometimes this toppled over into a posturing that was too self-conscious for its own good. This fascination with externals played into the more general Anglo-Catholic fondness for aesthetics. Anglo-Catholics were determined to make the setting of their Masses as perfect as possible. At its best this movement brought the beauty of holiness to slum parishes in England, and elevated the souls of the inhabitants through the splendour of the worship. At its worst, this became a fussy emphasis on form at the expense of content. Perhaps some Anglo-Catholics hoped that the power of the externals would convey the authority of the Church. They felt that Anglican doctrine and teaching was weakened by the absence of a sense of authority.

As part of his search for authority, Knox had come to doubt that he was really a priest. What are we to make today of Knox's anxiety over the validity of Anglican orders? On the one hand, Catholic hesitation about Anglican apostolic ministry has turned out to be prudent. Ordained ministry is just one of the Christian doctrines on which there is a wide variety of interpretation within Anglicanism. In 1950 Knox wrote: 'In the Church of England you could say what you like, and nobody took action – the merest suggestion of a heresy hunt was enough to bring out public opinion in arms.'[46] We may note that nothing has changed. Some would call it freedom of conscience, others might call it incoherence. On the other hand, today's perspective finds it hard to begin where Knox was beginning. Catholic-minded people do indeed want true, valid and real sacraments, just as Guy Lawrence sought when he went out to war. It is Catholic belief that in the sacraments we find Christ, woven into the rhythm of our living in an irreplaceable way. But in our more ecumenical age we are more open to respecting anyone whose life is a shining Christian presence in our world. Apostolic ministry is essential for the fullness of Christian life, but the question on the lips of people is often that of the Greeks who approached Philip in Jerusalem saying, 'Sir, we wish to see Jesus' (John 12.21). Later in life Knox himself approached the question of

Anglican sacraments in an eirenic way. A woman who wanted to become Catholic wrote to tell him how difficult she found it to make the formula of profession, with its implied vitiation of Anglican sacraments. Knox replied: 'As an Anglican, one errs not by believing wrong things but by failing to believe true ones, or failing to believe them with proper attention and precision. But it seems to me to be all right to make the profession [of Catholic faith] in that sense.'[47]

In general, conversion also implies loss. Certainly there is gain, but there is also a sense of leaving-behind, of bereavement, even. When he gave his last address in the chapel at Shrewsbury School Knox spoke on 'The Parting of Friends'. Few noticed the allusion to Newman's last sermon as an Anglican in the parish church at Littlemore, a sad occasion when Pusey sobbed aloud. There were those, including Knox's own family, with whom there would never again be the same easy relationship.

There was a change, too, in his sense of his Englishness. He remained a quintessential English gentleman who had come of age in the Edwardian era. He would always be English, and indeed his future ministry would bring together his faith and his English cultural heritage in a most fruitful way. But becoming a Catholic priest meant that his identity was now partly defined by a transnational loyalty. In 1918 near the end of his spiritual autobiography he wrote:

I am asked whether I find peace in being a Catholic – does it look like it? Rather it seems to me that in the disintegration of the world and of Europe in particular . . . which must follow the war, men will look for guidance to the two institutions which override the boundaries of country – International Socialism and the Catholic Church. And the forces of disintegration which will be at work will be in conflict most of all with the latter institution, because, being more centralized, it will be at once more formidable and more vulnerable. To feel every stab the Church feels, to rejoice in the triumphs she celebrates, that should be enough to keep a man's interests active, and his heart awake.[48]

This was not only a remarkably accurate prophecy, it was also a personal manifesto for the years ahead. As an apologist for the Catholic Church he would defend and commend the Catholic Faith. It would be the Catholic Church that would harness his heart and mind to new service.

Notes

1 *SA*, p. 152
2 Ronald Knox to Sligger Urquhart, 24 September 1914, Knox Papers, Mells Manor, Somerset.
3 J. E. Edmonds and G. C. Wynne (compilers), *Military Operations France and Belgium 1915* [Official History of the First World War] (London: Macmillan, 1927), p. 356.
4 Ronald Knox to Edmund Knox, 16th October 1915, KPM.
5 *SA*, pp. 191–2.
6 On enlistment, see Richard Holmes, *Tommy: The British Soldier on the Western Front 1914–1918* (London: HarperCollins, 2004), p. 138. On munitions, see Robin Prior and Trevor Wilson, *The First World War* (London: Cassell, 1999), p. 103.
7 Samuel Hynes, *A War Imagined: The First World War and English Culture* (London: Bodley Head, 1990), p. 42.
8 See Maisie Ward, *Father Maturin: A Memoir* (London: Longmans), pp. 73–5. Also online, *The Lusitania Resource* at web.rmslusitania .info:81/pages/saloon_class/maturin_basil.html
9 *SA*, p. 162.
10 *SA*, pp. 171–2.
11 *SA*, pp. 173–4.
12 Roger Lloyd, *The Church of England 1900–1965* (London: SCM, 1966), pp. 424–5.
13 *SA*, p. 168.
14 *SA*, p. 169.
15 Lloyd, *The Church of England 1900–1965*, pp. 128–9.
16 Alan Wilkinson, *The Church of England and the First World War* (London: SPCK, 1978), pp. 110–11, 118–19.
17 Lawrence to Knox, 28 May 1915 Knox Papers, Mells Manor, Somerset.
18 Macmillan to Knox, July [no day indicated] 1915, Knox Papers, Mells Manor, Somerset.
19 Kenneth Hylson-Smith, *The Churches in England from Elizabeth I to Elizabeth II*: Volume 2, *1833–1998* (London: SCM, 1998), p. 205.
20 Thomas Maloney, *Westminster, Whitehall and the Vatican: The Role of*

Cardinal Hinsley 1935–43 (Tunbridge Wells: Burns & Oates, 1985), pp. 84–86.

21 *SA*, 175–6.

22 For slightly differing accounts of this meeting, see *SA*, pp. 177–8 and Waugh, *RK*, p. 146.

23 EW, *RK*, p. 151.

24 Edmund Knox to Ronald Knox, 20 February 1917, pp. 3 and 7–8, Knox Papers, Mells Manor, Somerset.

25 Edmund Knox to Ronald Knox, 21 February, 1917, p. 7 Knox Papers, Mells Manor, Somerset.

26 Edmund Knox to Ronald Knox, 8 January 1917, p. 1 *verso*, Knox Papers, Mells Manor, Somerset.

27 Edmund Knox to Ronald Knox, 20 February 1917, p. 10, Knox Papers, Mells Manor, Somerset.

28 Edmund Knox to Ronald Knox, n.d. but probably 12 March 1917, p. 6, Knox Papers, Mells Manor, Somerset.

29 Edmund Knox to Ronald Knox, 8 January 1917, p. 2 *verso*, Knox Papers, Mells Manor, Somerset.

30 EW, *RK*, p. 141.

31 *SA*, p. 182.

32 Arthur Graeme West, *Diary of a Dead Officer: Being the Posthumous Papers of Arthur Graeme West* (London: Greenhill Books, 2007), p. 93 (8 August 1916) and p. 95 (15 August 1916). He was killed by a sniper in 1917.

33 'Prince of Wounds' appears in Siegfried Sassoon, *Diaries 1915–1918* (London: Faber, 1983), p. 28. For his caution regarding this poem, see Patrick Campbell, *Siegfried Sassoon: A Study of the War Poetry* (McFarland: Jefferson, NC 1999), p. 92. 'They' and 'Good Friday Morning' are in Siegfried Sassoon, *Collected Poems* (London: Faber, 1961), pp. 23–4. For the reference to God, see *Diaries*, p. 134.

34 Quoted in Wilkinson, *The Church of England and the First World War*, p. 116.

35 Nicholas Mosley, *Julian Grenfell: His Life and the Times of his Death 1888–1915* (London: Weidenfeld and Nicolson, 1976), pp. 265–6.

36 Jay Winter *The Great War and the British People* (Cambridge, Mass.: Harvard, 1986) drawing on detailed demographic research (see pp. 92–9) and quoting from page 98.

37 Hynes, *A War Imagined*, p. 244.

38 Evelyn Waugh (Donat Gallagher, ed.) *The Essays, Articles and Reviews of Evelyn Waugh* (London: Methuen, 1983), p. 348.

39 Ronald Knox, *The Essentials of Spiritual Unity* (London: Catholic Truth Society, 1918), paras 25–26.

40 Ronald Knox to Edmund Knox, 5th August 1917, KPM.

41 Nicholas Paxton, 'The Imperial Abbey at Farnborough, 1883–1920', *Recusant History* 28.4, pp. 585–6.

42 *SA*, p. 208.
43 *Catechism of the Catholic Church* (London: Geoffrey Chapman 1994), paragraph 890.
44 Ronald Knox, *Off the Record* (London: Sheed and Ward, 1953), pp. 67–8.
45 Compare, for example, the description of the Society in Michael Yelton, *Anglican Papalism: A History 1900–1960* (Norwich: Canterbury Press, 2005), pp. 221–4.
46 *SA*, p. xiv.
47 Ronald Knox, *Off the Record* (London: Sheed and Ward, 1953), p. 96.
48 *SA*, pp. 224–5.

A painting of The Old Palace by Bernard Gotch was presented to Knox at a farewell dinner in June 1939.

In 1938 Knox was 50 and had been at the Oxford chaplaincy for 12 years. *Photograph by Howard Coster © National Portrait Gallery, London.*

Knox with Evelyn and Laura Waugh in a family grouping, probably taken at Piers Court, Gloucestershire, around 1952. Knox was often a guest of the Waugh family.

Knox and Katharine Asquith at the entrance to Mells Manor, Somerset, the Asquith family home, where he moved in 1947.

6

Teacher and Preacher

All his life Knox had lived within an Anglican clerical ambience. It was the sea in which he swam. Becoming a Catholic meant not just a change of faith, but a whole change of horizons. There would be no more bright evenings full of banter and conviviality with other Anglo-Catholics. There would be no high-octane campaigns to entrench Catholic faith and practices in the Church of England. His circle of friends would necessarily change, and Oxford seemed to have gone for ever. Knox also needed to find accommodation. He no longer considered himself a priest and would therefore lose his exemption from conscription. In the autumn of 1917 the battle of Passchendaele had led to more fruitless bloodletting in the mud of Flanders, making British war nerves tauter than ever. Knox was distressed to hear that Cyril Alington, the Head Master of Eton, was stridently criticizing him for not joining the army. Alington, a histrionic character, was an Anglican priest and his criticism might have arisen from ill-feeling following Knox's conversion. Knox himself felt emotionally exhausted and left the decision about war service to the colonel in charge of his department, and to Cardinal Bourne.[1] The colonel refused to release Knox and he continued to work in the War Office.

Knox went to see Cardinal Bourne, Archbishop of Westminster, in October 1917. Knox was always overawed by Bourne. In a much-quoted phrase, Knox used an Etonian metaphor to describe how, when meeting Bourne, he often failed to convey what he sought. He felt overawed, he said, rather like a messenger 'taking a note round to some tremendous blood at school.'[2] In the normal run of things Cardinal Bourne would have sent him to the Beda College in Rome, which specialized in training mature men from the English-speaking world. This would have entailed a four-year course of studies in preparation for Catholic priesthood. It was normally required of convert Anglican clergy, and there was a steady stream of former vicars from England to Rome for this reason. Instead Bourne told Knox to study privately for ordination and to live with the Oratorian Fathers at Brompton Oratory. Bourne saw in Knox someone of remarkable intellect who already had a sound grasp of Catholic doctrine. Even so, it was a rare concession to allow private study for the priesthood. Waugh, in a caustic passage, has portrayed Bourne as dull and uninformed. Yet although Cardinal Bourne was a rather dry, cautious administrator, he was well aware of the tensions and changes in English society as the war dragged to its close.[3] There would be challenges and opportunities ahead for the English Catholic Church. Bourne's creative flexibility with regard to Knox's training hints at a desire to harness Knox's talents for the good of the Catholic Church in England.

What did the Catholic Church look like at the time of Knox's conversion? In 1918 there were fifteen dioceses in England. Some 2,450 diocesan priests and 1,300 priests from religious orders served around 1.8 million Catholics, a little over 5% of the population of England.[4] Catholics were concentrated in Lancashire, West Yorkshire, London and Tyneside. Catholic numbers had grown steadily since the mid-nineteenth century, boosted by Irish immigration. At the beginning of the First World War the Catholic Church was in the process of overtaking Nonconformity as the principal religious alternative to the Church of England.[5] English Catholicism presented a picture of both confidence and insecurity. The confidence came from a strong institutional ethos, certain of its message and proud of belonging to a global communion with an unbroken history. The insecurity came from knowing that English popular opinion had long been suspicious of the Catholic Church. Catholics were also aware of their uneven social structure. At the top was a small sliver of recusant gentry and nobility, educated at schools like Downside, Ampleforth and Stoneyhurst by elite religious orders. The middle class was also small but growing, fed by a steady stream of converts and by *embourgeoisement* of clever working-class children educated by teaching congregations like the Christian Brothers. The base of the social pyramid was a large urban working class, mostly Irish or of Irish descent, many of them crowded into the poorer areas of places like Liverpool or the East End of London.

Knox had left a church which, at many levels, had access to decision-makers in politics, newspapers, the civil service and local government. He had joined a church which did not relate to the body politic of England with the same ease as the Anglicans. David Mathew described the mid-Victorian Catholic Church as absent from whole sections of English life. He instanced 'the clerical and academic worlds, the new industrialism, the groups from which the Civil Service was then recruited. The great mercantile grouping of the City of London was alien soil.'[6] By 1900 there had been only modest progress in this respect, but Bourne sensed that the pace of social change would make new demands on the Catholic Church. He was right, because in the 1920s and 1930s there was strong growth in the suburbs and dormitory towns in southern England, to house the growing middle class. Catholic parishes had to be created to serve these areas. This would require in turn a clergy whose own education and sympathies enabled them to relate to professional people and civil servants. The pending resolution of the Irish situation would remove one major obstacle to fuller acceptance of Catholicism in England. There remained an English tendency to equate Catholicism with obscurantism, but Bourne must have hoped that Knox's vigorous mind would help to commend the intellectual vitality of Catholicism.

Some of the most important friendships in Knox's life continued. Harold Macmillan was in a nursing home in Belgrave Square recuperating from battle injuries. When Knox visited Macmillan there he had come between 12.00 noon and

1 p.m. to avoid Macmillan's fearsome mother, from whom Knox's visits were concealed.[7] Knox was also able to meet up with his former student Guy Lawrence who had joined the Grenadier Guards and was stationed at Chelsea Barracks. He and Knox would meet after Mass at the Oratory until Lawrence was sent back to the front. But tragedy struck once again. At the end of August 1918, Guy Lawrence was killed in action. On receiving the news Knox wrote to Sligger Urquhart saying that he was numbed, and that his heart seemed to have fused because of the strength of feeling it had to carry with this fresh loss. Yet, after two or three days of numb grief he knew a kind of comfort.[8] It was as if he had been prepared for the news. For a long time he had felt that fate was not on Lawrence's side. He wrote later to Harold Macmillan:

> I always have the feeling about my friends that some of them are born for tragedy and some are meant to succeed. I think Gi had always the aura of tragedy about him, and that one would have prophesied his not surviving the war. I used to worry about you terribly during the War, but not with the same hopeless sense that tragedy was appropriate to your nature.[9]

Guy Lawrence's death was another letting-go, part of the longer list of renunciations and losses that he had to accept. For Macmillan too it was a bleak moment. He wrote to Sligger Urquhart that after hearing of Lawrence's death he feared death himself less than ever. It seemed, he added, as if all the best company had gone to the life beyond.[10]

The fifteen months Knox spent living with the Oratorians was a stabilizing period, coming after the soul-searching of his conversion and the slaughter of nearly all his Eton and Oxford friends in the war. For a new Catholic, the time immediately after reception into the Church can seem something of an anti-climax. For Knox it was a time of repose, light and peace. He followed as far as possible the way of life of the Oratorians. His times of meditation and prayer were often periods of spiritual consolation. He was taken unawares when, during his confirmation by Cardinal Bourne in Westminster Cathedral, he had a numinous sense of the nearness of God's presence.[11]

With the end of the war there was no longer any need for his work at the War Office and he finished his assignment there in December 1918. In February 1919, Cardinal Bourne sent him to teach at St Edmund's College, Old Hall Green in Hertfordshire. By appointing Knox to St Edmund's, Bourne was strengthening the team there and signalling his desire to equip his people to play a greater role in the mainstream of national life.[12] St Edmund's had a venerable history. There had been a Catholic school on the site since 1769, its first chapel concealed in the loft over the dormitory, because Catholicism was still officially proscribed. From the Elizabethan era onwards it had been impossible to train men for the priesthood in England, or even to run Catholic schools. Schools and seminaries were set up on the Continent to serve the needs of the surviving English Catholic community. Then from 1789 onwards, the French Revolution brought a flood of refugees to England, among them the professors and seminarians from Douai which relocated to Old Hall Green in 1793. To the existing seminary there was now added a school for the children of established Catholic families. The combined school and seminary were relaunched as St Edmund's College. William Pitt the Younger had advised that there might be less opposition from Protestant circles if an existing institution were enlarged rather than a new one founded. St Edmund's constructed a new building between 1795 and 1799. It was an ambitious development in plain, late-Georgian style, three stories high with fifteen bays, and has been described by Pevsner as 'an enterprise comparable in scale only with college work at Oxford and Cambridge, but far exceeding what English public schools did at that time.'[13] Fifty years later Pugin derided the place, saying it looked like a 'priest factory'.[14] Pugin's response was to design a high-roofed chapel with a long choir separated from an ante-chapel by a magnificent stone screen. With its carved choir stalls arranged in collegiate style, tracery windows and large antechapel, the result did indeed resemble an Oxford college chapel. The chapel was built between 1845 and 1853; Pugin had died before it was finished, and never completed some of the designs. The chapel was an imposing pile, an assertion in stone and glass of the Catholic Church in England's continuity with the nation's Christian past as well as a sign of its determination that Catholicism should play its part in the life of the nation in the future.[15] Yet the grandeur of the school buildings concealed a constant struggle to find the money to run the place. There was ambition with limited means, and friction among the staff.

When Knox arrived at St Edmund's he found that the college treasured its continuity with the spirit of recusant Catholicism. Catholics who had maintained their faith through centuries of persecution were respected for their courage and steadfastness, a tradition reflected in the school motto, *Avita pro Fide*, 'For the faith of our forefathers'. Around 400 priests had been trained for England at Douai and a quarter of them had been martyred. With Catholicism proscribed and harbouring a priest a capital offence, the spirituality of the continuing Catholic community had of necessity been undemonstrative. They were a sober, reflective, discreet people with a touch of steel whose interior life was usually hidden. It was, in a sense, a simpler, more straightforward Catholicism that Knox met at St Edmund's and he noticed the difference. Living at St Edmund's helped him to let go of the assertive, rather perfervid catholicity that he had propounded on every opportunity within the Church of England. He was ordained priest in Westminster Cathedral by Cardinal Bourne on 5 October 1919. The ordination was 'on his own patrimony'. This meant that he would be subject to the diocesan bishop wherever he moved, but that he was free to move rather than tied to a particular diocese or a particular religious order. The *quid pro quo* was that he agreed to be responsible for his own maintenance, even in old age.

There were only around 130 boys in the school. Knox was appointed Latin master, and from 1922 onwards he was also professor of New Testament at the seminary which absorbed

more of his time. The teaching did not stretch him, but he
undertook it with the same conscientiousness he had displayed
when tutor at Trinity College and temporary master at Shrewsbury School. Once again there were the mnemonics and other
tricks as aids to memory and understanding. One long memory
poem about the Latin names of trees begins:

> When you find a bloke
> Using Latin speech,
> *Quercus* means an oak,
> *Fagus* means a beech.[16]

For two years, he composed a Latin play that was performed
to a dutiful audience of visiting parents and worthies, but not
even his touches of humour could lighten the moment. In
March 1925, the college was shaken by an explosion in the
early hours of the morning when the gas plant that supplied
the heating and the kitchens suddenly erupted in flames. There
was extensive damage but no injuries – and Knox commemor-
ated the moment in a humorous Latin poem which was
published in the school magazine. His mixture of seriousness
and fun came out in other ways, such as his successful attempt
to win the college record for the pogo stick. Cassock tucked
around his waist, biretta on his head, he bounced determinedly
up and down on the stone flags of the walkway. The college
president, Canon Edward Myers, heard the noise reverberat-
ing and came to investigate – and put a halt to the proceedings.[17] Knox's sense of humour was unimpaired. When the
youthful Christopher Hollis wrote to him from Eton asking for
a contribution to a magazine being brought out by some of the
boys, Knox wrote back politely declining, hoping that it would
sell well and 'be reasonably disrespectful of the school authorities.'[18]

His teaching duties were not onerous. He had already established a certain reputation for polemical writing, but the time
now available to him at St Edmund's, and his withdrawal from
the Anglican fray, meant that his ministry of writing was able
to flower. Through his books and articles, his influence was

to be felt in many parts of the Catholic Church and beyond. He wrote across a whole range of genres. Works on spirituality, apologetics, detective fiction, humour, popular journalism and even acrostics flowed from his typewriter. The polemical tone that had characterized much of his writing was now replaced with a style that was more measured and confident. His conversion turned his writing from the combative to the commendatory, more concerned to promote what was good than to rout the misguided.

Immediately after his reception into the Catholic Church, Knox felt compelled to explain himself and to justify his decision. He wrote his *Spiritual Aeneid* which appeared in 1918. Like Newman's *Apologia pro Vita Sua*, Knox's work is a mixture of biography, argumentation, and the re-hashing of past ecclesiastical battles. At that point he had not quite shaken off Anglican preoccupations. With the passage of time he looked back at this work with embarrassment. When a new edition was proposed thirty-three years later, he agreed reluctantly, writing to the publisher to say: 'I feel sick when I try to read it, and can't imagine anybody having a different reaction ... To me it's simply a period piece.'[19] Even so, it is written *con brio* and with that note of searching which marks many spiritual autobiographies from St Augustine to Thomas Merton. This gives it an underlying pathos. It was reprinted several times and clearly resonated with many of its readers. Other works followed swiftly. In 1923 he wrote *Memories of the Future*, purportedly the recollections of Opal, Lady Porstock, looking back from the year 1988. It was satire but his normally light touch deserted him here, and the rather leaden book was not helped by its dense print.

He had more luck in 1924 with *Sanctions: A Frivolity*.[20] In this novel Sir William and Lady Denham have taken a castle in the far north of Scotland for the summer. She, fearing boredom, has invited guests for a house party and the guests are expected to entertain their hosts and one another with stimulating conversation. Knox gives some deft touches of humour. The owners of the castle are 'Catholics, living in that part of Scotland where Catholicism is regarded as a congenital weakness rather than a morbid trait'. A peer is described as having been 'educated out of his prejudices without being educated into any principles'. The book does allow us to glimpse Knox's own changing appreciation of Catholic spirituality. A liberal Anglican priest, Canon Oxenhope, objects to 'the crude taste, the monstrous ornamentation, which distinguishes the Roman Catholic chapels in our country'. A Catholic guest replies: 'I suppose the truth is, if one's in love, she looks well in anything'. The move from Anglican aesthetic awareness to the more demotic Roman Catholic art and architecture has occasionally troubled some converts. Evelyn Waugh, on visiting the Jesuit house at Mount Street in Mayfair, recorded in his diary 'the ruthless absence of good taste'.[21] Knox shows his own increasing acceptance of a more quotidian Catholic sensibility, not only in the retort just quoted, but in a description he gives of Mass in the house chapel. A guest exploring the castle early one morning stumbles into the gallery above the chapel and finds Mass being celebrated. Stifling his first impulse to flee he stays:

> His experience of Catholic churches had always been one of mustiness and decay ... Here, the air of worship either borrowed or mirrored (he could not tell which) something of the freshness of the morning: it was vivid, real, and clean ... there was, too, an of-courseness about the proceeding ... There were silences, that stung the air more than speech; there was a sureness of touch, which made other more diffident approaches to the Unseen appear amateurish; there was matter-of-factness, which relieved the most elaborate gestures from any suspicion of masquerade. It neither invited nor repelled, neither welcomed nor excluded: it was simply there.[22]

The references here to the 'of-courseness', the 'matter-of-factness' show Knox having moved away from Anglo-Catholicism's preoccupation with form. Anglo-Catholic ritual could, indeed, sometimes achieve great beauty and solemnity, but in doing so it was prone to self-consciousness and even to fussiness. Knox was now at home in the more straight-forward Catholic approach. He felt the same about the sacrament of confession. As early as 1918 he wrote, 'Most converts, I suppose, find the Catholic confessional more homely and off-hand than the Anglican.'[23] The adjectives he chose may surprise non-Catholics ('homely', 'off-hand'), but they show someone who had already found a degree of freedom through his fellow believers' shared acknowledgment of human frailty. He already found himself at home in the Catholic Church.

Some of the topics discussed by the guests reflect the concerns of the period, such as eugenics. One clear note is the continuing emotional legacy of the war. As was noted earlier, the war left many in Britain with a sense that the 'old men' who had led the nation had betrayed its youth. The war also left a sense of a wrenching break with the past. Knox was obviously aware of this national soul-searching, for these themes come up in *Sanctions* and are voiced through Escrick, an angular, intellectual figure, who regards British society as 'hopelessly tainted with Confucianism', meaning the misguided adulation of its leaders. Another guest describes the way the war severed the nation's sense of continuity: 'The war judged us ... all our lives have been cut in half by four years, and we don't know which side of the division we belong to'. There is distrust of politicians, and disillusionment with politics comes up several times. The massive grieving after the First World War led some in Britain to an interest in spiritualism as they yearned to communicate with their war dead. Spiritualism was given publicity and some respectability when it was enthusiastically promoted by Arthur Conan Doyle. It was also utilized by Rudyard Kipling in his writing.[24] Both authors had lost a son in the war. Spiritualism appears in *Sanctions* where an anguished Lady Maud Sanquhar rejects a critique of spiritualism: 'You would take away from us what is to so many of us our only hope of seeing our dead again, the only thing that makes life worth living? I lost two brothers in the war ... and I should lose them again, this time irretrievably, if I could believe what you say'.[25] Sometimes Knox gives the impression of being unaware of social changes around him. *Sanctions* shows that he was attuned to the pain and sense of separation left by the war, and knew that some turned to spiritualism to fill the gap. However, ultimately the novel fails to ring true because the artifice of the house party becomes increasingly strained. Knox does not develop the characters sufficiently and puts impossibly erudite arguments into their mouths.

Knox was to return to the subject of spiritualism in his next novel, *Other Eyes Than Ours*. Here again there is a house party in which the assembled guests listen to what purports to be a series of broadcasts from the spirit world, through a kind of radio. Knox makes the content of the broadcasts orotund and vapid. The banality of the alleged messages is one of the reasons given to doubt their veracity. A French priest, the Abbé Bréhault, asks the spiritualist lady: 'If you have been corresponding all this long time with the dead, how is it that the dead have said nothing that is worth saying? That Shakespeare has written no more poetry; that Darwin has told us nothing about science which before we did not know?'[26] The link with the spirit world is eventually shown to have been a good-natured hoax; the host of the house party had arranged for his butler to make the 'broadcasts'.

Knox's forays into fiction were becoming more practised. *Memories of the Future* did not convince, *Sanctions* carried the reader part of the way. His fiction now took what might seem a surprising turn, and one that was financially quite successful. Knox turned to detective stories. He had always had an interest in detective fiction. His knowledge of the Sherlock Holmes stories was so profound that he had produced a detailed study of them, anchored in detailed, accurate knowledge of the stories, but citing spoof literary authorities. Here, once again, Knox's sonorous send-up sounds uncannily like today's post-modernist analysis:

Holmes may wear a squash hat, but Watson cleaves to his bowler, even at midnight in the silence of Dartmoor or on the solitary slopes of the Reichenbach. He wears it constantly, even as the archimandrite or rabbi wears his hat

... The bowler stands for all that is immutable and irrefragable, for law and justice, for the established order of things, for the rights of humanity, for the triumph of man over the brute.[27]

His analysis came to the attention of excitable fans of Sherlock Holmes and over the years Knox wearied of being an expert. Forty years later he wrote: 'I've got so bored with this rather humourless extension of the Holmes cult that I now try to disclaim all connexion with it. I mean, when a man sends you a life of Watson written in Danish, it gets past a joke.'[28]

Knox's turn to detective fiction had also been influenced by his friendship with G. K. Chesterton, whose *Father Brown* detective stories were best-sellers. Chesterton had been thinking about becoming a Catholic for years, for so long, in fact, that some of his Catholic friends had despaired that he would ever commit himself. Possibly Chesterton had known Knox since 1916 when the Society of Saints Peter and Paul published two pamphlets by Chesterton. In 1922 Chesterton was forty-six and a prolific writer whose work included biography, history, popular fiction, journalism and robust analyses of social questions. His vast literary output together with his rotund, shambling figure and quizzical face had made him something of a celebrity. Chesterton wrote to Knox proposing that they meet one Sunday in London, and in that letter already began unburdening himself with great honesty: 'I feel a monstrous charlatan, as if I wore a mask and were stuffed with cushions, whenever I see anything about the public G. K. C. it hurts me; for though the views I express are real, the image is horribly unreal compared with the real person who needs help just now.'[29] The self-revulsion he expressed in that letter seemed to arise out of exaggerated fears about ordinary human failings, such as the typical ardent imaginings of an adolescent schoolboy, to which, in fact, he refers. Chesterton met with Knox early in 1922 and questioned him about the process of becoming a Catholic. He had expected that reception into the Church would come first, followed by confession and instruction, but discovered from Knox that it was the other way round. Chesterton felt so agitated at the meeting that he could not express himself clearly, but Knox's measured calm and sure faith penetrated deep into his consciousness and helped him. Afterwards he wrote to Knox: 'The matter of our meeting has got into every chink of my thoughts, even the pauses of talk on practical things.'[30] He hoped to meet Knox again for instruction, and Knox offered to come to Chesterton's home at Beaconsfield in Buckinghamshire during the college vacation, but work commitments and the death of Chesterton's father made another meeting impossible. In the end Chesterton sent for Fr John O'Connor, a West Yorkshire priest whom he had known and admired since 1904 and with whom he kept up a steady correspondence. Many aspects of Chesterton's Father Brown were drawn from his friendship with O'Connor. Knox seems to have been disappointed that in the end it was O'Connor who received Chesterton into the Church, and in conveying his best wishes to Chesterton, Knox could not resist what sounds like a barbed comment: 'I'm awfully glad to hear that you've sent for Father O'Connor ... I must say that ... Father Brown's powers of neglecting his parish always seemed to me to be even more admirable than Dr Watson's powers of neglecting his practice; so I hope that trait was drawn from the life.'[31] O'Connor received Chesterton into the Church on 30 July 1922 in the temporary chapel of the Catholic Church in Beaconsfield, a converted ballroom with a corrugated iron roof.

As mentioned, Chesterton drew on his knowledge of Fr O'Connor when he created the clerical detective, Father Brown. Brown was an innocuous but perceptive priest who, through hearing confessions, had become acquainted with the more lurid side of human nature.[32] The first Father Brown mystery was published in 1911, followed by twenty-five others before the outbreak of the First World War when Chesterton set them aside. He wrote a further twenty-six stories between 1923 and his death in 1936. There is, however, a significant difference between the crime stories of Knox and those of Chesterton. Chesterton's Father Brown stories hint at the corruption that can be found in the human heart and the melancholy knowledge a priest has of human ambivalence. By contrast, in Knox's novels the murder to be solved represents not so much evil as an irruption of anomie and disorder into the world. The solution of the crime puzzle restores the world to its equilibrium. The solution comes from piecing together clues to which the reader is also party.

Knox's close reading of Sherlock Holmes, and the example of Chesterton's Father Brown stories, must have given an impetus to Knox's own desire to write stories about crime detection. But there was also the more general stimulus of the times. The inter-war years have subsequently been dubbed the 'golden age' of crime fiction. The first Agatha Christie crime novel was published in 1920; in 1923 Dorothy Sayers launched her series of novels based on the character of Lord Peter Wimsey. Radio was still in its infancy and there was no television: a public eager for diversion readily bought popular fiction. These novels largely avoided blood and gore, perhaps out of a reaction against the horrors of the war just past. Their attraction lay in the crime puzzle and the challenge to the reader to make sense of the clues. One scholar of crime detection points out that 'Solving the puzzle, however, often has a wider meaning, as the revealed criminal is also exposed as without moral sense and rejecting the practices of normal society.'[33] It was a combination that would appeal naturally to Knox, with his sharp intellect, love of puzzles and concern for morality. Knox was to write six murder mysteries, but only the first, *The Viaduct Murder* (1925), was published while he was at St Edmund's, at a time when he was still feeling his way in the genre. Four golfing friends find a mangled body on the golf course underneath a high railway viaduct, and these amateur sleuths try to solve the murder. The point of the story, it gradually emerges, is that the four were misled by preconceived ideas. Knox slips into his fiction the same argument he made in *Some Loose Stones* a little over ten years previously, namely that where understanding is led by theory it is likely to go badly astray. It will tend to overlook the obvious facts. Thus Hegelianism, of all things, comes in for a drubbing in *The Viaduct Murder*. One of the would-be sleuths, Alexander Gordon, complains that they were led astray through their belief that two of the suspects were actually one person. In this error they had been like those theorists who tried 'to make one thing out of matter and Spirit . . . that Spirit is a mode of matter, or the other way round' and they were 'stultifying experience for the sake of a formula'.[34] This stilted interjection does not convince, and the plot, intriguing though it is, falls short because of insufficient development of the characters. It is the same weakness that was noted earlier in *Sanctions*.

Ronald Knox also found himself recruited by the BBC. His first broadcast was on 25 November 1923, when he gave a religious address. Knox was friendly with George Marshall, Station Director of the BBC in Edinburgh. Knox often visited Edinburgh when en route to friends in the Highlands. On 15 January 1926, a broadcast by Knox from Edinburgh caused some listeners to panic and roused the ire of John Reith, who was head of the fledgling BBC. The script began with Knox imitating a lisping academic delivering a lecture on literature, which should have alerted listeners to the likelihood of the ensuing material being satire. Knox then proceeded via faux news items, which again should have alerted the listener: it was unlikely that Australia would be 569 for seven, while England would be all out for 173. But he then went on to give a spoof account of live coverage of social unrest. The announcer said that a crowd had gathered in Trafalgar Square and was in the process of sacking the National Gallery; he reported as the the crowd moved on to demolish the Houses of Parliament. The Savoy Hotel was blown up. Throughout it was repeated that the leader of the mob was 'Mr Popplebury, Secretary of the National Movement for Abolishing Theatre Queues', which again should have calmed any trepidations in the listener.[35] But the broadcast gained verisimilitude from the cool, professional tones in which Knox 'reported' the events. He seemed to have forgotten that listeners would tune in and out without necessarily hearing, or recognizing, the clues. He took for granted that the preposterousness of what he was saying would reveal its inherent satirical content, but the BBC began to receive a flood of anxious phone calls. The BBC had to issue a statement, which was broadcast, explaining that it was all in jest: 'The BBC regrets that any listeners should have been perturbed by this purely fantastic picture, but we should remind listeners that in this case, as in all similar cases, a preliminary warning was given that what followed was to be taken as entertainment and not seriously.' The incident was widely reported in the press. The *Daily Mirror* headlined it 'That BBC Scare', the *Daily Express* criticized it in an editorial and the London *Evening Standard* called it a blunder. Mr John Reith, Managing Director of the BBC soothed the Board of Directors in his monthly report:

> The outstanding item of the last month was the unexpected. Father Ronald Knox's broadcast aroused much public attention, but Press criticism only produced an increase in the number of appreciations received by us, i.e. 2,307 appreciations as against 249 criticisms, of which 194 were immediately directed against Father Knox.[36]

It was a delicate time in the BBC's fortunes. The first public broadcasts had only begun in 1922, and at the beginning of 1926 the broadcaster was in the process of establishing a monopoly in which it transformed itself from the British Broadcasting Company to the British Broadcasting Corporation. A. J. P. Taylor notes that disturbing views were rarely aired during this period.[37]

Knox's intent had been light-hearted, but, without realizing it, he had tapped into a widespread fear that society was disintegrating. This was a time when unemployment was rising sharply, industrial relations were poor and Bolshevism seemed to be making headway. Five months after the broadcast the country would be caught up in the tragedy of the General Strike. Against this backdrop some aspects of Knox's broadcast seem ill-judged. He aimed to provide a parody of a news report, but in effect he was articulating deep-seated fears. It is evidence that Knox was a little lacking in worldly wisdom, but it also points to an element of social isolation in Knox. There is a paradox here. On the one hand he was becoming a national figure in Catholic circles and even beyond. On the other hand his social experience was very limited. His writings would increasingly nourish the Catholic community and commend the Catholic faith to the wider public. Yet he had little understanding of the lives and struggles of working-class people. A priest with such knowledge would have thought twice before choosing a demonstration of the unemployed as material for a satirical skit. Eventually, however, the furore died down, and further invitations to broadcast came his way.

The articles he wrote for the popular press appeared regularly in the London *Evening Standard* and in the *Weekly Dispatch*. Often they were musings on the ordinary incidents and demands of life, sometimes whimsical in nature, sometimes with a lightly disguised seriousness. The light touch and the evident good humour draw the reader along. Almost anything could set off his train of thought: recovery from an attack of jaundice, the dating of Easter, a proposal to ban smoking, a limerick, the country paths of Hertfordshire, proverbs of the past, the sound of the cuckoo. Many of them deal with trains, such as one on the etiquette of seating yourself in a railway carriage:

Don't spread coats, hats and dispatch-boxes about so as to create a dummy army of imaginary travellers. This habit, often found, I am sorry to say, in people of otherwise irreproachable character, is a criminal one ...

During the journey, don't sing, whistle, hum, cut your nails, spit, throw orange-peel on to the floor, or otherwise behave as if you were alone when you aren't ... Beware especially of trying to talk shop to clergymen. (I am always mistaken for an Anglican at first ... But a certain lack of enthusiasm betrays me; and then they tell me they have no prejudice against Roman Catholics. I should hope not; it would be very disgraceful if they had. What would they think if I told them I had no prejudice against commercial travellers?)[38]

The broadcasting and writing for the popular press carried a quietly implicit message, that Catholicism was part of the ordinary life of the country. Catholic priests had variously been seen as slightly subversive or faintly exotic. As the Catholic Church moved slowly into the national midstream, people could hear or read Knox and find that a priest could be remarkably like them. As his niece, Penelope Fitzgerald pointed out, although his articles showed how a reasoning mind could argue for Christianity, they also showed 'that a normal, pipe-smoking, income-taxed Englishman, not a Jesuit, not a mystic, no black cloaks, no sweeping gestures, could become a Roman Catholic priest.'[39]

The ministry of writing, the frequent invitations to preach at special occasions and the occasional broadcast meant that Knox was not limited to life as it was lived at St Edmund's. Even so, he began to yearn to get away. It is sometimes suggested that there was not enough there to stretch him intellectually, but it also needs to be said that St Edmund's was not a happy place. Some of the tension arose out of the overlapping layers of authority. The college had a president of the overall ensemble who was responsible ultimately for both school and seminary, but there was also a headmaster for the school. In addition Cardinal Bourne took a keen interest in St Edmund's and regarded himself as the ultimate arbiter of its fortunes. He was determined that the school should rise to the level of England's great public schools and to this end he reorganized it on the house system found at Eton, despite there not being enough funds to see such a bold plan through to its fulfilment. Some of the resulting tensions were felt in staff relations that were fraught with ill-feeling. One president had been persuaded to resign in July 1916; his successor left after a breakdown in 1918; a vice-president was similarly forced out in 1926.[40]

In this atmosphere of souring of relations and inbuilt tension, Knox felt more than ready to move on. It seemed that the Catholic chaplaincy at either Oxford or Cambridge would suit his talents ideally. Since 1895, appointment to these chaplaincies had been in the hands of the Universities Catholic

Education Board, a committee of fifteen clergy and laity established by the bishops. Knox's appointment to Cambridge had been mooted in 1922, but Cardinal Bourne had advised Knox that it would require more money than Knox would be able to find. Both chaplaincies required men who could provide out of their own resources. In the spring of 1926, it became clear that the Oxford chaplaincy would soon be vacant and that Knox was a strong candidate. Knox was frustrated to find that Bourne was reluctant to let him go. Knox wrote to Sligger Urquhart in terms of near despair about Bourne's position. Knox pointed to new staff appointments to St Edmund's which meant that he would no longer be essential to the teaching staff there, and concluded: 'Meanwhile my temper has gone long ago, my literary style is rapidly vanishing, I never preach a new sermon, and I find that I can't depend even on my health.'[41] Urquhart met with Bourne and persuaded him to let Knox go. He also lobbied members of the Universities Board. Money was no longer an issue. By 1926 Knox's herculean efforts at the typewriter meant that he was in a more assured financial position. He made around £1,300 a year. Of this about £15 a week came from articles for the London *Evening Standard* and *The Universe*, a Catholic weekly; he made another £3 each week from acrostics.[42] In the mid-1920s this amounted to a comfortable income. Cardinal Bourne believed that the priests on the staff of St Edmund's needed no more than £40 a year, their board and lodging, and whatever they could earn by supplying for parish clergy when the latter went on holiday and hired seminary priests as stand-ins.

In July 1926, Knox was appointed Catholic chaplain to students at Oxford University. The President of St Edmund's, Canon Myers, congratulated Knox but added that he believed Knox to be going into a hornet's nest. Apparently Knox managed to hold back the reply that if so, he had been well trained for it by his time at St Edmund's. But we may contrast this with what he wrote later in a letter to Cardinal Hinsley: 'So far as personal relations are concerned, I have none but the warmest memories of St Edmund's.'[43]

Notes

1 Knox to Sligger Urquhart, 7 February 1918, KPM. Alington later became Dean of Durham.

2 Quoted in EW, *RK*, p. 167.

3 Edward Norman, *Roman Catholicism in England: From the Elizabethan Settlement to the Second Vatican Council* (Oxford: OUP, 1986), p. 110.

4 *Catholic Directory 1918* (London: Burns and Oates, 1918), p. 572.

5 Gerald Parsons, 'Victorian Catholicism' in G. Parsons, ed., *Religion in Victorian Britain* Vol 1: *Traditions* (Manchester: Manchester University Press/Open University, 1988), pp. 180 and 193.

6 David Mathew, 'Old Catholics and Converts' in George Beck, ed., *The English Catholics 1850–1950* (London: Burns and Oates, 1950), pp. 225–6 and 242.

7 Knox to Urquhart, 17 March 1918, KPM.

8 Knox to Urquhart, 2 September and 16 September 1918, KPM.

9 Knox to Macmillan, n.d. but early June 1929, Macmillan Papers, Bodleian Library, Box 65 fo. 9.

10 Macmillan to Urquhart, 5 September 1918, Macmillan Papers, Box 452 fo. 152.

11 EW, *RK*, p. 169.

12 Cf. David Mathew, *Catholicism in England: The Portrait of a Minority: Its Culture and Tradition* (London: Eyre and Spottiswoode, 2nd edn, 1947), pp. 257 and 274.

13 Nikolaus Pevsner, *Hertfordshire* (The Buildings of England; revised edition by Bridget Cherry; London: Penguin, 1978), p. 366.

14 A. S. Barnes, *The Catholic Schools of England* (London: Williams and Norgate, 1926), pp. 115–16.

15 Rosemary Hill considers St Edmund's chapel to be 'one of Pugin's best and best-realized buildings' (*God's Architect: Pugin and the Building of Romantic Britain*, London: Allen Lane, 2007, p. 341).

16 'Tractate on Tree Names in Virgil', KPM, dating from *c*. 1919.

17 The poem, with several Latin neologisms, is reprinted in W. T. Gribbin (ed.), *St Edmund's College Bicentenary Book* (Old Hall Green, Herts: Old Hall Green Press, 1993), p. 128.

18 Hollis, *Along the Road to Frome*, p. 246.

19 Quoted in EW, *RK*, pp. 165–6.

20 Ronald Knox, *Sanctions: A Frivolity* (London: Methuen, 1924).

21 Michael Davie (ed.), *The Diaries of Evelyn Waugh* (London: Penguin, 1979), p. 320.

22 Above quotations from pages 3, 9, 192 and 123 of *Sanctions*.

23 *SA*, p. 60.

24 Quoting from *Sanctions*, pp. 24 and 30; see also pp. 90 and 95. On Spiritualism, see Jay Winter, *Sites of Memory, Sites of Mourning: The*

Great War in European Cultural History (Cambridge: CUP, 1995; Canto edition, reprinted 2000), pp. 58–9 and 71–4.

25 *Sanctions*, pp. 146–50.

26 Ronald Knox, *Other Eyes Than Ours* (London: Methuen, 1926), p. 52.

27 *Essays in Satire*, pp. 164–5. The Holmes study had originated as a paper he wrote in 1911 and read to many student groups. After its first publication in 1912, Arthur Conan Doyle wrote to Knox complimenting him on his detailed knowledge of the stories (EW, *RK*, p. 122).

28 Knox to Woodruff, 14 October, no year but probably 1953, Douglas Woodruff Papers Box 4 folder 25, Georgetown University Library Special Collections.

29 The letter is printed in EW, *RK*, pp. 207–8.

30 These undated letters of Chesterton to Knox are in the Knox Papers at Mells, and in substance have been printed in Maisie Ward, *Gilbert Keith Chesterton* (London: Sheed and Ward, 1944), pp. 391–5.

31 Quoted in Ward, *Chesterton*, p. 395.

32 Joseph Pearce, *Wisdom and Innocence: A Life of G. K. Chesterton* (London: Hodder, 1996), pp. 92–3.

33 Stephen Knight, 'The Golden Age' in Martin Priestman (ed.), *The Cambridge Companion to Crime Fiction* (Cambridge: CUP, 2003), p. 88.

34 Ronald Knox, *The Viaduct Murder* (Merion Station, PA: The Merion Press, 2001), p. 155.

35 The script is reprinted as 'A Forgotten Interlude' in *Essays in Satire*, pp. 277–87.

36 Reports from newspapers and Reith's report to directors, folder C1/18/1–Hoaxes, BBC/WA. The BBC was still a company. Reith's title changed to Director-General the following year.

37 A. J. P. Taylor, *English History 1914–1945* (Oxford: Clarendon Press, 1986 rev. edn), p. 233. On fears of social disintegration, p. 177.

38 Ronald Knox, *An Open-Air Pulpit* (London: Constable, 1926), p. 111.

39 Fitzgerald, *The Knox Brothers*, p. 174.

40 See the memoir St Edmund's College Archives, held at Archives of the Archdiocese of Westminster: 'Notes on St Edmund's College' by John Vance, January 1960 in Bickford and Vance papers, 14/31/v12; also Ward Papers II 15 (4) and III 1, 22–30 and 45.

41 Knox to Urquhart, 20 March 1926, KPM.

42 Knox to Urquhart, 24 June and 21 July 1926, KPM.

43 EW, *RK*, p. 203; Knox to Hinsley, 22 June 1938, KPM.

7

Oxford Again

Knox's return to Oxford as Catholic chaplain brought him into a highly visible ministry of pastoral care coupled with writing and broadcasting. In Oxford he would know the sudden, unwelcome glare of publicity, and he would have to wrestle with occasional bouts of melancholy.

Knox went to live in a palace, at least in name. There had been a society for Catholic students at Oxford since 1878, which became known as the Newman Society, with its own trustees. The Newman Society was autonomous and yet essential to the good functioning of the chaplaincy. In 1917 the Newman trustees purchased the Old Palace for the chaplaincy. This run-down building gave the Catholic chaplaincy a central and visible location in the university at the corner of St Aldate's and Rose Place, near Christ Church. The Old Palace also gave the chaplaincy the patina of antiquity. The five bays of the building were adorned with fine plastering and wood-work, evidence of its early seventeenth-century origins. Although completed in 1628, the Old Palace possibly incor-porated foundations and woodwork dating back to the first Bishop of Oxford, Robert King, who moved to the site in 1546. It was known as 'The Old Palace' because of this epis-copal association. This was Knox's home in Oxford, but it was also his place of work where he counselled, exercised hospitality and celebrated Mass for the students. Central to his work was that most difficult of disciplines, a ministry of avail-ability, where a priest has to create an impression that others can come and talk to him at their convenience. Half-way through Knox's time as chaplain it was said of him that in term time he was always to be found in the Old Palace, 'there to be invaded'. Almost anyone could run up the short flight of stairs 'and seat themselves beside a man . . . whose rather shy courtesy will never give them any abrupt hint to depart.'[1]

The external grandeur of the palace did not match the inconvenience of life there. True, there were some splendidly ornate plaster ceilings. But there were rats in the walls, chimney smoke sometimes came out of the floorboards, and the ceilings were low. One bedroom had been condemned by the university as unsuitable for an undergraduate; Knox slept in it himself. Guests were sometimes shocked at the spartan bathroom with two baths and the expectation of common ablutions. When Evelyn Waugh came to dinner in the summer of 1936 he recorded: 'Shown into infamous bedroom without looking-glass, chest of drawers or wash-hand-basin; hideous oak beams, a crooked floor . . . distant bathroom . . . Changed in frightful discomfort.' He pronounced the food repulsive.[2]

A university chaplain's task of keeping faith alive and flourishing among students is usually a challenging one. Free for the first time from the conformity imposed by parents and schools, students often adopt a sceptical attitude towards religion. Christopher Hollis remembered that in the mid-1920s 'The overwhelming majority of [Oxford] undergraduates were . . . agnostic. To them, Holy Communion was something that one gave up when one left school, in much the same way that one gave up wearing the school uniform.' His chaplain at Balliol was a pathetic figure, who begged unavailingly for 'anybody who believed in anything' to come to the college chapel.[3] The Catholic chaplaincy had been established in the hopes that it would safeguard Catholic students at Oxford against this kind of religious indifference. It also had to guard them against the blandishments of establishment religion, because the chapel services in each college offered not only worship of God but a sense of church and nation linked in a seemingly eternal Englishness. Early in the nineteenth century the question of safeguarding Catholic faith had hardly arisen, because Oxford required undergraduates to subscribe to the Thirty-Nine Articles of the Church of England. This effectively excluded Catholics and Nonconformists, until the 1854 Oxford University Act allowed them to proceed to a first degree. Then in 1871, the Universities Tests Act had opened nearly all the degrees and offices to men of any religion. Existing colleges had to maintain Church of England services in their chapels and provide religious instruction for Anglican undergraduates.

The Catholic Church in England came under the purview of Propaganda Fide in Rome. Despite the more open attitude to Catholics at Oxford, Propaganda Fide ruled in 1867 that Catholics should not attend Oxford or Cambridge. It was believed that such mixing together could lead to 'an intrinsic and very serious danger to purity of morals as well as to faith.'[4] In 1873 the bishops of England and Wales reaffirmed the ban, but Catholics who belonged to the upper classes began sending their sons to Oxford like their peers from Eton, Harrow and other public schools. The contacts to be made, and the quality of the education on offer, were highly appealing. The bishops never sought to discipline anyone who transgressed.[5] In 1895 Pope Leo XIII removed the prohibition, with the stipulation that special lecturers should be appointed to give Catholic students sound instruction. When the Universities Catholic Education Board established the Oxford chaplaincy in 1897 it decided that half-hour conferences or addresses at the Sunday Mass would fulfil the papal requirement. Knox's role as chaplain combined, therefore, pastoral and apologetic aspects. He had to keep a discreet eye on the welfare of the students, and provide sound teaching about the Catholic faith.

He also exercised a ministry of hospitality. Throughout the academic year he held three dinner parties a week to which he invited Catholic students, trying to get to know as many of them as he could. In the course of an average year he would entertain 240 guests to lunch or dinner.[6] In the Michaelmas term he would begin by inviting each Catholic fresher in turn. He was candid about the response to these gatherings. He wrote:

I never quite know what mixture of gratification, embarrassment and boredom an Old Palace invitation brings with it to the ordinary man. But I am sure it is a good thing to make a universal gesture of friendliness, even if some of the people affected seem to make absolutely no response.[7]

An appalled upper class response to one of these invitations was portrayed in Evelyn Waugh's novel *Brideshead Revisited,* in which Charles Ryder calls round to see Sebastian Flyte at Christ Church on a Sunday morning. He finds Flyte returning from Mass, who tells him:

I've been to mass at the Old Palace ... I haven't been all this term, and Monsignor Bell asked me to dinner twice last week, and I know what that means. Mummy's been writing to him. So I sat bang in front where he couldn't help seeing me and absolutely shouted the Hail Marys at the end; so that's over.[8]

The fictional Lord Flyte did not welcome the invitation and the implied scrutiny of the chaplain that went with it. But there were many who were glad of the invitation and the sense of solidarity that the chaplaincy provided. The chaplaincy was particularly important for Catholic students who did not come from the small circle of Catholic public schools. Public school men met others from their school at Oxford and therefore had a ready-made circle of friends. Students from elsewhere might arrive knowing no one at all and the chaplaincy was a good way to get to know others. In *Brideshead Revisited* Flyte also objected to his mother's plan that he should go and live with Monsignor Bell. He could not, he said, envisage himself 'helping at tea parties for shy Catholic freshmen.'[9] Knox's hospitality also included a small number of students who lodged with him. This helped make ends meet but it was also a shrewd move on his part, for it meant that visiting students would find a welcome at the chaplaincy from others to whom they could readily relate.

The number of students under Knox's pastoral care at

Oxford was modest. The university itself was much smaller than it is now. In 1936 there were only 4,848 undergraduates in residence. Of these 256 appeared on Knox's list of Catholics. This did not include the 60 or so women undergraduates who were regarded as under the pastoral care of the Sisters of the Holy Child Jesus.[10] There were three Masses on a Sunday. The first at 8.15 a.m. was normally said by Knox himself; a Jesuit priest would then say the 9 a.m. for the townspeople of the district; the 10.30 a.m. or conference Mass would often be taken by one of the Dominicans from Blackfriars. The use of visiting priests to celebrate allowed Knox more time to buttonhole students and oil the wheels of the chaplaincy generally. Knox fretted constantly about what he regarded as the laxity of the students about going to Mass; but in fact, the rate of Mass-going was high, much higher than the religious observance of their peers. It seems that on any given Sunday between half and two-thirds of Catholics were at a chaplaincy Mass.[11] It is true that there was an element of compulsion, as Catholics were excused the occasional college chapel attendance required of other students, on condition that they went to the chaplaincy, but even allowing for this the attendance rate was high. In the tradition of the day, however, only about a third of the students received communion. The normal expectation was that an adult communion required confession beforehand to make sure the person was in a state of grace.

In 1933 the question of communion suddenly thrust the chaplaincy and Knox into the roar of controversy. It involved a Christ Church student called Richard Rumbold, the son of an Irish officer. His egoistical, violent father had bullied and despised him for what he considered to be effeminacy. His mother was mentally ill and committed to an asylum before committing suicide. Both parents had impressed the Catholic faith upon him, but Rumbold began to doubt and even resent what had been commended to him by such obviously unstable people. The Catholic faith also conflicted with his growing acknowledgement of his own homosexuality. His friends included Harold Nicolson and the writers Richard Aldington and William Plomer, the latter being a relation. While at Christ Church, Rumbold revived the defunct Literary Club. He had an innate flair for publicity and re-launched the club with a talk by Lord Alfred Douglas, whose notoriety attracted a large audience. Later speakers would include Frieda Lawrence and W. B. Yeats. But the tensions within Rumbold were building up, and he poured them into his first novel *Little Victims* (1933) which he wrote as an undergraduate. In his own words,

> I was impetuous. I had not the emotional self-mastery and patience to work out the theme with care, and the novel degenerated into a bitter cathartic outpouring in which I lashed out bitterly against everything within my experience – my parents, the Roman Catholic Church, public schools and the Oxford aesthetes. I also spoke with frankness about my emotional problems . . .[12]

The book won him immediate *réclame* and some notoriety, since it was obviously autobiographical. In May 1933, shortly after the book appeared, Rumbold went to the 8.15 a.m. Mass at the chaplaincy where as usual Knox was the celebrant. Rumbold did not know that Knox had been contacted beforehand by Archbishop Thomas Williams of Birmingham, in whose diocese Oxford was situated. Williams had received complaints about the book and wanted Rumbold to issue a public retraction. Knox had advised against this course of action, but Williams had insisted that Rumbold could not receive communion unless he repented. Spotting Rumbold in the chapel, Knox sent a message to him asking him not to come up for communion until they had a chance to talk together. More in a spirit of bafflement than of rebellion Rumbold ignored the message and at communion went up and knelt at the altar rail with the other students. In the pre-conciliar mode the communion plate was held under the chin of the communicant in case the host dropped as the priest placed it in the communicant's mouth. When it came to Rumbold's turn, Knox took the communion plate away and passed it to the next student along the rail. In the hothouse atmosphere of Oxford this action could hardly fail to be noticed by others, and implied at least a temporary excommunication of Rumbold, who was hurt and incensed. His response was to contact the Oxford and London newspapers telling them that he had been humiliated in front of his fellow students. The story of the excommunicated undergraduate author was swiftly taken up and in the next few weeks Rumbold received hundreds of press cuttings. The incident was even reported in the international edition of *Time Magazine*.[13]

The incident must have been distressing to Knox. Twenty years previously he too had been a skilful publicist. Now he preferred a quiet life to the extent, throughout his time as chaplain, of refusing to have a telephone installed at the Old Palace. Knox wrote to Rumbold explaining the order he had received from Archbishop Williams. Knox, it should be remembered, had sought a pastoral solution before the whole affair blew up. But Archbishop Williams had an unpredictable side which sometimes led to errors of judgement. Shortly before this incident he had appeared at a public meeting in Birmingham which had been organized to condemn Nazi persecution of the Jews. Williams did indeed issue a condemnation, but he must have astounded the audience at the end of his speech. In closing he said that if the Jews in question were Communists, then the Nazis had his sympathy even if their methods were wrong.[14] As for Rumbold, although he had stirred up the subsequent publicity, he felt deeply that he had been rejected by the Catholic Church. And not only by the Church – the novel itself lost him many friends at Oxford and elsewhere who disliked his depiction of the decadence of the aesthetes. He went on to become a courageous and successful RAF pilot in combat over Europe, but he was grounded in 1941 after another impulsive act when he flew his plane under the Menai Bridge.

Knox faced constant money worries. The Board gave him £220 per annum but that was hardly enough and he had to subsidize the chaplaincy out of his own pocket. Parents of the Oxford Catholic students were asked annually for donations to its work, but less than a third of them contributed anything. Knox's writing proved to be a steady and necessary source of income, particularly his detective stories. He once complained to the secretary of the Universities Catholic Education Board: 'I am writing detective stories hard, and only just making ends meet.'[15] Despite the shortfall of money, there was a pressing need for a new chapel. In the system he inherited, Newman Society meetings for social and educational purposes were held in the chaplain's room on the first floor of the Old Palace. Services were hold in the chapel which was on the second floor. The chaplain's room would be packed with seventy students on Sunday evenings for Newman Society meetings, while on Sunday mornings the chapel on the floor above would also be uncomfortably full. An appeal was launched to raise money for an extension, and the new chapel and Newman room were completed in 1931. The extension was built on the site of a former stable next to the Old Palace. This extended the chaplaincy footprint along Rose Place and provided a new meeting room on the ground floor with a chapel above it. Knox gave £500 to the building fund, plus, for a considerable period, the chapel collections and his Mass stipends.[16] The chapel could accommodate 140 people, something like twice the number of its predecessor.

Here part of the paradox that was Knox emerged. In his Anglican days he had pressed for church architecture to be baroque, so that it would reflect the full glory of Counter-Reformation Continental Catholicism. Papalist Anglo-Catholics rejected what they called 'British Museum religion', which was a more moderate Catholic style based on pre-Reformation English Catholicism. As Peter Anson put it, for the more extreme Anglo-Catholics, 'Anglican worship must be brought into line with that of the Church of Rome. The ideal was to create an un-English and Continental atmosphere.'[17] Yet now that Knox was a Catholic the chapel he designed for Oxford was severely simple, with a plain, wood-panelled sanctuary, an unfussy altar and light streaming in through the clear windows. Knox later recalled that

When ... the architect brought me a nice set of Gothic

plans, I told him I was sorry, but I didn't want anything which couldn't be turned into tea-rooms later on. But it was to be a little chastening, a little sombre; you were not to forget, as you knelt there, that Oxford and the Catholic Church had got along well enough, these many centuries past, without you.[18]

The small, functional Oxford chapel was not there to feed the senses of the undergraduates with an aesthetic religion. Compared with the grand college chapels, the chapel at the Catholic chaplaincy was a very modest affair. But Knox valued this, because it would be a reminder that in penal times the ancient faith had been proscribed and driven underground. In good times and in bad Catholics before them had clung to their faith through the Mass, and its reminder of Christ crucified and risen from the dead. In effect, he was telling the students to go to the heart of their faith, and not to dwell on external signs. The faith had survived the penal era, when Catholics had worshipped with a necessary simplicity. This was the faith for which their forebears had suffered and even died. Knox's question to the students was simple: would they play their part in keeping the faith alive and passing it on?

To help in this latter process Knox worked out a well-rounded scheme of instruction for the conferences at the 10.30 Sunday Mass. The talks lasted half an hour and took place after the gospel, making an unusually long interruption in the course of the eucharist. This placing of the conference was inherited from Knox's predecessor, Mgr Barnes, but it clearly had the intention of stopping students from 'hearing Mass' and then sloping off before the conference. Some of the talks were given by Knox himself, some by visiting speakers. The topics were structured in a three-year cycle with the intention that an undergraduate would, across the time of his degree, hear the major ground of his faith covered, together with some moral issues. The cycle started with the existence of God, moving to the nature and mission of Christ. The Church was taught in terms of the four marks – One, Holy, Catholic and Apostolic – and in terms of its authority as the organ of revelation.

There were other courses on the Four Last Things (Death, Judgement, Heaven and Hell), on science and miracles, on the Mystical Body of Christ, on the history of the Church and the role of the Holy See. The ninth and final term in the cycle covered sex and marriage.[19] Reading Knox's conferences today is a remarkable experience because of their freshness and directness, despite the occasional dated reference. After a scholarly survey of Knox's apologetic technique, Milton Walsh concludes that, 'By his contemplation of creation and the events of daily life, Knox was able to engage his audience. There is a quality of gentleness and human sympathy in his apologetics giving them an atmosphere of Wisdom, not simply erudition.'[20] Knox had the knack of composing his talks in such a way that what he had to say would come across as a word addressed not only to the whole congregation, but to each person present. Even the middle-aged Waugh could be affected this way. Once, on a visit to Oxford in 1943, he coincided with a return visit by Knox and felt that every word of Knox's conference seemed directed at him.[21]

Take, for example, Knox's address on one of the four marks of the Church, the Church as Holy. The very title seizes the attention: 'The Unholiness of the Church'. Typically throughout a Knox conference or sermon there would be little touches like these, squibs to keep the listener alert, dovetailed neatly into the flow of the talk. Thus Knox approached the holiness of the Church by raising the question of whether Catholics were less holy than others: it was true, he said, that Catholics seemed to be well-represented among the miscreants in prison and elsewhere. But this was because 'the Catholic feels the truth of his religion as something independent of himself, which does not cease to be valid when he, personally, fails to live up to its precepts.' It was still part of a rogue's identity, even if he came from the rougher or more lurid walks of life: Catholicism was a robust faith. As for the students, they had to remember that at a place like Oxford where they were a small minority and mingled freely with others, they were responsible for the reputation of their faith. They could not make the Church more apostolic or more catholic: they could, however, extend the area of the Church's sanctity by the quality of their daily living. Knox was well aware that Catholics at Oxford were a minority, and he wanted to strengthen their sinews when it came to upholding Catholic values rather than the shifting values of the day:

> You find here a crowd of people of your own age, superficially of the same culture as yourselves, and it seems natural to go on doing what you have been accustomed to do, swimming with the stream ... You feel rather small, coming into such a world of new experience, and very naturally; lots of your friends seem so much cleverer, and so much more experienced in the ways of life than you. And it is the easiest thing in the world for you to pick up, without noticing it, something of their hopelessly vague attitude about religion and the world, about right and wrong, about what matters and whether anything matters ... You fall into slack ways, and worldly ways, and riotous ways, out of mere human respect, because people up here seem to do that sort of thing; weak fools, throwing away with both hands your Catholic birthright. But the Master whom we follow was holy, separated from sinners; and he has made his Church holy; and his will is to find that holiness visibly reflected, for all the world to see, in you.[22]

It was a bracing call to holiness, linked to a sense of Catholicism as something distinctive in the life of the community. He also showed a shrewd understanding of how a student felt trying to find a place for himself in collegiate life. Central to Knox's understanding of spirituality was the necessity of choosing. Following Christ meant belonging to a distinctive community with values that sometimes cut across those of the world. And yet, we may wonder at Knox's statement that Christ was *separated from sinners*. Of course Christ was holy and sinless. Yet he took the risk of being involved in the world, and one of the complaints made against him was that he ate and drank with notorious sinners (Mark 2.16 and pars). If Knox's ability to present the call to holiness was a strength of his chaplaincy, it was a lack of social involvement that was its weakness, which is the more remarkable when it is recalled that he was at Oxford during some of the most turbulent years in British social history.

Initially, there would have been comparatively little interest in such issues at the beginning of his chaplaincy ministry. When Knox returned to Oxford as Catholic Chaplain in September 1926, many of the students were uncomprehending about the state of the nation. In May 1926 the nation had been convulsed by the General Strike; in September the miners were still on strike and living in desperate circumstances. One reason for the comparative political indifference was the legacy of the war. The survivors were determined to enjoy themselves and to blank out the bad memories. After 1918 many students felt that the world had seen enough of politics. Oxford undergraduates at this time included the stellar talents of W. H. Auden, Louis MacNeice and Cecil Day-Lewis. Auden and MacNeice remembered 1926 as a time of comparative insouciance. MacNeice wrote in his autobiography that students took part in strike breaking and regarded the strike as 'an occasion for a spree; a comic phenomenon due to the Lower Classes; a comet that came from nowhere and dissolved in rubble and presaged nothing to come.'[23] Auden portrayed himself and his peers as uninterested in political and social issues at this time: 'We were far too insular and preoccupied with ourselves to know or care what was going on across the Channel. Revolution in Russia, inflation in Germany and Austria, Fascism in Italy ... went unnoticed by us. Before 1930 I never opened a newspaper.'[24] There was also the question of Oxford's exclusiveness. Although the number of scholarship students was growing steadily, many students still came from the public schools, and some students were prone to crude snobbery. We glimpse the rawness of this in an account of three years at Oxford (1928–1931) written by a mineworker who won a scholarship offered by his union's pension fund. His account included incidents where students from leading public schools openly mocked and ostracized students from working-class backgrounds.[25] Part of the challenge of the Catholic chaplaincy was to create a spiritual home where class was not an issue.

The shock of the stock market collapse in 1929 and the economic depression of the early 1930s began a change in the Oxford conscience. As mass unemployment hit Britain, many Oxford students were radicalized and the student community tended to be more left-wing and critical of the government, as became clear when the Oxford Union passed its notorious resolution in February 1933, 'That this House will in no circumstances fight for its King and Country'. An historian of Oxford writes about this period that 'Economic depression at home and rising international tension abroad were beginning to pierce undergraduate complacency.' One of the consequences was that 'the temper of Oxford in the early 1930s was noticeably more radical than it had been.'[26] There was a greater moral earnestness, and some of the students were involved in projects to help the unemployed.

Little of the *Sturm und Drang* of Oxford politics in the 1930s penetrated the walls of the Catholic chaplaincy. What social content there was usually came through the parallel work of the Newman Society, which occasionally invited speakers on contemporary topics. In 1931–1932, for example, J. B. Morton came to speak on Poland, Eric Gill on 'Labour-Saving Gadgets', Eric Strauss on psychotherapy, and Bruce Lockhart on events in Germany, where the Nazis had recently come to power. This, however, was an exceptional year in terms of the number of contemporary topics. Knox later described the Old Palace as 'An old place *[sic]*, where the near-Left political language of the early thirties found no conspicuous echo.' He made it clear that with hindsight he regretted the fact that the chaplaincy did not show a greater awareness of some of the pressing social concerns of the day.[27] Initially there was a contrast here with the Cambridge Catholic chaplaincy. During the General Strike of 1926, Fr Lopes had been shocked to hear of undergraduates volunteering as strike breakers and had warned, 'If there is ever a class war in this country the universities of Oxford and Cambridge began it in 1926.'[28] But Fr Lopes left in 1928 and the next but one chaplain, Mgr Alfred Gilbey, followed a far more conservative style.

Knox had his own reasons for steering the chaplaincy away from social and political issues. He felt that Catholic students at Oxford in the 1930s were well served by the Dominicans and the Jesuits when it came to tackling the issues of the day. The Dominican house of studies at Blackfriars had been re-established in 1921. The Dominican provincial, Fr Bede Jarrett, intended not only that student Dominicans should read for Oxford degrees and attend lectures, but also that the Dominicans should be able to contribute to the life of the university.[29] Blackfriars quickly became a centre of forward-looking preaching, and friendships were formed between the friars and members of the university. The Dominicans were particularly influenced by French writers such as Jacques Maritain and Emmanuel Mounier. In opposition to both Communism and Fascism these French philosophers propounded an intensely personalist social ethic, in Maritain's case drawing on a Catholic understanding of the virtues. Like the Dominicans, the Jesuits took culture in their stride, and the Jesuit centre of Campion Hall was only a few yards away from the Old Palace. Its Master from 1933, Fr Martin D'Arcy, was a friend and confidant of Knox. D'Arcy was well informed of current trends in society. Even non-Catholics were admirers of D'Arcy. Louis MacNeice wrote of D'Arcy,

> He alone among Oxford dons seemed to me to have the glamour that medieval students looked for in their masters. Intellect incarnate in a beautiful head, wavy grey hair and delicate features; a hawk's eyes. I suspected his religion, of course, but it at least, I thought, has given him a *savoir-faire* which you do not find in these wishy-washy humanists . . .[30]

D'Arcy was an acute reader of cultural trends. He had been one of the first to praise MacNeice's poetry, in a review in *The Oxford Outlook*, and later, in 1932, he was a helpful interlocutor between MacNeice and T. S. Eliot.[31] D'Arcy's brilliance so impressed the students that in 1934 he was elected to the Standing Committee of the Oxford Union. D'Arcy was not content to limit himself to narrowly-defined Catholic interests but wanted to demonstrate Catholic interest and involvement in many areas of cultural life.

Knox was reluctant to be seen as proselytizing through the Oxford chaplaincy. It was D'Arcy who acquired the reputation of a fisher of men. Frank Pakenham, the future Lord Longford, was Student in Politics at Christ Church when he felt drawn to the Catholic Church and sought out Fr D'Arcy for advice and initial instruction. Of D'Arcy he wrote: 'He stood out in my mind as the one man capable both of understanding my personal problems and of providing an objective answer to the dominant agnosticism of the time.'[32] Someone else who gravitated to D'Arcy was Quintin Hogg, later Lord Hailsham and Lord Chancellor, who had been brought up to believe that the Pope was anti-Christ and the Jesuits his shock troops. After initial hesitation, he sought D'Arcy's friendship, often turning to him for advice in later years at times of crisis. D'Arcy helped him return to the Christian faith, by showing him that Christianity, Catholic or Protestant, was intellectually respectable.[33] Despite such successes, D'Arcy was careful not to press too hard. In 1937 Vita Sackville-West (Vita Nicolson) wrote to D'Arcy in good-humoured exasperation about her son Nigel Nicolson, who was then at Oxford: 'Nigel has an enormous admiration and respect for you, and his only grievance against you is that he "can never get you to talk to him about religion"! He says that you have tried, but you "sheer off". Now, of course I quite understand why you "sheer off". Your position in Oxford must require great tact and circumspection.' But she asked, please could he talk about religion with her son?[34]

With D'Arcy at Campion Hall and Knox at the chaplaincy, it was something of a golden age for Catholics at Oxford. Looking back at Oxford some twenty years later, Waugh certainly thought so.[35] The Knox-D'Arcy partnership worked well, for Knox regarded himself more as a shepherd than a fisherman, and was happy to send most of his inquirers about the faith to Blackfriars or Campion Hall for instruction. One of those Knox did receive into the Church himself was Arnold Lunn. Lunn, who had been Knox's contemporary at Balliol in the 1930s, was achieving fame as the organizer and promoter of alpine winter sports in which he invented the modern slalom and introduced skiing into the Olympic Games. In 1924 Lunn had written a book, *Roman Converts*, in which he puzzled over why eminent Englishmen, including Knox, had become Catholics. In 1930 he wrote to Knox suggesting that they co-author a book in which Lunn would raise objections to Catholicism and Knox would reply. The result of their epistolary exchange was *Difficulties* (1932). It had a wide readership and two subsequent editions appeared. From today's perspective it is a rather pedestrian work. Knox always sought to explain things in ways that would make sense to contemporary readers. But he found it hard to understand the mind and feelings of those who struggled to reconcile the reality of suffering with a good and omnipotent God. Moreover, Lunn was respectful and already half-attracted to what he was ostensibly attacking. For two years after the book, Lunn continued to read and think and in July 1933 Knox received him into the Church in the chaplaincy at Oxford. Knox, said Lunn, was the greatest influence in his conversion, but D'Arcy, Douglas Woodruff and his own reading had also played their part. He believed even so that rational arguments were far more important than were generally realized, and hence Knox's work in this respect would always matter.[36] Lunn became a lifelong friend and a frequent visitor to the Old Palace. He wrote later that Knox gave himself with single-minded determination to the task of reinforcing the faith of the undergraduates, who regarded him 'not only with great affection but also great respect and this in spite of an informality – many of his university friends addressed him as "Ronnie" – which shocked his more conservative colleagues.'[37]

It is hard to ascertain when Knox first met Evelyn Waugh, but it was probably through Fr D'Arcy. After a brief period of instruction in the summer of 1930, D'Arcy had received Waugh into the Catholic Church at the Jesuit church in Farm

Street, Mayfair, on 29 September 1930. When Campion Hall was built in 1934 on its present site, Waugh contributed to the costs by writing a biography of Edmund Campion and donating the profits to the hall. In the preface he expressed his gratitude to D'Arcy as the one to whom, under God, he owed his faith.[38] In August 1933 Waugh, D'Arcy and others had joined a Hellenic cruise. On the return journey Waugh was invited to visit the Herbert family who were staying at their villa near Portofino on the Ligurian coast of Italy, which Mary Herbert had inherited from her husband, the Conservative MP and adventurer Aubrey Herbert. Before Waugh's arrival, Mrs Herbert had been given a favourable account of him by Ronald Knox, who was also staying at the villa.[39] This was fortunate, because during this visit Waugh met Laura Herbert, the daughter of Aubrey and Mary, and was captivated by her. They married in 1937 after the annulment of Waugh's first marriage. So Waugh owed a debt of gratitude to Knox, and although it was D'Arcy who presided at the wedding of Evelyn and Laura, in time Waugh grew closer to Knox.

The Spanish Civil War of 1936–1939 sharply divided political opinion in Britain and the division of opinion was felt in Oxford. English Catholics were well aware of the hatred shown towards the Church by the extreme Left in Republican-controlled areas, and the resulting massacres of priests and nuns. Although there were some differences between the English bishops, they united in seeing the Spanish Civil War as a struggle in which ordinary Catholics were wholly justified in supporting the rebels. This message, together with stories of Red atrocities, was conveyed from the pulpit and through the Catholic press. Labour Party and trade union activists found that Catholic areas were less likely to support campaigns for Republican Spain. Catholic fear of Communism was one contributory factor to Catholic support for Franco, although in addition some right-wing Catholic intellectuals believed that Franco was bringing a new social and political order that would apply Catholic principles.[40] Not all Catholics felt this way. The most significant dissent came from the

Dominicans in Oxford, who voiced their doubt about Franco and the Nationalist cause through their journal *Blackfriars*. The Dominicans were always open to French influence and here they were following the lead of Jacques Maritain, who refused to see the Spanish Civil War in terms of the conflict between Christianity and Communism. Knox felt that Franco had been justified, and said so, rather reluctantly, in one of his conferences.[41] It created a permanent division between Knox and Maurice Bowra, the influential Classics don (and from 1938 Warden of Wadham College) who had always suspected Catholicism of being authoritarian.[42] In general Knox wanted to steer away from such partisan declarations which could so easily divide his little flock.

His comparative indifference over political issues has to be seen in the context of his love for the Catholic faith and his conviction that it offered all that was necessary to live a full life in the world. Catholicism was, therefore, a primary commitment. Other commitments such as political ones might be made in the light of faith, but they were not required for the fullness of life. Catholics, he told his students,

> are in this position of advantage, that instead of having to look about the world and find for ourselves some loyalty which will make life worth living for us, we are provided, from our cradle upwards, with such a loyalty all ready made. It does not in the least prevent us from adopting other loyalties if we will, from attaching ourselves to any reputable movement or adhering to any sensible philosophy. But it makes that unnecessary; so long as we retain the Catholic faith we have always one interest, one loyalty, one enthusiasm in the world to keep us alive ... it does also take us out of ourselves by throwing our reliance on a Personality, the Personality of Jesus Christ; it does also take us out of ourselves by identifying us with a movement, whose triumphs are our triumphs, whose anxieties are our anxieties ...[43]

We would be wrong to conclude that Knox's approach ignored

the pressures and problems of the 1930s. Knox said in a sermon (probably to students in July 1938) that Catholic culture included traditions about state and society, marriage and family, the values of life and the duties of life. This gave Catholics a philosophy which might mean opposing the dangerous trends such as, in Germany, 'that militant nationalism which endangers the peace of Europe.' Salvation, said Knox, did not depend upon an active interest in politics.

> But this I do say, that in so far as you are an active Catholic, really try to appreciate the Catholic culture and what it stands for ... you will find yourself in the full stream of the life of your generation, you will know the joy of conflict, without which there is little savour in living ... The question is whether you will be a spectator merely, or whether there will be a part of yourself in the issues that are being fought out during your generation.[44]

This was not flight from the world. Rather, it saw Catholic faith as fundamentally constitutive of a person. An active, confident Catholic identity would lead in turn to an engagement with the world. It seemed to work this way for Patrick O'Donovan, then a student at Christ Church, who found that his fellow students gave his faith a great battering. O'Donovan found that the priests at Oxford helped him make the transition to a more open yet still confident faith. His friend and contemporary Robert Kee believed that O'Donovan's Catholicism 'gave him an ordered structure from which to view fairly effortlessly the world ... I was both less sure of myself and less well-informed than he was.'[45] Knox's approach is understandable, although it rather sidestepped the challenge of working out how Catholic principles were to be applied in an agonistic world. How to read the signs of the times was a challenge in the 1930s. Oxford, at the time, was a perplexed place, with Communists and Fascists, among others, bidding for student sympathies, knowing that here the minds of the country's elite could be captured. Malcolm Muggeridge wrote sardonically that, during this period, 'Fathers in clubs complained that their sons had become Communists at Oxford.'[46] Mosley's British Union of Fascists was also trying to recruit Oxford students. At a BUF meeting in Oxford addressed by Mosley in May 1936, Frank Pakenham had been repeatedly punched and kicked by Fascist stewards, whose behaviour appalled many in Oxford and helped turn them against Fascism.[47]

Also vying for the loyalties of students was a very different movement, the Oxford Group, a non-denominational pietist movement headed by an American evangelist, Frank Buchman. The movement encouraged its adherents to pray together in small groups where they also practised public confession of sin. This self-scrutiny all too often elevated the trivial and ignored deeper issues. The element of public confession also carried the risk of prurience. Devotees were expected to seek direct divine guidance. In the 1920s Buchman visited both Oxford and Cambridge, and, according to Owen Chadwick, 'found ready hearers among groups of undergraduates. They were not content with the cynicism of post-war Britain or with the university of Evelyn Waugh. They saw the churches quarrelling over trivialities.'[48] In the 1930s the Oxford Group was able to recruit well in Oxford, holding meetings in Oxford town hall and hiring whole colleges in the summer for summer house parties. One of the more surprising recruits was B. H. Streeter, Provost of Queen's College, whose arguments in *Foundations* had been so strenuously opposed by Knox some twenty years previously.[49] In the novel *Still Dead* of 1934, Knox hints at the Oxford Group through references to a laird who seeks 'guidance' and a visitor who belongs to devotional groups called 'Circles'.[50] He worried that some of his Catholic students might be weaned away. He complained about the Oxford Group to his friend and publisher Maisie Ward. He told her that they were notorious for exploiting every sign of interest shown by others and he feared that there would soon be news of Catholics having joined the movement.[51]

Against this Oxford backdrop of competing loyalties Knox preached the timeless wisdom of the Catholic faith. This

concentration on the spiritual did not arise out of ignorance of
the real world. Knox's preaching would have nourished the
students spiritually, and given them a sense of perspective
about the social issues of the day. But we may wonder
whether this same approach might also have had the effect of
abstracting them from the realities of the world. If so, it was
in keeping with the mainstream of English Catholic tradition
at this time, of which Bishop David Mathew could write airily
in 1935: 'Politics play little part in the Catholic community as
such . . .'[52] Although Catholics of every political hue could be
found, there was also a broad strain of Catholic indifferentism
when it came to party politics.

Writing had always been important to Knox. In his first year
at the Old Palace he completed a book explaining the Catholic
faith to those who knew little about it and wanted to understand more. This book, *The Belief of Catholics*, was quickly
reprinted. What is striking is that Knox tries to put himself
into the mind of a non-believer, and in doing so he stresses
that Catholicism must capture the mind as well as the heart.
He argues, therefore, for the existence of God from nature,
giving not only the five traditional Thomistic proofs of the
existence of God but also arguing for God from the phenomenon of human self-consciousness. In recent years there has
been renewed interest in theology in this approach, and Knox
sounds remarkably contemporary when he writes that 'this
spiritual principle, the self-conscious life within man' is not
accounted for by any natural element but points to God.[53]
When explaining salvation history he opens with the record of
Christianity in early non-scriptural writers such as Pliny,
Tacitus and Josephus. Only then does he turn to the scriptures,
and special revelation. Here and there a pungent Knoxian
aside breaks through. He dismisses claims that Christian
doctrine is still uncertain, for 'If Christianity is still in process
of formulation after twenty centuries, it must be an uncom-
monly elusive affair.' He insists that the Church is right in
requiring converts to understand what they believe: 'It is their
duty to satisfy their own minds . . . about God's existence, the

authority of Christ, etc. before they can expect the grace of faith to come to them.'[54] In a passage that probably reflects his own journey, he adds that after all the probing, assessing and questioning, a person has to make an act of commitment.

However paradoxical it may seem, it does need a resolution of the will to put the verdict of the intellect into execution. Mere brainwork will not bludgeon you into changing your creed; especially since such a change of creed involves practical consequences – the submission to ceremony, the adoption of new devotional habits, strained relations with your family or your old friends, and so on. Nothing is more certain as a matter of experience ... than that a voluntary step is still needed *after* you have become intellectually convinced that Catholicism is true.[55]

The intellect might lead the mind to assent, but still a decision had to be made. And others might find, as he had himself, that there was a price to be paid in family relationships, and even, perhaps, in the wider community. So the decision might require an element of steel.

This combination of will and intellect underlay what we might call Knox's spirituality. He wanted students and other Catholics to understand the Church's doctrinal teaching, to know how it was formed and why. A good grasp of Catholic doctrine would give them the strength to commit themselves to the Catholic faith and to renew that commitment in the countless choices and decisions that would lie ahead of them. His conferences on Catholic doctrine can sometimes seem a little daunting in the solidity of their content. Even though he shaped his conferences and sermons carefully, their doctrinal content could be unsparing. He paid his listeners the compliment of believing that they could absorb solid teaching. In his day this would not have seemed unusual. Compared with our own times it seems old-fashioned and even reactionary, because the divorce of spirituality from theology has led to an emphasis on spirituality. Faith thus becomes the cultivation of feelings. It is an individualistic pursuit rather than sharing in a corporate life. Aidan Nichols has drawn attention to the poverty of a religion of sentiment, and the need for English Catholicism to be more centred on its own doctrinal teaching: 'A Church that retains some power of moral uplift through its ceremonies and ministrations will make no evangelical headway in a high culture ... if in the meanwhile it has lost the intellectual argument.'[56] Knox saw this quite clearly. It was their duty, he told students, to try to convert heretics, because if you possess spiritual truth then you must necessarily want to impart it to others. Not, he added, that he wanted them to make indiscriminate attempts to convert those they sat next to in the hall of their college: 'No, your duty is to defend the faith to the best of your power where you can see it is being misrepresented, and to help your friends when they begin to take an interest in the Catholic religion.'[57] It is the measure of Britain's dilution of its Christian heritage that today, such confidence in one's own faith would probably be criticized as intolerance or damned as fundamentalism.

But what was the cost of this certainty for Knox himself? That he believed in Catholic truth from his heart, there is no doubt. Yet it had required an act of will to make the leap, as well as intellectual conviction, because there would be a cost for him. We catch a glimpse of that cost, oddly enough, in the first detective novel that he wrote while at Oxford. *The Three Taps* is about the suspicious death of a wealthy businessman staying at a country inn. The insurance company with which he had a policy sends its detective, Miles Bredon, to investigate, for if the death is a murder the company must pay out £500,000. If it is a suicide, it will pay nothing. There is a conundrum in the question of murder or suicide. When the body was discovered, the door was locked from the inside, so how could it be murder? On the other hand, the gas tap was found to be turned off, so how could it be suicide? Compared with *The Viaduct Murder*, this mystery is fast-paced and holds the reader's attention. In the middle of the story Miles Bredon visits the fictional Catholic Bishop of Pullford. At the meal table he discovered that the bishop's secretary is a former vicar who has converted to Catholicism. Bredon the detective knows the place where this man used to be rector and finds himself envisaging how it used to be for the former Anglican:

> Yes, you could put this man in clerical clothes, and he would fit beautifully into that spacious garden; you saw him, with surplice fluttering in the breeze, going up the churchyard path to ring the bell for evening service; that was his atmosphere. And here, unfrocked by his own conscience, he was living as a hired servant, almost a pensioner, in this gaunt house, these cheerless rooms ... You wondered less at his silent habit, and his melancholy airs of speech.[58]

It is difficult not to feel that in part Knox was referring to his own feelings – a nostalgia for the past, a sense of loss as well as of gain, and the realization of emotional poverty. And is that reference to a 'gaunt house ... cheerless rooms' a reference to the Old Palace, or perhaps to St Edmund's, Ware? By this point Knox had been a Catholic for ten years. He was back at Oxford, with national recognition of his talents, and responsibility for the elite of the nation's youth. He had time to write and occasionally to broadcast. It might have been thought that there would be little room for a sense of loss. This passage seems to hint otherwise. If so then Knox was true to his own teaching: he was intellectually convinced of the Catholic truth, but it required also, from time to time, the gritty exercise of his will.

Other Bredon detective stories followed: *The Footsteps at the Lock* (1928; reprinted four times in two years), *The Body in the Silo* (1933), *Still Dead* (1934) and *Double Cross Purposes* (1937). Knox acquired a following of loyal readers. Some are still in print, including some translations into other languages. The Italians, especially, seem to enjoy his detective books. The settings of these books varied. In *The Footsteps at the Lock*, for example, there are some lyric descriptions of Oxford countryside along the banks of the Thames. But for all the ingenuity of the puzzles, there is always a sense of the characters being underdeveloped and the plot proceeding too much by discussion and too little by events. Yet perhaps this dissection of the crime by brainy sleuths was precisely the appeal of these books. It is sometimes said that the detective story of this period was an escape from the amorphous sea of subjectivity that characterized modernist literature. An article written in 1929 explained that

> We have revolted from an excessive subjectivity to welcome objectivity; from long-drawn-out dissections of emotion to straightforward appeal to intellect; from reiterated emphasis upon men and women as victims either of circumstances or of their glands to a suggestion that men and women may consciously plot and consciously plan . . . most of all, from a smart and easy pessimism which interprets men and the universe in terms of unmoral purposelessness to a rebelief in a universe governed by cause and effect. All this we find in the detective story.[59]

If this analysis is correct, then it tells us that Ronald Knox's detective stories were very much of their time, and that they appealed to those for whom modernist literature was quite simply too tortuous. Their longing for a narrative with a clear moral and rational landscape, in which the protagonists were accountable for their deeds, played into Knox's strengths. And, we might note, his own sense of propriety.

It is notable too that his detective stories won him both a modest but important financial return and a recognized place among the best-known writers of the genre. In 1928 he was invited to co-edit *Best Detective Stories* and in the introduction laid down ten rules which he believed should be followed by practitioners of the craft. The criminal must be named early in the story, but we must not be able to read his thoughts; all supernatural agency is ruled out; no more than one secret room or passage; no hitherto undiscovered poisons may be used, nor any appliance requiring long scientific explanation; no Chinaman must feature in the story (at this time writers tended to produce a Chinese man as an archetypal scheming villain); no accident or unaccountable intuition could help the detective; the detective must not himself commit the crime; any clues had to be instantly produced for the reader; the detective's duller friend ('the Watson') had to be transparent; twins were not allowed.[60] In 1929 he joined others in the newly founded Detection Club, a kind of guild of detection fiction writers. Other members included Dorothy Sayers, Freeman Wills Crofts, E. C. Bentley and Agatha Christie. G. K. Chesterton, another member, was elected its first president.[61] His skill was recognized by the BBC too, which asked him to join in writing a detective story called 'Behind the Screen' in which each instalment would be by a different author. His was the last instalment broadcast on 14 July 1930, and he had to bring together the clues and narrative woven by (among others) Agatha Christie and Dorothy Sayers. It says a good deal that the BBC entrusted this most difficult of the episodes, the *dénouement*, to Knox.[62]

Knox was well known to the BBC, which had been broadcasting religious talks and services since 1923. The Catholic Church accepted an invitation to join this new development, but found itself with a particular difficulty. Cardinal Bourne and others felt that the Mass was too sacrosanct to be broadcast to casual listeners, and anyway the fact that it was in Latin would have left many listeners unable to understand. There was also pressure from the BBC for the Catholic Church to avoid anything divisive and to restrict itself to a centralist Christian message. The first Catholic broadcasts were studio services, for which the BBC found it difficult to find good Catholic preachers. Knox and the Jesuit Cyril Martindale were two of the most popular.[63] Knox declined BBC requests to broadcast more often, pleading other commitments, although it is clear that he was reluctant to participate in frivolous debates. He turned down an invitation to a debate on the question 'Should the BBC be abolished?' when the BBC particularly sought Knox because they wanted to be defended by someone with a sense of humour. He declined other invitations to debate whether domestic pets should be abolished (1924), and about capital punishment (1927) when the BBC hoped that he would argue for and Margery Fry against. He did accept an invitation to produce a humorous commentary on events of the week in March 1934, called 'Seven Days Hard'. Previous commentators had included Bernard Shaw, J. B. Priestley, Beverly Nichols and Dorothy Sayers. After the broadcast Knox wrote to Iremonger at the BBC: 'My "fan mail" included a very nice letter from my Archbishop, so it seems I wasn't unorthodox!' Other invitations to broadcast came and the BBC indicated that it wanted to hear Knox on the air at least once a year.[64] He contributed to a series called 'Revisited' in which well-known persons revisited places where they had grown up. In his case he visited Birmingham, recalling the street familiar to him as a small boy in the late 1890s. He remembered the frock-coated sidesmen of his father's church, St Philip's; crowds shouting as they mobbed an eminent statesman, who escaped, it was said, only by disguising himself as a policeman; the electric trams on the Bristol Road, with their strange lunging motion; and how you had to make sure you had on a clean collar if you visited the people of Edgbaston.

On Easter 1938 the BBC wanted him to speak on 'What happened on Easter Morning'. However, that Holy Week he was in Dublin to preach a retreat at the University Church. The BBC accordingly went to some trouble to arrange a link with Irish Radio, so that he could broadcast to Britain from a Dublin studio on Easter Sunday, 17th April. In his address Knox restricted himself to scripture, weaving together the six different sources in such that way that they corresponded. It was deftly done, even if it would not meet the standards of today's biblical scholarship because of the way he harmonized the different accounts. The starkly central fact of the story, he pointed out, was the empty tomb, a fact that was deeply embarrassing to the opponents of Jesus. To contradict the story of the resurrection all they had to do was to produce the body, but they could not do so. Of course, it was possible that the disciples themselves had stolen the body in a deliberate fraud to give the impression that their Master had risen from the dead.

What you have to decide is, whether such a notion is consistent with the behaviour of those same people two days before, at the Crucifixion, running away and leaving their Master to face his persecutors alone, and with the behaviour of those same people, in the years which followed, suffering imprisonment and dying in support of a story which they had made up to deceive the public.[65]

It was a stout defence of tradition, clear in exposition and cast as an appeal to his listeners to believe in what Christians had always believed. It was typical, too, of Knox's style, with its strong reliance on scripture, interpreted from a Catholic perspective in a way to make the message as acceptable as possible to all people of good will.

Oxford was in many ways a time of fulfilment for Knox. He was held in great affection by his students, for whom his ministry of availability was always on offer. Many years later one of his former students wrote, 'He was someone we could always go to: not because he preached well or wrote well, but because he was always young and always seemed to understand. He was a fountain of refreshment on which we could always draw.'[66] He was well known and respected in the university itself, valued for his wit and his humanity. For example, at Eights Week each May the Oxford Union featured a debate usually on a humorous topic and Knox was the guest speaker several times. In 1939 he spoke for the ninth and last time at an Eights Week debate and the university newspaper the *Isis* described his speech as 'not a success but a triumph'.[67] He was sought after by the BBC. He had an entry in *Who's Who*. In 1936 he was made a domestic prelate to the Pope, a largely symbolic honour which meant that he would now be addressed as Monsignor Knox. He was the author of books on many different topics, in a variety of genres. Yet, as so often in life, the outer success was not matched by an inner serenity. Evelyn Waugh alluded to a growing sense of depression felt by Knox as the 1930s progressed, and attributed it to a mixture of ill-health and loneliness.[68] Knox also found, as many do in their forties, that new and nourishing friendships are hard to come by. Certainly there were those in his life whose company was oxygen for him, such as Harold Macmillan, Laura Lovat and latterly, Daphne Acton. He and Macmillan kept in touch by correspondence and by visits. When Macmillan lost his Stockton constituency to a Labour candidate in the election of 30 May 1929, he wrote to Macmillan commiserating: 'I have to write this cheap consolation to you, because it is a long time since I was in the position to have any ambitions, or consequently any disappointments, of my own. But good Lord, how few people in the world there are to whom I can write with any real feeling of intimacy.'[69] Macmillan was one of the few. Other factors may be assumed to have played a part in Knox's melancholy. One was a spate of bereavements. Sligger Urquhart died in September 1934, having been Dean of Balliol since 1918. Urquhart was not only the Catholic elder statesman in Oxford University, he was also a good friend to Knox. In Knox's Anglican days his discreet friendship had given Knox a sense of security, knowing that there was an influential Catholic on whose sagacity and goodwill he could rely. At the time of conversion, a lonely period, he had leaned heavily on Urquhart. Knox owed the chaplaincy itself to Urquhart's lobbying. In June 1936, G. K. Chesterton died, and Knox preached at a memorial requiem Mass attended by 2,000 people in Westminster cathedral on June 27th. There was a further bereavement in the summer of 1937, when his beloved housekeeper Mrs Lyons died.

A particularly significant death must have been that of Knox's father Bishop Edmund Knox, who died in January 1937 aged 89. All the losses took their toll, but we may wonder especially at the effect of his father's death. Ronald knew that his father, a convinced evangelical, disagreed strongly with his son's Catholic convictions and indeed even in his old age had been a strong opponent of catholicizing tendencies in the Church of England. Bishop Knox had rallied evangelicals to help persuade parliament to defeat a proposed revision of the Book of Common Prayer in 1927 and 1928.

The bishop particularly condemned the Catholic belief in the real presence of Christ in the eucharist, which he believed was being promoted by the revisions proposed for the Prayer Book. As a Reformation Church, he said, the Church of England must deny that God was in the consecrated elements.[70] Ronald Knox, on the other hand, was saying Mass daily and had based his life on the reality of Christ's presence in the eucharist. In his autobiography Bishop Knox wrote warmly of his adult children's accomplishments. But he described Ronald as being 'in charge of a Roman Catholic house, the Old Palace at Oxford', an obvious obfuscation. It made his son's position seem analogous to that of the head of college. He could not bring himself to say that Ronald was a Catholic priest. Edmund Knox admitted that his children's inability to share his evangelical faith was a source of sorrow and pain: 'Here I find the saddest of the experiences and remembrances of my life, records of the most humiliating of my failures.'[71] One wonders if Ronald read those words, and what he felt if he did. He does not seem to have been a frequent visitor to his father in his retirement at Bromley, south of London, which might point to something unresolved in their relationship. His father was simply being true to his own principles just as Ronald was true to his. But it must have been painful for Ronald to have known that his father deeply distrusted and disliked the faith to which he had given his life. After his father's death, Ronald discovered that he had been left nothing in his father's will. Of this he wrote later to a friend: 'I've always honoured my father for his consistency in not leaving me anything.'[72] The jaunty note here scarcely hides the pain. Perhaps there was even a subconscious fear that his father disliked him because of his Catholicism. It was virtually impossible for them to explore this tension between them and to resolve it. Feelings ran too deep, and the emotional reserve of their class and upbringing was too strong to be overcome.

There were other reasons for Ronald Knox's bouts of depression from around 1937 onwards. By then he had been university chaplain for over ten years. The life of a university chaplain has particular strains. One of them is the peculiar intensity of the pastoral work which has to run within the constraints of university terms. Three times a year the chaplain has to accomplish within ten or so weeks programmes that a parish priest can spread over a whole year. Thirty years after Knox, one of his successors as chaplain found the same struggle with a cyclical mood of bleakness. Michael Hollings, Catholic chaplain at Oxford throughout the 1960s, wrote that 'towards the middle of every term such a black mood of tiredness, feeling of failure and disillusion came down that I personally felt like packing the whole work up . . . The few successes get totally obscured by the suicide incidents or the apparent falling away of good young men and women.' Nor did it help that Knox's personality was, as he admitted, inclined to be Pelagian.[73] A Pelagian believed that salvation had to be won by one's own efforts. He had to resist this temptation to strain constantly for effect, with its concomitant gloom at any failure.

There is also the question of the bereavements Knox had endured twenty years earlier during the First World War. When he walked along Broad Street past Balliol, did he remember the times of laughter and companionship with Charles Lister and Patrick Shaw-Stewart? When he went in to dine at Trinity, did he see in his mind's eye Guy Lawrence and other students he had coached and encouraged? All had been cut down in their youth during the war. When Waugh's biography of Knox was published, the All Souls don and professional Cornishman A. L. Rowse asked him if Knox had given the impression of great sadness. Waugh said yes, and added that Knox never got over the loss of his friends during the war.[74] Rowse may well have exaggerated Waugh's comments, and indeed seems almost to have relished them, but Knox did show signs of depression in his last few years at Oxford.

Some of Knox's inner feelings can be discerned in two of the conferences he gave known as the 'freshers' raspberry'. The name came from the bracing mixture of advice and exhortation to the first year students which these talks contained. They were always given in the second term, i.e. the Hilary term. The students were abjured not to get drunk, not to sink into debt, to avoid bad company and to keep up their religious duties. In the 1934 'raspberry' Knox made his points with lightness of touch.

I always notice, going about the streets of Oxford in October, what a lot of bright, healthy complexions one sees. That's the freshers. It doesn't happen at any other time of year; by now, you have mostly acquired that pallor which is characteristic of the undergraduate; it is perhaps most charitable to assign it to the influence of the Oxford climate . . .
    You should make sure you are not drifting into a set you don't, really, want to drift into. Here's one lot who are quite nice people, but their tastes and habits have made them stupid – much stupider than you want to be. Here is another lot who are clever, to be sure, rather cleverer than you are, but you can see for yourself that they are cynics, laughing at everything that other people hold sacred. Cast in your lot with them, and your faith will suffer . . . Here is another lot who spend more money than you could afford to spend . . . Here is another lot who are rather good value until about six o'clock in the evening, but after that hour to be seen sober in their company would make you a marked man.

Three years later the 'raspberry' was written as he was coming out of one of several bouts of influenza. The tone was heavier, there were elements of self-pity and too much ranting. He complained to his students that they were too bovine, 'the great wedge of what you may call beta query gamma Catholics who go down each year from this University and remain beta query gamma Catholics after doing so.' He scolded them: 'All except about half a dozen of you, I suppose, are deliberately neglecting God. I say, ARE neglecting God, not WILL neglect.'[75] And more of the same. He had had a good innings at Oxford, and it had been a creative period when both his pastoral and his creative gifts had been harnessed. But it was time to go.

Notes

1 Annual chaplaincy report 1937, Universities Catholic Education Board at Archives of the Archdiocese of Westminster (UCEB/AAW). This description of Knox was written by Douglas Woodruff.

2 From a letter to Katharine Asquith. Quoted in Walter Drumm, *The Old Palace: The Catholic Chaplaincy at Oxford* (Dublin: Veritas Publications, 1991), p. 77. But compare EW, *RK* 'The cooking was excellent' (222).

3 Hollis, *Road to Frome*, pp. 85 and 79. Hollis himself became a Catholic while at Oxford.

4 Quoted in Drumm, *The Old Palace*, p. 28.

5 Owen Chadwick, *The Victorian Church* Part II (London: Adam and Charles Black, 1970), pp. 455 and 457. The bishops however could dispense from the ban.

6 Knox to Wilfred Woollen, Secretary to the Universities Catholic Education Board, (UCEB) 10 December 1932, AAW.

7 From a typescript, *The Whole Art of Chaplaincraft* which Knox wrote for his successor in 1939. KPM. (Quotations here are taken from lengthy extracts in Drumm and EW, *RK*.)

8 Evelyn Waugh, *Brideshead Revisited* (London: Penguin, 2000; first published by Chapman and Hall, 1945), p. 59. On the title page Waugh inserted an Author's Note: 'I am not I; thou art not he or she/they are not they.' But several characters in the novel suggest aspects of persons from real life (e.g. Harold Acton, Maurice Bowra). Is 'Bell' here a playful dig at Knox? It could have been that in 'Monsignor Bell' Waugh had Knox in mind. It could also refer to Knox's predecessor, Mgr Arthur Barnes who was Catholic chaplain while Waugh was at Oxford. But Waugh was not a Catholic at that time and would hardly have known Barnes, whereas he knew Knox.

9 Waugh, *Brideshead Revisited*, p. 139.

10 Annual chaplaincy report 1937, UCEB/AAW. Overall total of undergraduates from *Whitaker's Almanac 1937*.

11 See, for example, the figures for a Sunday Mass in 1938 which would indicate that up to two-thirds of the Catholic students were present at a chaplaincy Mass that day. Waugh, *RK*, p. 238.

12 Richard Rumford [*pseudonym*, Richard Rumbold] *My Father's Son* (London: Cape, 1949), p. 163.

13 *Time* 19 June, 1933. For Rumbold's account of the incident, see *My Father's Son*, pp. 162–5 and his diaries edited by William Plomer, *A Message in Code* (London: Weidenfeld and Nicolson, 1964), pp. 31–2, as well as the entry in the online *Oxford Dictionary of National Biography*.

14 Aspen, *Fortress Church*, p. 215.

15 Knox to Woollen, 24 October, no year but ?1932, UCEB/AAW.
16 F. De Zulueta, Memorandum, 'The Oxford Chaplaincy' n.d., UCEB/AAW.
17 Anson, *Fashions in Church Furnishing*, p. 317. See also Nigel Yates, *Anglican Ritualism in Victorian Britain* (Oxford: OUP, 1999), pp. 337–8.
18 Ronald Knox, 'The Oxford Chaplaincy' in Philip Caravan, ed., *Occasional Sermons of Ronald A. Knox* (London: Burns and Oates, 1960), p. 269.
19 Knox, 'Chaplaincraft', KPM.
20 Milton Walsh, *Ronald Knox as Apologist* (San Francisco: Ignatius Press, 2007), p. 247.
21 *The Diaries of Evelyn Waugh* (Michael Davie, ed.), p. 538.
22 Knox, 'The Unholiness of the Church', *In Soft Garments: A Collection of Oxford Conferences* (London: Burns Oates, 1942), pp. 74–80.
23 Louis MacNeice, *The Strings are False* (London: Faber, 1965), p. 101.
24 From an article in the *New Yorker* of April 1965, quoted in Samuel Hynes, *The Auden Generation: Literature and Politics in England in the 1930s* (London: Bodley Head, 1976), p. 401 n. 26.
25 Roger Dataller, *A Pitman Looks at Oxford* (London: Dent, 1933), pp. 104–6.
26 V. H. H. Green, *A History of Oxford University* (London: Batsford, 1974), pp. 193 and 194. See also Christopher Hollis, *The Oxford Union* (London: Evans Brothers, 1965), p. 182.
27 Annual chaplaincy report 1933, UCEB/AAW; and Knox, 'The Oxford Chaplaincy', *Occasional Sermons*, p. 269.
28 Maurice Couve de Murville and Philip Jenkins, *Catholic Cambridge* (London: Catholic Truth Society, 1983), p. 132.
29 Aidan Nichols, *Dominican Gallery* (Leominster: Gracewing, 1997), pp. 8–9.
30 MacNeice, *The Strings are False*, p. 128.
31 Jon Stallworthy, *Louis MacNeice* (London: Faber, 1995), pp. 141 and 163.
32 Frank Pakenham, *Born to Believe: An Autobiography* (London: Cape, 1953), p. 97.
33 Geoffrey Lewis, *Lord Hailsham: A Life* (London: Cape, 1997), p. 29.
34 Vita Nicolson to Martin D'Arcy, SJ, 8 July 1937, Jesuit Provincial Archives.
35 Waugh, *Essays, Articles and Reviews*, p. 431.
36 Lunn to Knox 1 July 1949, Sir Arnold Lunn Papers, Georgetown University Library Special Collections, Box 2 folder 37. See also Speaight, *Ronald Knox the Writer*, pp. 90–3.
37 Arnold Lunn, *And Yet So New* (London: Sheed and Ward, 1958), pp. 9–10.

38 Quoted in Christopher Sykes, *Evelyn Waugh: A Biography* (London: Collins, 1975), p. 145.

39 Sykes, *Waugh*, p. 135.

40 Tom Buchanan, *Britain and the Spanish Civil War* (Cambridge: CUP 1997), pp. 176–88, quoting from 180. Cf. James Flint, '"Must God Go Fascist?" English Catholic Opinion and the Spanish Civil War' *Church History* 53.3 (1987) 373–4.

41 EW *RK*, p. 228.

42 Leslie Mitchell, *Maurice Bowra: A Life* (Oxford: OUP, 2009), pp. 199–200.

43 Knox, 'Faith Lost and Found', *In Soft Garments*, p. 91.

44 Knox, 'Church and State', *Occasional Sermons*, pp. 216–17.

45 Patrick O'Donovan, *A Journalist's Odyssey* with personal recollection by Robert Kee (London: Edmond Publishing, 1985), pp. 104 and 8.

46 Malcolm Muggeridge, *The Thirties: 1930–1940 in Great Britain* (London: Hamish Hamilton, 1940), p. 211.

47 He described this in a letter to *The Times* (11 July 1936, p. 15). See also 'Police and Fascist Meetings, 6 June 1936, p. 6; also C. M Bowra *Memories 1898–1939* (London: Weidenfeld and Nicolson, 1966), p. 347.

48 Owen Chadwick, *Hensley Henson: A Study in the Friction between Church and State* (Norwich: Canterbury Press, 1994), p. 212.

49 Garth Lean, *Frank Buchman: A Life* (London: Constable, 1985), pp. 159–60. Streeter and his wife were killed in a plane crash in Switzerland in 1937 returning from an Oxford Group centre in Germany.

50 Robert Speaight, *Ronald Knox the Writer*, p. 42.

51 Knox to Ward, n.d., Sheed and Ward Family Papers, Notre Dame University Library, folder CSWD 16/15.

52 Mathew, *Catholicism in England*, p. 261. For a different perspective, arguing that ultramontane English Catholicism was committed to 'mainstream politics', see Jeffrey Paul von Arx, 'Catholics and Politics' in V. Alan McClelland and Michael Hodgetts (eds), *From without the Flaminian Gate: 150 Years of Roman Catholicism in England and Wales 1850–2000* (London: DLT, 1999), pp. 245–71, especially 266–7. But this seems to apply primarily to issue-based politics.

53 Ronald Knox, *The Belief of Catholics* (London: Ernest Benn, 1927; reprinted 1928), p. 70.

54 Knox, *Belief of Catholics* quoting from pages 20, 42, and 50.

55 Knox, *Belief of Catholics*, p. 173.

56 Aidan Nichols, *The Realm: An Unfashionable Essay on the Conversion of England* (Oxford: Family Publications, 2008), p. 134.

57 Knox, 'The Unconscious Catholic', *In Soft Garments*, p. 104. On this page he also refers to 'the Buchmanites'.

58 Ronald Knox, *The Three Taps* (London: Methuen, 1927), pp. 80–1.

59 Laura Marcus, 'Detection and Literary Fiction' in Martin Priestman

(ed.), *The Cambridge Companion to Crime Fiction* (Cambridge: CUP, 2003) p. 249, quoting from Marjorie Nicolson, 'The Professor and the Detective' in Howard Haycraft (ed.) *The Art of the Mystery Story*.

60 In the American edition, Ronald Knox and H. Harrington (eds), *The Best English Detective Stories of 1928* (New York: Horace Liveright, 1929), pp. 12–15.

61 Pearce, *Wisdom and Innocence*, p. 367.

62 Miss H. Matheson to Knox, 9 May 1930, R Cont 1, Talks File 1 1924–1941, BBC/WA.

63 Kenneth Wolfe, *The Churches and the British Broadcasting Corporation 1922–1956: The Politics of Broadcast Religion* (London: SCM, 1984), Chapter 4 and p. 150.

64 See correspondence in R Cont 1, Talks File 1, 1924–1941, BBC/WA BBC/WA, especially 17 April 1934, Knox to Iremonger; also 15 November 1935, Iremonger to Knox.

65 Script, 'What happened on Easter morning?' 17 April 1938, National Service, p. 8; BBC/WA.

66 David Walker, *The Tablet* 31 August 1957, p. 159.

67 Hollis, *The Oxford Union*, p. 201.

68 EW *RK*, p. 239.

69 Knox to Macmillan, n.d. but early June 1929, Macmillan Papers, Bodleian Library, Box 65 fo. 9.

70 Randle Manwaring, *From Controversy to Co-Existence: Evangelicals in the Church of England 1914–1980* (Cambridge: CUP, 1985), p. 35. For Bishop Knox's leading role among evangelicals, see also pp. 20–2.

71 E. Knox, *Reminiscences of an Octogenarian*, p. 300.

72 F. W. Chambers *Ronald Knox and the Converts' Aid Society* (London: CAS, 1960), p. 12.

73 Michael Hollings, *Living Priesthood* (Great Wakering, Essex: McCrimmon, 1977), pp. 40–1; Ronald Knox, *Off the Record*, p. 164.

74 Richard Ollard, *A Man of Contradictions: A Life of A. L. Rowse* (London: Allen Lane, 1999), p. 260. Rowse, however, held strongly anti-Catholic views and these seem to have coloured his conversation with Waugh.

75 The two 'raspberry' conferences are printed as an appendix to Drumm, *The Old Palace*, quoting here from pages 152, 155–6, 161 and 168.

8

A Quiet Country Living

Knox's departure from the chaplaincy at Oxford came after a year of preparation. He was aware that his energies were not rising to the task. In December 1938 he wrote to inform the Universities Catholic Education Board that he would be leaving the following summer. He added:

> I must confess I have been feeling for some time that the chaplaincy at Oxford would be better for a change. It is the kind of work in which routine counts for a minimum; it is of necessity personal and experimental. And in such work it seems to me, the enthusiasm of a new and untried man for his own methods will always be valuable, even if he has to learn from his own mistakes ... there is also something to be said for youth when a man has to put up with the manners of the young.[1]

It is a testament to how the robust cheerfulness of the student world had left its mark on him. He went to Oxford wedded to routine and to the exquisite politeness of Edwardian manners. These things were always part of him, but in Oxford he also had to learn how to relate to a younger generation, with its informality, its moods, its candour and its preoccupations. It had been an experience of growth, but it had also taught him his limitations.

Knox now needed a place to live where he could pursue his research and writing. This became possible when Daphne Acton invited him to join the household of the Acton family as their chaplain. Moreover, in Daphne Acton, he found a confidante who helped him come out of his shell. He never found it easy to express his emotions. He had missed the emotional nourishing of a mother, whose death had consigned him to a childhood spent in the company of an uncle and aunts. Later, as a brilliant student of the classics, he was steeped in a tradition of Roman stories which emphasized a rugged, stoical masculinity, and anyway, his social class had discouraged any show of the emotions.[2] Ten years of friendship with Lady Acton would bring a gentle thaw in his life.

Daphne Acton née Strutt was the daughter of the fourth Lord Rayleigh. Both her father and grandfather were well-respected physicists. Her family background was part-agnostic, part-Protestant and antithetical to Catholicism. In 1931, at the age of twenty, she married the third Baron Acton, the youthful head of one of the leading Catholic families in England. She became chatelaine of the family's stately home at Aldenham in Shropshire. At first she did not share her husband's religious sympathies but her second child, a daughter, died in infancy in March 1935, and in grief she began a process of searching. Little by little she became curious about Catholicism. Lord Acton's sister Marie, known as Mia, was married to Douglas Woodruff, editor of *The Tablet*, an influential Catholic weekly. The Woodruffs took in hand Daphne's Catholic education themselves, but by the summer of 1937 decided that she needed to meet a priest as part of her formation in the faith. They arranged to introduce her to Ronald Knox at their house in Berkshire. Knox was dreading the meeting but immediately found himself charmed. Waugh, who knew Daphne Acton well, wrote later that in her Knox had found:

A girl of strong and original intellect, certainly; a tall, elegant beauty, but one who looked younger than her twenty-five years; was as shy as himself and fermenting with a radical, spontaneous humour in which there were echoes of the laughter of his lost friends of 1914.[3]

This, then, was someone with a slightly anarchic sense of humour, which chimed perfectly with Knox's own, someone who could get him laughing again. But equally important, she had a first-rate intellect, an inquiring mind and could hold her own in debate. When the Woodruffs and Knox went on a Hellenic cruise, Daphne came also (both Knox and Douglas Woodruff were on-board lecturers for the cruise). Knox and Daphne Acton spent a great deal of time in each other's company during the voyage. She gave him, says Waugh, 'an infusion of strength and hope' and as for her, she was 'wholly captivated by him'. In a moment full of the symbolic language of love, each threw overboard something criticized by the other. She threw away a lipstick that he disliked, and he jettisoned his most recent detective novel, *Double Cross Purposes*.[4] This platonic but intense relationship flourished despite the difference in their ages. In 1937 he was forty-nine; in November of that year she turned twenty-six. In April 1938 Daphne Acton was received into the Catholic Church in the chapel at Aldenham. Knox was already spending the greater part of the Oxford vacations there.

In the mid-1930s his stream of literary inspiration had seemed to shrivel and he produced very little that was noteworthy. Now, during a stay at Aldenham, the blockage was swept away and in a spate of creativity he produced one of his best-known works, *Let Dons Delight*. It was written during the summer vacation of 1937 and was published to acclaim in February 1938. It came from a lifetime's reading of English history, literature, classics and theology, and from his personal acquaintance with Oxford life. *Let Dons Delight* is set in the fictional Simon Magus College, Oxford, where the author has gone to dine on a Sunday evening and falls asleep in the common room while the dons gather round the port. He dreams a sequence of eight conversations between the dons of Simon Magus at intervals of fifty years between 1588 and 1938. The first episode takes place as the Spanish Armada is awaited; the last episode mentions the Spanish Civil War. One of the young fellows at the beginning of each section appears as an aged senior in the next. Each time the curtain rises, there are changes in faith and society, and the conversation discusses these as well as the petty rivalries of Oxford life.

The common room barbs fly back and forth, particularly about the detestableness of Cambridge.

Part of the genius of the book is Knox's mastery of the idiom of each period, including imagined dialogue put into the mouths of real historical figures. For example, there is a conversation between Boswell and Johnson which is so convincing in form and content that, as Robert Speaight comments, 'The reader rubs his eyes; can this really have been made up?'[5] Knox concludes each chapter with faux source notes that are themselves a delight. For example, the 1638 episode ends with an alleged extract from *Athenae Oxonienses*, a history of Oxford and its personalities written by Anthony à Wood and published *c*.1692. The book and its author are real; Wood has been much criticized for mixing history with acerbic commentary. The 'extract' written by Knox claims to be about an Anglican academic called Elias Fulwell who suffered under Cromwell and became a bishop after the Restoration. Fulwell is the product of Knox's mind, but done so brilliantly that, as with the Boswell-Dr Johnson conversation, the reader begins to wonder whether it might be real after all. Solemnly claiming to be quoting from Wood, *Let Dons Delight* tells us that Fulwell became rector at Little Matchett

> where, finding the chancel fallen into great disrepair; the dampishness of the walls (by reason of the roof gaping here and there) breeding everywhere ... nothing but mildew and pestilence, the walls scribbled on, the grease from the candles standing in great pools, and all the furniture of the benches &ctr. set kim-kam here and there; this stout and public-spirited person made a great purge of these and other sluttish negligences by which the worship of God had hitherto been profaned. Causing the Communion table to be set in its right place, together with proper and comely rails at the entering of the chancel ... All which things were cast up against him before the Grand Committee for Religion (as 'twas called, but should rather have been called the Grand Committee for sneaking and factious sycophancy) set up by

the Parliament after the King's Cause was lost in these parts.[6]

It is a brilliant pastiche of Wood's *Athenae Oxonienses*.

As one era succeeds another it becomes clear that there is an overarching theme, subtly woven through the conversations. Even the name of the Oxford College is a clue. In the biblical book of Acts, Simon Magus was a magician in Samaria impressed by the gifts of the Spirit shown by the apostles. He offered them money to give him the same power, and for this he was roundly rebuked by St Peter (Acts 8.9–24). A recurring feature in each episode of *Let Dons Delight* is how to balance the demands of truth versus the demands of the state. England had been convulsed with regime change from the Tudor period through to William and Mary. Oxford fellows were nearly all clergy, and were sometimes torn between self-preservation and spiritual principle, because a change of monarch meant a change of ecclesial loyalty. In the 1838 episode, when disestablishment is being mooted, the objection is raised that the Church of England contains within itself many differences of outlook. One of the dons fears that these different groupings might not hold together if the Church of England was disestablished. Another don dryly replies that it depends whether disestablishment includes disendowment: 'So long as there are any emoluments remaining, I believe you will find churchmen sticking closer together than you think.'[7] Knox's point is far more serious than poking fun at Anglicanism. Throughout, in piquant prose, he raises the question of the Erastian nature of the Church of England. If the Church depends upon the state for its validation, can the Church be said to teach any enduring truth? In the conversation set in 1738, when the provost of Simon Magus supports state control of the church, one of the dons replies:

Then, Sir, if I had lived under Queen Mary, I would have done right to burn Cranmer in the street yonder, because her bishops ordered it? But if I had lived under Queen Elizabeth, I had done right to hang the massing-priests, now the new bishops ordered different? . . . So the bishops must be obeyed, but only if the Crown is our warranty that they are true bishops?[8]

Knox's real theme is the despiritualization of England. Religion had been reduced to being the handmaid of the state, and over the centuries its credibility had eroded.

Let Dons Delight closes in 1938 with the final conversation taking place in the common room where, significantly, for the first time there is no priest participating in the conversation. The scientist, the economist and the philosopher debate together but find little common ground in their search for mutual understanding. The philosopher asks the economist, 'Do you believe in a duty of the mind to love truth . . .?' The economist replies that terms such as truth and honesty are most often the language of hypocrisy.[9] Knox is implicitly raising a further question, namely how truth can be sought if there is no belief in an objective truth. This was a prescient question, given today's postmodern claims that all human understanding is contingent upon changing structures of power, with no absolute values. Once more we note how Knox seems to anticipate a post-modern perspective. *Let Dons Delight* deploys humour and history to ask how faith and society have interacted in English life. The effect is to leave an unspoken question. Did the Reformation cut most of English Christianity away from its living roots? And if so, where is the common perspective that will bind English society together? Without that the scientist, the economist and the philosopher will always be talking past each other rather than to each other.

In mid-1938 Cardinal Hinsley heard that Knox would be leaving Oxford at the end of the following academic year. Hinsley wrote offering him the presidency of St Edmund's, Ware. 'I know something of your innate modesty,' wrote the cardinal in his own hand, 'but I also know that the Catholic world does not share your opinion of yourself.' No one, he added, could fulfil the post as well as Knox, and his appointment would give prestige to the college. Knox was in a dilemma. He intended to move to Aldenham, where he would not only enjoy the company of Daphne Acton but have the time to write. His conscience told him that he should listen to the voice of Catholic authority coming from the premier bishop of England. After consulting his friends and his confessor Knox replied to Hinsley pleading unsuitability. Knox wrote that he was too inefficient and a poor disciplinarian. The responsibility would make him too anxious and nervous. There were, he admitted, selfish reasons for saying no:

> I started a book in 1918, *[Enthusiasm]* of which I have still no more written than some four or five chapters. And if I don't write soon, some of the things I feel I could write, I shall have become too rusty and perhaps too flabby to write them at all ... I could not find the time, the leisure, or the peace of mind for effective literary work, such as might be of benefit to the Church.[10]

The strength of Knox's desire to find the time and space to write was clear, and Hinsley gracefully accepted this demurral. In June 1939 a farewell dinner for Knox was held at the Randolph in Oxford, its high-ceilinged Victorian dining room lined with academic portraits and college coats of arms. Guests included Evelyn Waugh, Professor J. R. R. Tolkien, Professor F. de Zulueta (Regius Professor of Civil Law) and Douglas Woodruff. Supporting the toast by Douglas Woodruff, Evelyn Waugh said that in the thirteen years Knox had been chaplain, 'he lent a lustre and prestige to the Catholics of Oxford such as they had not known since days of the Reformation.' If a Catholic coming to Oxford had asked where could be found 'scholarship, humour, wit, taste, courtesy and stability of opinion ... we could proudly and appropriately point to the Old Palace.' Knox was presented with a cheque, a first edition of the Rheims-Douai version of the Bible, a silver tankard and a painting of the Old Palace.[11]

In August 1939 Knox moved to Aldenham Park. The house stood on a small rise at the end of a long, straight avenue approached through wrought-iron gates. The original Georgian house had been encased in stone and given sombre plate-glass windows. To one side were red brick stable buildings, and on the other a detached chapel on a terrace, built about 1870. The house had been the home of the first Lord Acton, Regius Professor of History at Cambridge and a friend of Gladstone. But Acton's magnificent library had been bought after his death by Andrew Carnegie and given to Cambridge. The inside of the house was rather austere. Once again the outbreak of a war affected Knox's plans. It was feared that mass bombing of British cities by the Luftwaffe was imminent, and so even before the formal declaration of hostilities, children were being evacuated to the countryside. The Actons had arranged for the girls and sisters of the Assumption Convent, Kensington, to come and live at Aldenham. Lord Acton went off to join the Shropshire Yeomanry. It was decided that Knox would live in the priest's house beside the chapel. Knox would now be chaplain not only to the family but also to the school and the Assumptionist sisters. Knox was disappointed. He had hoped to be able to spare all his energies for a new translation of the Bible, which he would undertake single-handed. During the next few years he did not neglect the school, and he tried his best to help Lady Acton with her many duties on the Aldenham estate.

The outbreak of war had created its own demands. At the invitation of Macmillan publishers, Knox wrote a pamphlet as part of their series on the war. He described Nazi persecution of the Catholic Church in Germany, Austria and Poland, and emphasized the Nazi takeover of youth movements and schools:

> The aim of the Nazis has been, from the first, to capture the imagination and loyalties of youth; and to capture these for a perverted, though carefully elaborated, world-view. There is no room in the same child's head for the principles of Christianity, however languidly acquired, and for the racial ideology which has Hitler as its rule of faith, and the world-domination of the German race as its end.[12]

He wrote this in 1940, when it was not as widely understood as it is now that racism was intrinsic to Nazi ideology. His writing was not his only contribution to the war effort. Despite his lack of practical skills, he did what he could to help on the land. Like every farm in the country, the 1,000 acre Aldenham estate was under great pressure to produce as much food as possible. In 1939 Britain was importing nearly half its food, and, to do so, maintained the largest merchant fleet in the world. Some 2,500 ships were at sea at any time. By the end of 1940 German U-boats were taking a terrible toll on British merchant marine, food was rationed, and Britain had to grow or rear as much of its own food as possible. The Ministry of Agriculture launched a slogan 'Dig for Victory'. Even the verges of trunk roads were ploughed up.[13] Knox helped with the farmwork, mainly the pigs. He and Lady Acton still dressed for dinner. Isabel Quigly was one of the schoolgirls at Aldenham and remembered that 'From the muddiest and most bedraggled of outdoor gear they changed into evening dress, she making a glamorous appearance on the main staircase in what seemed like ball dresses, he in a cassock with tiny puce buttons all down the front, puce socks and buckle shoes.'[14] Knox accepted a BBC invitation to give a series of talks on 'The World We're Fighting For'. He took great care to use simple language and concepts. His premise was that to fight for what was right and just meant in turn that you had to have a belief in the eternal justice of God, otherwise you were on shifting sands of human sentiment. Knox referred in passing to the Nazi racism of blood and soil, and to its worship of the state. But the talks were weakened by his argument for the existence of God, where he waffled and seemed to stray from the title of the series.[15]

He showed the same kind of care towards the schoolgirls from the Assumption Convent that he had shown towards the students at Oxford. In particular, he took great pains to explain the meaning of Catholic faith and practice in language that they could understand. We know this because after the war a series of sermons about the eucharist was published under the title *The Mass in Slow Motion*. Each of the sermons takes the girls step by step through the Tridentine Mass, explaining the meaning and significance of the words and gestures. He repeatedly uses the metaphor of a sacred dance to describe what we now call the Extraordinary Form of the Mass. Knox's text faithfully preserves the sense of being addressed, and again, there are the little touches of humour to keep his audience interested. The Introit is 'the point at which you have to find your place in the missal, to shew the girl next to you that you are pretty well up in these things.' The beginning of the Creed, the *Credo* always, says Knox, seems to take organist and choir unawares, and they fumble for a moment, 'as if this sudden announcement that the priest believes in one God had taken them all by surprise.' At the point in the Creed ('incarnatus est') where the congregation knelt in the pre-conciliar Mass, '*You* weren't following, of course, you were day-dreaming ... if the girl behind you hadn't suddenly butted you with her nose in the small of the back, it's arguable that you would have forgotten to go down on your knees at all.'[16] The humour, though, is not the point in itself, rather, it is the way he establishes and keeps a rapport with teenage girls as he explains the Mass. Knox himself was surprised to discover that he could communicate with such an age group. Indeed, one girl, recovering from illness at home, had insisted on returning early to Aldenham because she did not want to miss 'one of Ronnie's talks.'[17] Knox combined simplicity of exposition and depth of meaning. He explains the meaning of each prayer. For example, he draws their attention to the offertory prayer which the priest makes as the bread and wine are being prepared for the altar. This prayer ends with an invocation of the Holy Spirit.

You know how, when you are making a fire at a picnic, you want everything to be quite still until you have got your match lit and the first twigs crackling and then you want a puff of wind ... which will gradually spread the flame, go on spreading the flame, until the fire is really going. So it is with this burnt-sacrifice of ours; we want the Holy Spirit to be gently breathing on it from the first moment when it is really ready, kindling our hearts and making them glow, while he kindles our material offerings of bread and wine into a supernatural flame, which is Christ's Body and Blood.[18]

Studying these sermons is a reminder of how mistaken it is to dismiss the Tridentine Mass as something incomprehensible, as though our forebears in the faith sat baffled in the pews. True, Knox was especially gifted, but in this glimpse we have of the girls following the Mass in their missals, we also catch a glimpse of the power of the liturgy to draw its participants into the timeless mysteries of the eucharist. Perhaps, though, we also glimpse a numinousness which is less easy to attain today. At the words of consecration, says Knox

Don't make too much of that glance which you give when the Host is elevated, and of the prayer which goes with it; let it be only a momentary burst of recognition. Then relax the effort of your mind, and let yourself be carried away on the stream of intercession which is going on all round you when Jesus Christ is there ... let Our Lord do the praying for you ...

... we present to God the oblation we are making to him out of his own gifts to us; his own gifts of bread and wine – but what a change has come over them! Bread, that was meant to sustain our bodies just for a few hours, now ready to bring us eternal life; wine, that might be used to cheer us up for just an evening, now implanting unfailing health in our souls! ... We must offer to give them back, offer to share them with him, before we can reconcile ourselves to the idea of actually consuming them, the Body and Blood of Christ.[19]

Pre-conciliar spirituality encouraged this intense interiority during the celebration of the Mass. As we can see, Knox calibrated it precisely, so as to accompany the unfolding action.

Today's Mass encourages a more active involvement, yet

we would be pushed to say that today's Catholics have a more intense sense of the holiness of the Mass and of the divine presence. The idea that the old liturgy minimized participation is also challenged by more recent analyses. Sheridan Gilley points out that after Vatican II participation was redefined in terms of verbal participation, which depreciated the previous means of participation in the Mass. This had taken place 'visually through the elevation of the Host, aurally through the ringing of bells to punctuate the rite, and by gesture, in kneelings and crossings and bowings of the head' – all of them, he points out, ways that the poor could participate, and those less confident in speaking aloud.[20] *The Mass in Slow Motion* was a publishing success, so it clearly met a need. His publisher wrote to Knox informing him that the book was producing impressive sales figures. Knox replied with a postcard: 'Sauline I presume, not Davidic.' Sheed replied: 'Just passing from the Sauline into the Davidic.' The reference was to 1 Samuel 18.7: 'Saul has slain his thousands, and David his ten thousands.'[21]

As can be seen, Knox thought carefully about how to explain and commend the Catholic faith. But his heart was in his new translation of the Bible. It seems that he began to think seriously about a new translation some time in 1937. In itself this desire was surprising, because study of the scriptures was not a key element in Catholic devotion at this time. Knox wrote:

In my experience, the laity's attitude towards the Bible is one of blank indifference, varied now and again by one of puzzled hostility. The clergy, no doubt, search the Scriptures more eagerly. And yet, when I used to go round preaching a good deal, and would ask the P. P. for a Bible to verify my text from, there was generally an ominous pause of twenty minutes or so before he returned, banging the leaves of the sacred volume and visibly blowing on the top. The new wine of the gospel, you felt, was kept in strangely cobwebby bottles.[22]

Priests and members of religious orders studied the scriptures, of course, as part of their formation. But the Mass and extra-liturgical devotions played a greater role than the Bible in lay spirituality. Nearly every English Catholic home in the 1930s would have had a rosary; fewer would have had a Bible. Where scripture was pondered it was usually as material for prayer and meditation. The epistle and gospel at Mass were in Latin, which could be followed in an English translation if you had one of the missals with the Latin on one side and the English on the other. Even this had only been allowed since 1900, when prohibitions against translating the missal were allowed to lapse.[23]

Despite this unpromising background, Knox was accurate in discerning the moment. Standards of education among Catholics were rising all the time, and Catholics were mixing more and more with the wider population. This called for a better-informed laity, able to talk about their faith with confidence. It was, moreover, a boom time in vocations for the religious life, especially among women, where the formation programmes often included a good grounding in scripture. Some of these factors may have influenced the Catholic bishops of England and Wales when Knox sought their permission to undertake his translation. They were also aware that the American bishops were proposing a fresh translation. In 1855 an earlier proposal for a new translation to be undertaken by Newman had been dropped when it was discovered that the Americans were already at work on one. The English bishops were determined not to be upstaged again, and in November 1938 Cardinal Hinsley had written to Knox on behalf of all the bishops giving their approval for the project In terms of warm approbation: 'We have confidence in you as the one man who can give us an English text readable and understood of the people.'[24] This gave Knox not only official backing but a graceful exit from the chaplaincy. In January 1939 *The Tablet* announced: 'Monsignor Ronald Knox has been entrusted by the hierarchy with the preparation of a new version of the Sacred Scriptures. He is accordingly resigning the work of the Catholic chaplain to the undergraduates of

Oxford at the close of the summer term.'[25] Later still, when Knox's process of translation was well under way, he was encouraged by the publication in September 1943 of Pope Pius XII's encyclical *Divino Afflante Spiritu*. Pius XII made it clear that the Catholic faith was rooted in scripture as well as in tradition, and encouraged the use of scripture for personal spiritual growth. He commended the work of exegetes and translators who were at the service of the Church. Most translators would have been members of a scholarly team, working, for example, at the oriental institutes established to promote the study of ancient scriptural languages and texts. It was a huge task for one man to undertake on his own.

There already was a well-known translation of the Bible for English Catholics known as the Douai Bible or the Rheims-Douai Bible. It was a translation undertaken in exile by the English Catholic community in France. The New Testament translation was published at Rheims in 1582 and the Old Testament at Douai (or Douay) in 1609. This translation was adapted in the eighteenth century by Bishop Richard Challoner who also ironed out many Latinisms and provided explanatory notes. Where English-speaking Catholics turned to a Bible, it was almost always this translation. But there were two problems. First, the haphazard process of authorizing this translation had given rise to many variant editions. Different bishops had given their approval to different publishers who engaged in what one authority has called 'free manipulation of the text'. In 1837 the future Cardinal Wiseman had lamented:

It had been well if Dr Challoner's alterations had given stability to the text, and formed a standard to which subsequent editors had conformed. But, far from this being the case, new and often important modifications have been made in every edition which has followed, till, at length, many may appear rather new versions, than revisions of the old. [26]

This process of modification was evident even in the edition of 1914 published by Burns and Oates. The agreement of the bishops to Knox's proposal was probably motivated in part by the desire to establish a standard translation.

It was also an opportunity to go beyond the language of the Douai translation. In his revisions Bishop Challoner had sought, wherever possible, to conform the text to the language of the Authorized Version, but this meant that the translation was increasingly dated. Knox described the Authorized Version as being written 'in a language of its own: a hieratic language, deeply embedded in the English mind and perhaps indispensable to the ordinary Englishman's religion; but not a model to be imitated, because its idiom is foreign to us.'[27] To help him, the bishops had appointed a commission, but its terms were very vague. It became clear early on that there was a divergence of opinion within the commission. Some wanted a completely new translation. Others wanted simply a revision of the Douai Bible. Fr Martindale was in the latter group. He hoped that Knox would not change what he called the 'consecrated phrases' of the Douai version. Knox replied that there were no 'consecrated phrases' and, on the contrary, he proposed a thoroughgoing revision.[28] It seemed at first that Knox would have great difficulty in getting his proposals past Martindale, but then fate intervened. Martindale was visiting Denmark when the Nazis invaded in April 1940 and was subsequently interned. Another trenchant critic was Archbishop Peter Amigo, Bishop of Southwark, who was temperamentally opposed to any change. However, there had been a tense relationship between the Westminster and Southwark dioceses, with each bishop alert to assertions of authority by his London neighbour. Hinsley rose wrathfully to Knox's defence, and Amigo subsided. It should have been a warning to Knox, however, about how risky his undertaking was. He was attempting single-handedly to provide what would become an official alternative translation of the Bible, for use in England and Wales. The Catholic Church during this era preferred initiative to come from the centre, and was cautious about change. These troubles were not good auguries for the future but he pressed on. He worked from the Latin text of the Vulgate approved by Pope Clement VIII and issued in 1592.

This was the foundational text of scripture which was also the prescribed text for Catholic biblical studies. But Knox also consulted the underlying Greek texts, and he learned biblical Hebrew in preparation for his translation of the Old Testament.

Knox's translation of the New Testament appeared in a limited edition in April 1944. It was an immediate success and sold well. Even so, the bishops hesitated to give it their corporate backing. Knox almost snapped at this point, and wrote a long plaintive letter to Hinsley's successor, Cardinal Griffin. It is a bizarre letter, pointing out, as it does, that Anglicans will rejoice to see a convert rebuffed by his bishops, proof of the folly of going over to Rome.[29] The note of self-pity here points to his exhaustion at having to push against the inertia of the authorities. Eventually, after more revisions, a hardbound version of his translation of the New Testament authorized by the bishops came out in 1945 with a commendatory preface from Cardinal Bernard Griffin who praised Knox's 'masterly command of the English language and limpid style'.[30] And yet, Knox's translation is almost forgotten today. Although he conveyed the scriptural text in elegant English, his style was too stilted, too self-conscious even, at times. Here are two examples from Knox, the opening of the gospel according to John, and the beginning of Paul's famous hymn to love in 1 Corinthians 13. For comparison, the RSV version is given afterwards in brackets.

John 1.1–3:
At the beginning of time, the Word already was; and God had the Word abiding with him, and the Word was God. He abode, at the beginning of time, with God. It was through him that all things came into being, and without him came nothing that has come to be.
(*RSV*: In the beginning was the Word, and the Word was with God, and the Word was God. He was in the beginning with God; all things were made through him, and without him was not anything made that was made.)

1 Corinthians 13.1:
I may speak with every tongue that men and angels use;
yet, if I lack charity, I am no better than echoing bronze,
or the clash of cymbals.
(*RSV*: If I speak in the tongues of men and of angels, but
have not love, I am a noisy gong or a clanging cymbal.)

Knox's translation suffers in this comparison. We note an old-
fashioned word like 'abode'. There is the more cautious
'charity' rather than love for the Greek *agape*. An 'echoing
bronze' makes little sense today. The phrasing is awkward.
Christopher Sykes sees evidence here of Knox's failing
powers, and says of the translation that it is 'distressingly
genteel'. It is a fair criticism. Knox had tried too hard for a
polished work. He believed that a translation should be more
than functional, for it should 'represent the original, in a
graceful, a genuine, a solid form; the rendering, like the original, is to be a literary production.'[31] Despite its shortcom-
ings, Knox had achieved his aims of providing a translation
that was in clearer and in more contemporary language than
the Douai Bible. Its success was a sign of the times. The interest his translation aroused, and its good sales, showed that
Britain now had an increasingly well-educated Catholic laity,
who wanted to be biblically literate. They also wanted to be
able to explain and defend their faith, using a more lively
translation. Such were the sales that Frank Sheed believed the
royalties to have been 'vast'. But Knox gave the royalties to
the Church, because, Sheed guessed, 'he could not bring
himself to make money out of the Word of God.'[32] The drive
within him to undertake this translation may also point back
to his childhood. Was he still unconsciously his father's child?
Knox had grown up in an evangelical family, with that love of
the Bible which characterized convinced Protestants, between
whom and the Catholics a wide gulf yawned. In those days it
was impossible to conceive of an evangelizing pope like the
future John Paul II. Knox's translation would soon be eclipsed
by the English version of the Jerusalem Bible, first published
in 1966 as the Vatican Council opened the floodgates of

change in the Catholic Church. In fact, Knox had expected that new translations would follow, all of them in a more modern, directly narrative form: 'The germ is spreading, and there will be more translations yet. Indeed, it is doubtful whether we shall ever again allow ourselves to fall under the spell of a single, uniform text, consecrated by its antiquity.'[33] Knox had shown that demand was growing among Catholics for a translation of the scriptures in the language of the day, and he saw it as a sign of the times.

During the war the circle of the Knox siblings was broken for the first time. By the end of 1942 his brother Dillwyn was seriously ill with cancer. Dillwyn, a Classics fellow at King's College, Cambridge, also had a distinguished career as a cryptographer in both world wars. He was part of the team that broke enemy codes through coming to understand how the German Enigma cipher machine worked. From the time he entered adulthood Dillwyn had been a religious sceptic. As he lay dying Ronald waited and prayed, hoping, perhaps to save his soul. But Dillwyn was as steadfast in his non-belief as Ronald was in his faith. 'Is Ronnie still out there bothering God in the passage?' he asked.[34] He died at the end of February 1943. Harold Macmillan, by now Minister Resident in North Africa, sent Ronald his condolences from Algeria. Knox replied that he had found Dillwyn's last days and funeral a grim experience, and went on to muse about the years 1912–1914, wondering whether historians might look back and see those as the peak years for Britain.[35] It was nostalgia perhaps, but it showed his sense of time slipping away, and his feeling that, for him, the best was in the past.

Daphne Acton would always be close, but slowly the war brought changes in their friendship too. Initially their relationship had been difficult for her. Twenty years later she told Evelyn Waugh: 'The fact that Ronnie was even older when I first met him than I am now, as well as being full of grace, meant that he could behave with effortless chastity, whereas I found it more of a strain . . . but I daresay he knew, as I was always having scruples and fussing.'[36] But the exigencies of the war years had given new outlets for her energies and she was no longer as absorbed with Knox as she had been. Women everywhere were learning new skills as part of the war effort, and like many women at that time Lady Acton became a proficient tractor driver, ploughing the land with gusto. She also became more absorbed with her growing family. Catherine was born in December 1939, Richard in July 1941, and Charles in January 1943. In 1943 Lord Acton was posted to Italy, and his return from war service in 1945 and the end of the war brought a new dynamic to the life of the house. Daphne Acton's deep friendship with Knox had been therapeutic for them both, but now things changed again. He was no longer as central to the operations of the household as he had been when it contributed to the war effort. The school returned to London. He was like many people in Britain for whom the end of the war brought a time of disorientation in which they struggled to find new roles. He found it harder to accept with his customary aplomb the noise and confusion of a burgeoning young family. Waugh says that Knox sometimes 'felt estranged from the young lives teeming around him.'[37]

No one seems to have realized quite how depressed he had become, and as sometimes happens, spiritual and emotional pain ran together. At the end of 1945 he wrote to the Catholic author Caryll Houselander, having just finished reading her book *The Reed of God*. He wrote to praise her but in doing so he allowed a rare glimpse of his emotions. He told her that he found her spiritual writing valuable, not least because at one point she had depicted a spiritual state very much like his own. If we turn to the reference which he gives, we find that Houselander was writing about spiritual aridity, but in view of what Knox told her, this passage speaks to us of his hidden desolation at this time. She had written: 'The lyrical young Christ that was the youth of our soul has gone away, leaving us a dyspeptic old man, lonely in a cluttered room of his own making, a forgotten invalid sitting in a timeless twilight of mediocrity.'[38] It is startling that Knox could liken himself to so broken a figure. He seems to have been suffering spiritually and emotionally. The Christ who had once seemed so close seemed now distant. He felt lonely and dull-witted. When Waugh's biography of Knox was published it was this aspect of Knox's character that attracted most interest, and some criticism for Waugh.[39] Some who knew Knox personally could not square the light-hearted, charming Knox they knew with the man depicted by Waugh as struggling sometimes in the slough of despond. Yet both states, in turn, were real.

The sense of God as distant is not a sign of loss of faith; in fact, periods of spiritual aridity are part and parcel of the life of faith. Sometimes aridity occurs during the process when the soul lets go of a more limited notion of God and moves into deeper waters. There is loss before there is discovery. Sometimes, as with Mother Teresa of Calcutta, the spiritual aridity is an affliction, a cross to be borne. In Knox's case, the sense of God as having gone away seems to have been a phase through which he had to pass. The associated emotional difficulties, however, were not a phase but part of a longer term shift in his personality. He was not a solitary by nature, rather, someone who became shyer with the passing of the years. When the more brash confidence of his youth faded Knox found emotional negotiation difficult. He had little formative experience from his childhood to draw upon, having grown up with elderly relatives and in boarding schools. Katharine Asquith noted that he had a great gift for friendship, but was frightened of indulging it. Yet when he said an extra collect at Mass in the Mells chapel, it was always for friends: 'I knew so surely it would come that I kept a marker in the place.'[40] This was a man of hidden feelings. After Knox's death, Waugh showed Fr Martin D'Arcy Knox's statement that he would always be cheered by a walk and conversation with D'Arcy. D'Arcy was astonished. He told Waugh that he had admired and liked Knox, but had never realized that the affection was mutual and hence had been rather reticent in inviting himself to visit Knox at the Old Palace.[41] The element of inner withdrawal became more prominent as Knox grew older: it was shown in his love of routine and his dislike of change, and in his reluctance to travel. Yet this was not alienation. He continued to be a sought-after preacher and giver of retreats. His friends continued to enjoy his company. But with the move to Mells in 1947 there is a sense of a change of gear, of his absorption in the task of translation and of his moving in a smaller circle. Perhaps Knox's tendency to depression was an unspoken part of his friendship with Waugh, whose brusque ebullience concealed his own bouts of melancholy.

News of the atomic bombs dropped at Hiroshima and Nagasaki in August 1945 dismayed Knox and led him to wonder about the new world order that this presaged. It was a surprising reaction in a man who had taken so little interest in political and social controversy. His first thought was a letter to *The Times* but instead he turned to the writing of a small book, *God and the Atom*. The book was composed quickly, perhaps too quickly, because his argument is not always easy to follow. This uncharacteristic lack of clarity might have been caused by the passion behind the book, or it might be another sign of his depression at this time. For Knox, the atomic bomb was both an amoral error of judgement and a symbol of something deeper that had entered into the human psyche. Religion by its very nature tutored humankind in self-restraint. Nuclear weapons meant power on a vast scale and thus the temptation to remove all restraint: 'That is why, I repeat, I wish the Allied Powers, with the world at their feet and the Atom Bomb in their hands, had said No.' Restraint, said Knox, was often a haphazard affair, involving instincts, impulses, prejudices, phobias, and other factors, held together by repression. If the band snapped then the result was insanity.[42]

For someone who was such a conventional Catholic, his approach sounds surprisingly Freudian. In fact, Knox's approach is sometimes explicitly Freudian. The book is divided into sections headed Trauma, Analysis, Adjustment and Sublimation, and he referred to a 'Hiroshima Complex' in which the world had been left in doubt and uncertainty about the moral order and the natural order. As part of his research for the book he consulted Sir Edmund Whittaker, Professor of Mathematics at the University of Edinburgh. There is a note of prescience in Knox's ruminations about the new physics. If at the nuclear level there was uncertainty rather than fixed structure, he asked, what did this say about God? 'The scientists tell us in so many words that they do not bother about the causes of things any longer; the very word has passed out of their vocabulary.'[43] At the very heart of nature it was now seen that there was not order, but indeterminacy. Knox had shrewdly spotted that the new physics could bring with it a rethinking of how to explain the relationship of God to the world. Since then theologians have shown increasing interest in quantum physics, wondering whether it reveals a universe more open to providential action.[44]

The immediate aftermath of the war proved difficult for all the residents of Aldenham as they shared the privations of the rest of the nation. Britain was exhausted, and there seemed no end in sight to the need for belt-tightening. Rationing continued, and there was a new emphasis on growing food for export to help the balance of payments crisis. Taxation rose to new levels, because the incoming Labour government had to pay off war debts as well as implement its own programme of social reform. The winter months of early 1947 were particularly hard. Heavy snowfalls across the country hampered the distribution of coal from the mines, and power stations ran short of fuel for their generators. By mid-February there were power cuts for up to five hours a day. Broadcasting hours were reduced, many magazines failed to appear and most forms of external lighting were forbidden. Unemployment tripled to 1.75 million.[45] It was a bleak and depressing time for a country hoping to recover from the privations and devastation of war. Before the war, Lord Acton had been a stockbroker in Birmingham but after the war had decided to devote himself to farming full-time. By early 1947 he had decided to sell up and emigrate to Southern Rhodesia, where he bought a farm named Mbebi in the Mazoe area.

Knox would have to find a new home. Here he was helped by the enduring links woven by the friendships of his student days in Oxford forty years earlier. Through his closest Balliol friends he had come to know Katharine Horner, a famous beauty of the Edwardian era who, with her lively mind, could hold her own in any company. Her brother Edward Horner had been part of the same close-knit Balliol set as Knox and Charles Lister. In 1907 Katharine Horner had married Raymond Asquith, whose father H. H. Asquith was the serving Prime Minister. Raymond had been killed in the war, in September 1916 at the battle of the Somme, leaving her with three small children. Raymond had taken a double first in Classics and Law at Oxford, and had the choice of careers either in politics or at the Bar. His death, and the death of her brother Edward in November 1917, left Katharine Asquith bereft. In 1919 she found a confidant in Hilaire Belloc, a friend of her late husband. They had their great grief in common. Belloc's wife had died in 1914 when he was only forty-three, and left a wound in his life that never healed. His son Louis was another victim of the carnage of the First World War. After recovering from a gas attack at the Somme, Louis had retrained in 1917 as a pilot with the Royal Flying Corps. In August 1918 he had taken off on a sortie but never returned. His body was never found. Katharine Asquith and Hilaire Belloc would meet and talk for hours, and exchanged long letters, as they shared their grief. He arranged for memorial plaques to be placed in Cambrai cathedral to commemorate his son Louis and her brother Edward Horner. When he told her that suffering could benefit the soul, she disagreed: suffering was an invitation to despair and could only injure the soul. In his reply Belloc said that the soul carried an awareness of eternity, and the pain of bereavement had to be seen against this deep self-awareness: 'We are not creatures of change and loss, but their victims for a time.' The pain of separation had to be carried into this promise of an eternal happiness.[46] Katharine Asquith became interested in the Catholic faith through hearing how it had helped Belloc through the darkest hours. She was received into the Catholic Church in 1923.

Daphne Acton was troubled at the thought of what would happen to Knox when her family moved to Rhodesia. First she sounded out Knox about a possible move to the Asquith family home at Mells in Somerset, and then she approached Katharine Asquith, who was pleased at the suggestion.[47] After a short retreat at Downside, Knox moved to Mells in October 1947. The Tudor manor at Mells had belonged to the Horner family for some 400 years and had been the home of her mother, Frances Horner, with whom Katharine had gone to live after Raymond's death. Lady Horner had been a famous Liberal hostess in her younger days. Katharine's conversion to Catholicism had not been welcomed by either the Asquiths or the Horners. H. H. Asquith's family background had been Nonconformist and, according to one Catholic historian, Asquith's 'cool sharp distaste for Catholicism was rooted in his Nonconformist origins.'[48] The Horners were faithful Anglicans and their manor abutted the beautiful parish church at Mells, whose 104-foot high pinnacled tower soared above the village. There was a striking monument to Edward Horner in the church.

After Lady Horner's death in 1940 Mells became a place of Catholic conviviality where Belloc, Waugh, Knox and other Catholic friends of Katharine Asquith enjoyed her hospitality and delighted in the sparkling conversation. Downside Abbey, the Benedictine powerhouse, was only eight miles away. The Catholic MP Christopher Hollis and his wife came to live in the village. There was no Catholic church there, but after her mother's death Katharine Asquith converted a garden building into a chapel. Mass was said by a Benedictine monk who would come over periodically from Downside, until Knox's arrival, when Knox celebrated Mass daily. One of the visitors recalled later: 'The Mass he said was of such beauty of diction and prayer, it made one pray with him and through him. We said the Rosary every evening in the Mells chapel ... He prayed, unconscious of all around him ... He had come into harbour and was at peace.'[49] The setting helped him find that peace. Mells Manor was a beautiful and peaceful place, tactfully modified by Lutyens in 1900. Roses and wisteria climbed up the old grey stone walls which were flecked with gold lichen. Lupins and lilies nodded at the windows. The house and its hospitality duly worked its magic on Knox. Within six months of the move Evelyn Waugh came on a visit and described him as looking 'plump and cosseted' and much more at ease.[50]

Life at Mells was an ideal solution for him. Here his needs could be provided for. There was company when he wanted it, and privacy when he wanted that. It was a family setting, but without the intensity that had once been present at Aldenham. He was respected and loved. Knox's friend and confessor Fr Hubert van Zeller was nearby at Downside Abbey. He was still in touch with the wider world, through his reading and through the invitations to preach on special occasions. Knox also had his correspondence. Each day he received ten to fifteen letters from people in many part of the world asking his spiritual advice.[51] He was conscientious in his replies, and regularly had to buy sheets of stamps from the post office to fuel his correspondence. Yet there was a sense of his life winding down, of projects completed rather than of fresh projects undertaken. He continued to work on the Old Testament translation and finished it in 1948. A good deal of work still lay ahead of him. Committees of experts continued to examine his translation and made recommendations, some 1,500 being accepted by Knox and incorporated into his translation.[52] A complete definitive Bible in the Knox translation appeared in 1955. It was printed on Oxford India paper with type composed by the Cambridge University Press, although Burns and Oates were the actual publishers. At a celebratory lunch at the Hyde Park Hotel, Cardinal Griffin was in the chair and the Minister of Education, David Eccles, was one of the guests.[53]

Another project completed at Mells was his scholarly work *Enthusiasm* which studied those who, claiming special inspiration, had broken with the wider fellowship of the Church. The book turned out to be too wide in scope. Although he specialized in the seventeenth and eighteenth centuries, his survey included the Pauline Church in Corinth, the Middle Ages and the Anabaptists. Moreover, the book had been written over a period of thirty years (he had started it in 1918) and so inevitably some internal development took place as his own thinking shifted over the years. He admitted as much. In the foreword, taking the form of a letter to Evelyn Waugh, he wrote:

> When the plan of the Book was first conceived, all those years ago, it was to have been a broadside, a trumpet-blast, an end of controversy ... here, I would say, is what happens inevitably, if once the principle of Catholic unity is lost! All this confusion, this priggishness, this pedantry, this eccentricity and worse, follows directly from the rash step that takes you outside the fold of Peter ... But somehow, in the writing, my whole treatment of the subject became different; the more you got to know the men, the more human did they become, for better or worse; you were more concerned to find out why they thought as they did than to prove it was wrong. The result, I am afraid, is a hotch-potch.[54]

Having commenced with the belief that the illuminists about whom he was writing were lamentably wrong, he came to a more nuanced understanding. He concluded that in itself enthusiasm was not a wrong tendency but a false emphasis. It exaggerated some aspect of interior religion at the expense of the more balanced teaching of the institutional Church. In particular Knox looked askance at the work of John Wesley and his fellow evangelicals. Knox believed their spiritual legacy to be dangerous, because English religious expectation had, ever since, valued experience over doctrine. The English religious sensibility believed something to be true because of deeply held feelings: 'You did not place your hope on this or that doctrinal calculation; you *knew*. For that reason the average Englishman was, and is, singularly unaffected by reasons ...' His assessment was not entirely negative. He warned that while the Catholic Church was always being renewed by God and carried within itself spiritual treasure, yet its spiritual energies could burn low; where it became too complacently institutional it could lapse into mediocrity.[55] He had undertaken the book in the white heat of his own conversion, determined to be the hammer of heresy; he concluded it with greater charity and perspective. As he wrote to a correspondent, 'The wholeness of Christian life, as one sees it from inside the Church, is or ought to be something in which both the charismatic side of religion and the institutional side of religion are integral parts, not conflicting forces.'[56] This was a witness to his own interior journey. He believed no less than before in the fullness of Catholic truth, yet he could also see that the fruits of the Spirit were widely shared, and that the Catholic Church had benefited from those like St Francis who had felt impelled by God.

Knox still received invitations to preach on special occasions, but he accepted fewer of these. In 1951 he was the preacher at a Mass broadcast from Westminster Cathedral as part of the Festival of Britain. He made a rare foray abroad in 1954 when he travelled with Katharine to Zanzibar to visit her son Julian, the Earl of Oxford and Asquith, who was Administrative Secretary there. Knox had preached at the wedding of the Earl and Anne Palairet at Brompton Oratory in 1947, and his connection with the family went back to his student days in Oxford and his friendship with Edward Horner. Knox went on from Zanzibar for a happy visit to the Actons at their farm in Rhodesia, where he found them flourishing and the family still growing. Back in Britain he continued to be sought after as a guest speaker and preacher. He had always been welcomed back to the Oxford chaplaincy, and a volume of his later conferences there was published under the title *The Hidden Stream*. Other collections were published: of short articles he had written for the Fleet Street press, of sermons, of addresses given at weddings.

It was a time for friendship also. In the post-war years his friendship with Evelyn Waugh ripened, and indeed Knox was held in high esteem by Waugh, who in 1950 tried to get Knox made a cardinal and then sought an honorary Oxford doctorate for him.[57] Their shared Catholicism has perhaps obscured the reality that their friendship was a case of the attraction of opposites. Waugh was blunt sometimes to the point of abrasiveness, enjoyed creature comforts and craved social recognition. Knox was reserved, lived simply and preferred a deeply private life. Each admired the writing of the other. When Waugh's novel *Helena* came out in 1950 Knox read it aloud to the household at Mells in the evenings, and later he and Katharine Asquith listened to it again when it was broadcast.[58] He would stay with Evelyn and Laura Waugh at their home, Piers Court, near Stroud in Gloucestershire, and later, after they moved in 1956, at Combe Florey in Somerset. Sometimes the Waughs would visit Mells. Evelyn Waugh was not generally inclined to put himself out for others, but he was extremely kind and caring to Knox. Knox was only fifteen years older than Waugh, but seems to have given him the father figure that he had always lacked. Waugh had been unloved by his own father, and repeated the pattern in being distant and sometimes oppressive with his own children.[59] The relationship with Ronald Knox was a filial relationship in which he showed uncharacteristic altruism and indeed love.

Another literary figure who visited Mells was the poet and autobiographer Siegfried Sassoon, who lived a short distance away across the county border at Heytesbury in Wiltshire. Sassoon, who was two years older than Knox, had served as an infantry officer in the First World War and had become something of a national figure after he risked court-martial to make a public protest against the war. His poems were often caustic about the war, in which he was wounded and awarded the MC. Afterwards he continued to write and live like a country gentleman, but by the early 1950s he was aware of drifting rudderless through life. Although he had married and was the father of a son, his past lovers included the aesthete Stephen Tennant.[60]

Sassoon had known Katharine Asquith since the late 1930s. He began visiting her at Mells in 1954 and came to know Knox well through those visits.[61] He was somewhat awed by Knox and never raised his spiritual search directly with him. But Knox seems to have discerned Sassoon's turmoil. In 1956 some of Sassoon's more recent poems appeared in a collection entitled *Sequences* which made clear his questing. In a poem 'Faith Unfaithful' he wrote:

> Mute, with signs I speak:
> Blind, by groping seek;
> Heed, yet nothing hear;
> Feel; find no one near.[62]

An atmosphere of loneliness, doubt and spiritual searching pervades the poems. In January 1957 Sassoon received a letter from Mother Margaret Mary McFarlin, one of the Assumption sisters at the Convent in Kensington. She had read the poems, was moved by them and was praying that he would sense God's presence shining through the darkness. Sassoon replied by return and a stream of correspondence followed, during which he also visited her. As he opened up his heart, she suggested that he might consider becoming a Catholic. Was this contact, with its important consequences, as coincidental as it might seem? Knox had known Mother Margaret Mary from the years the Assumption Convent school had spent at Aldenham. She was well read and interested in contemporary literature. Sassoon's biographer Jean Moorcroft Wilson thinks it likely that Knox had prompted Mother Margaret Mary's letter to Sassoon. If so, it was typical of Knox to find a discreet way of helping Sassoon articulate his spiritual needs, without any element of coercion. Knox declined to undertake Sassoon's instruction in the Catholic faith, instead referring him to Downside Abbey, where Sassoon was received into the Catholic Church on 14 August 1957. Possibly Knox was deterred by his own failing health, although it has also been suggested that by now he was temperamentally opposed to 'such an exchange of intimacies.'[63] Even so, Knox and the atmosphere at Mells were crucial in the conversion. Sassoon read and re-read Knox's essays and sermons, and wrote later that Knox had been for him 'a life line toward illumination in my crepuscular contemplations ... [an] incomparable expositor of alive religion ... he *gave* with both hands – spiritual help, scholarship, entertainment.'[64] Sassoon once described Catholicism to one of his closest friends as 'so civilised', a word which, as Jean Moorcroft Wilson pointed out, had also been applied to the conversation at Mells, adding: 'There is little doubt that Katharine Asquith and her circle there gave Catholicism a social as well as an aesthetic appeal for Sassoon.'[65] Which is another way of saying that through Mells, Asquith and Knox, Sassoon found a credible faith and a source of community.

Knox's Catholicism did not mean that he was hostile to the Church of England. At Mells he enjoyed the friendship of the Anglican rector. He accepted invitations to address the clergy of the local rural deanery, and the students of Wells Theological College. Both invitations gave him great pleasure, as did a visit from John Betjeman who came to open a fête in the grounds of the Manor in aid of the parish church.[66]

By the end of 1956 it became clear that there was something seriously wrong with Knox's health. In January 1957, an operation in London revealed cancer of the liver which had metastasized. An intestinal obstruction was removed, but the problem of the liver cancer remained. In March, Katharine Asquith asked Waugh to take Knox away for a short break. At Knox's request they stayed at the Imperial Hotel, Torquay. The out-of-season resort was empty and it rained, and Knox's spirits sank further. Laura Waugh joined them for a week and then all three moved to another hotel at Sidmouth, after which Waugh took Knox back to Combe Florey for two weeks.[67] Back at Mells he found that drink tasted like ink. He often had to go and lie down in the middle of a meal to avoid being sick. He felt a kind of torpor stealing over mind and body, and was deeply thankful for the help and support of friends.[68]

Knox had earlier accepted an invitation to give the Romanes Lecture in the Sheldonian Theatre at Oxford. This public lecture had been held every year since 1892 and could cover any subject in art, science or literature. Previous Romanes lecturers had included some distinguished figures: Curzon, Balfour, John Masefield, G. M. Trevelyan, Winston Churchill and Julian Huxley. Knox knew that it would be his farewell to the university with which his own history had been so intertwined, and was determined to give the lecture. On June 11th, the day of the lecture, Fr Hubert van Zeller accompanied him to Oxford. Even before they set out 'his colour was bad and he was speaking with pauses between the sentences'. After the two-hour drive, when they arrived at Oxford, he 'was looking ghastly and hardly saying a word.'[69] Knox did not know it, but a doctor had been stationed near the rostrum in case something went wrong. His services were not needed. From the beginning of the lecture Knox gained strength and spoke, sitting down, for more than an hour. He spoke wittily on the problems of translation, outlining the difficulties, calling for translations that were both elegant and yet practicable. If a translation was to be accessible, then it would be unlikely to be useful for longer than fifty years. He was greeted with thunderous applause at the end. Knox stayed with J. C. Masterman in the Provost's Lodging at Worcester College. He stayed up talking until 11 p.m. with friends from various colleges, mostly Trinity. Van Zeller had intended to stay elsewhere but an alarmed Provost discreetly pressed him to stay the night, worried by Knox's condition.

The next day van Zeller escorted Knox to Downing Street where he was the guest of Harold Macmillan, by now Prime Minister. They had stayed in touch throughout the 1930s, visiting and writing one another, and presumably the contact had continued as Macmillan rose in public life after the war. A consultation with Sir Horace Evans, physician to the Queen, had been arranged by Macmillan. It revealed that nothing could be done. The next day Macmillan took him in the Prime Minister's car to Paddington Station.

'I hope you will have a good journey,' Macmillan said, at the moment of farewell.

'It will be a very long one,' replied Knox.

'But, Ronnie, you are very well prepared for it.'[70]

When he arrived back at Mells, Knox was exhilarated that he had succeeded in what he had meant to do.

He wrote to friends telling them of the diagnosis, asking their prayers that he might persevere. He was, of course, a person of faith, but too honest to himself to deny that in the face of death, like any other human being, he might be tempted to despair. Many people from all walks of life wrote to him assuring him of their prayers, and from Rome Pope

Pius XII sent a relic, and a word of praise for Knox's translation of the Vulgate.

By early July he was bedbound. Laura Lovat came down from Scotland. Before she went back, Knox gave her his copy of the *Imitation of Christ*. It had belonged to her brother Charles Lister and had been with Lister when he died. Knox told her: 'After my death, I want you to give it to Harold [Macmillan] and to tell him what affection and admiration I have always had for him. I am too weary to write all this to him, so you must do it for me.' Katharine Asquith and Magdalen, Countess of Eldon (daughter of Laura Lovat) took it in turns to watch by his bedside day and night. He was moved into a big room on the first floor. The windows were wide open because of the summer heat. The magnolia was in full flower against the wall of the house. Sometimes Knox would gain inner strength by gazing on a relic of the martyr St John Southworth. For a time, to ease his discomfort, Katharine Asquith resorted to his childhood delight in hearing Robert Louis Stevenson read aloud. Knox worried that he was causing unnecessary trouble to Katharine.

Visitors included a housemaid he had visited regularly in a mental home. Harold Macmillan rang to ask if he could come down or do anything for him, but Knox was already too ill. He died on the evening of 24th August. His body was taken to Westminster Cathedral and on 29th August William Godfrey, Archbishop of Westminster, presided at a solemn requiem offered by Bishop George Craven, his auxiliary. The cathedral was full, with Harold Macmillan in the front row – it was a rare event for a Prime Minister to attend a Catholic Mass. The Archbishop of Liverpool was present, along with the Bishops of Southwark, Brentwood, Clifton and Motherwell. The preacher was Fr Martin D'Arcy. D'Arcy spoke of Knox's combination of tradition and apostolic endeavour. Knox had used his gifts to commend the faith, seeking always to express it in ways that would help the people of his day hear and respond to the faith that was both ancient and ever new. Through his translation of the Bible, Knox sought to ensure 'that the word Roman in Roman Catholic should no longer feel foreign.'[71] That the Catholic faith, in other words, should be seen as what it always had been, part of English life and English culture.

Laura Lovat waited and then, as Knox had requested, sent his copy of the *Imitation* to Harold Macmillan. Macmillan replied: 'Nothing has given me more pleasure than that you should have given this to me – it brings back so many memories. As you know, Ronald Knox was my dearest friend for very many years.' [72]

Knox was buried on 30 August 1957 in the churchyard at Mells, in a pastoral English setting. The front of his gravestone commemorates him as priest, scholar, preacher, writer and translator. Less noticed is the reverse side, which contains the symbols of priesthood, a chalice and a host, and a simple inscription taken from Colossians 3.3: 'You have died, and your life is hidden with Christ in God.'

Notes

1   Knox to Woollen, 22 December 1938, UCEB/AAW.
2   On this aspect of the classics, see Linda Colley, *Britons: The Forging of a Nation 1707–1837* (London: Yale, 1992), pp. 167–8.
3   EW *RK*, p. 249.
4   EW *RK*, pp. 250–1.
5   Speaight, *Ronald Knox the Writer*, p. 77.
6   Knox, *Let Dons Delight*, p. 70.
7   Knox, *Let Dons Delight*, p. 177.
8   Knox, *Let Dons Delight*, p. 129.
9   Knox, *Let Dons Delight*, pp. 270–1.
10 Hinsley to Knox, 10 June 1938; Knox to Hinsley, 22 June, 1938, KPM.
11 *The Tablet* 17 June 1939, p. 790. Drumm, *The Old Palace*, pp. 180–1, mistakenly ascribes the speech cited to Woodruff.
12 Ronald Knox, *Nazi and Nazarene* (London: Macmillan, 1940), p. 18.
13 John Keegan, *The Second World War* (London: Arrow/Random Century, 1990), pp. 104–5; Peter Hennessy, *Never Again: Britain 1945–1951* (London: Vintage, 1993), p. 47.
14 Isabel Quigly, 'Obituary: Daphne, Lady Acton' *The Independent* (London) 29 March 2003.
15 Ronald Knox *et al.*, *The World We're Fighting For* (London: SCM, 1941).

16 Ronald Knox, *The Mass in Slow Motion* (London: Sheed & Ward, 1948), pp. 16, 50, 52.

17 Martin D'Arcy funeral panegyric for Ronald Knox, *The Tablet* 31 August 1957.

18 Knox, *The Mass in Slow Motion*, p. 72.

19 Knox, *The Mass in Slow Motion*, pp. 114–15.

20 Sheridan Gilley, 'A Tradition and Culture Lost, to be Regained' in Michael Hornsby-Smith (ed.), *Catholics in England 1950–2000* (London: Cassell, 1999), p. 33. He is drawing on the work of Michael Archer in *The Two Catholic Churches*.

21 Maisie Ward, *Unfinished Business* (London: Sheed & Ward, 1964), pp. 321–3.

22 Ronald Knox, *On Englishing the Bible* (London: Burns Oates, 1949), p. 17.

23 James White, *Roman Catholic Worship: Trent to Today* (New York: Paulist, 1995), pp. 85–6 and 90.

24 Quoted in EW, *RK*, p. 269.

25 *The Tablet* 14 January 1939.

26 Hugh Pope, OP, *A Brief History of the English Version of the New Testament* ... (London: Bibliographical Society, 1940) quoting Wiseman, p. 351; on free manipulation of the text, p. 70.

27 Ronald Knox, *On English Translation* (Oxford: Clarendon Press, 1957), pp. 5–6.

28 EW, *RK*, p. 285.

29 EW, *RK*, pp. 300–1.

30 Cardinal Bernard Griffin, Preface, *The New Testament of Our Lord and Saviour Jesus Christ Newly Translated from the Vulgate Latin* ... (London: Burns Oates and Washbourne, 1945), p. v.

31 Christopher Sykes, *Evelyn Waugh: A Biography* (London: Collins, 1975), p. 313; Knox, *On English Translation*, p. 4.

32 Typescript note after Knox's death, Sheed and Ward Family Papers, Archives of the University of Notre Dame, folder CSWD 16/15.

33 Knox, *On Englishing the Bible*, p. vii.

34 Quoted in Fitzgerald, *The Knox Brothers*, p. 256.

35 Knox to Macmillan, 25 May 1943, Macmillan Papers, Bodleian, Box 283 fo. 249.

36 Acton to Waugh, 25 August 1958, Evelyn Waugh Papers, British Library Manuscripts, Add 81046.

37 EW, *RK*. p. 304.

38 Knox to Houselander, 18 December 1945, Sheed and Ward Family Papers, Archives of the University of Notre Dame, folder CSWD 16/15; Caryll Houselander, *The Reed of God* (London: Sheed and Ward, 1944), p. 73.

39 See Angus Wilson quoted in Humphrey Carpenter, *The Brideshead Generation: Evelyn Waugh and his Friends* (Boston: Houghton Mifflin, 1990), p. 454.

40   Asquith to Waugh, 3 October 1958; Evelyn Waugh Papers, British Library Manuscripts, Add 81046 and 81047.
41   D'Arcy to Waugh, 18 June 1958, Evelyn Waugh Papers, British Library, Manuscripts Add 81052.
42   Ronald Knox, *God and the Atom* (London: Sheed and Ward, 1945), pp. 83–5, quoting from 83.
43   Knox, *God and the Atom*, p. 42.
44   See, for example, John Polkinghorne, *Quantum Physics and Theology: An Unexpected Kinship* (London: Yale University Press, 2007) and other books by the same author.
45   David Kynaston, *Austerity Britain 1945–1951* (London: Bloomsbury, 2007), p. 194.
46   *Letters from Hilaire Belloc* (Robert Speaight, ed.) (London: Hollis and Carter, 1958), pp. 112–14, quoting from 113.
47   Katharine Asquith to Evelyn Waugh, 23 November 1958, Waugh Papers, British Library.
48   Mathew, *Catholicism in England*, p. 272.
49   From a typescript memoir (anonymous, but by Lady Eldon) in the Sheed and Ward Family Papers, Archives of the University of Notre Dame, folder CSWD 16/15.
50   Evelyn Waugh, *Mr Wu and Mrs Stitch: The Letters of Evelyn Waugh and Diana Cooper* (Artemis Cooper, ed.) (London: Hodder, 1991), p. 102.
51   Interview with Hon. John Jolliffe, 10 February 2009.
52   EW, *RK*, p. 311.
53   Tom Burns, *The Uses of Memory: Publishing and Further Pursuits* (London: Sheed & Ward, 1993), p. 135.
54   Ronald Knox, *Enthusiasm: A Chapter in the History of Religion* (Oxford: OUP, 195), pp. v–vi.
55   *Enthusiasm* pp. 547 and 590–1, quoting from 547.
56   *Off the Record*, p. 64.
57   Norman Page, *An Evelyn Waugh Chronology* (London: Macmillan 1997), pp. 116 and 119.
58   Katharine Asquith to Waugh, October 1950 and December 1951, Evelyn Waugh Papers, British Library Manuscripts, Add 81047.
59   On Evelyn Waugh not being loved by his father, see Alexander Waugh, *Fathers and Sons: The Autobiography of a Family* (London: Headline, 2004), pp. 219. See also p. 273, 'Neither Laura nor Evelyn was thrilled to have children.'
60   Tennant is sometimes said to be one of the real-life characters from whom Waugh derived inspiration for his creation of the fictional Sebastian Flyte. Others are variously said to be Waugh's source material: Harold Acton, Brian Howard, Alastair Graham and above all Hugh Lygon of the Beauchamp family.
61   These and following details from Jean Moorcroft Wilson, *Siegfried*

Sassoon: The Journey from the Trenches (London: Duckworth, 2003), pp. 384–96.

62 Siegfried Sassoon, *Sequences* (London: Faber, 1956), p. 51.
63 Wilson, *Journey from the Trenches*, p. 390, quoting Julian, Earl of Oxford and Asquith, from an interview.
64 Letter from Sassoon to Dame Felicitas Corrigan, OSB, 14 April 1960. Felicitas Corrigan (ed.), *Siegfried Sassoon: Poet's Pilgrimage* (London: Gollancz, 1973), p. 185.
65 Wilson, *Journey from the Trenches*, p. 396.
66 Christopher Hollis, *The Tablet* 31 August 1957, 159.
67 Norman Page, *An Evelyn Waugh Chronology*, p. 158.
68 Knox to Douglas Woodruff 12 May and 1 July 1957, Douglas Woodruff Papers, Box 4 folder 25, Georgetown University Library Special Collections.
69 These details from an untitled typescript by Fr van Zeller, KPM, n.d. but probably 1958.
70 Harold Macmillan, *Winds of Change: 1914–1939* (London: Macmillan, 1966), p. 43.
71 *The Tablet* 31 August 1957, 173.
72 Most of the details of Knox's last few days, including the later letter from Macmillan, come from the typescript memoir by Lady Eldon in the Sheed and Ward Family Papers, Archives of the University of Notre Dame, folder CSWD 16/15.

9

In Retrospect

The Catholic Church was not really foreign to England. For over a thousand years it had been part of the warp and woof of English history, until the turmoil of the Reformation era had marginalized Catholicism. Thereafter the myth of Catholic foreignness took deep root. It did not help that two of the countries against which England vied for supremacy, France and Spain, were Catholic. Even the poorest, least educated elements of the population tended to know about the Armada, and about Guy Fawkes's 'gunpowder, treason and plot.' Linda Collings has shown how a sense of divinely ordained deliverance from Catholicism created a pan-British consciousness which helped meld together the constituent nations of the United Kingdom. She tells us that in the eighteenth century, 'The slang adjective most commonly applied to Catholics was "outlandish", and this was meant quite literally ... They did not belong, and were therefore suspect.'[1] Catholic emancipation from civil disabilities was enacted in 1829, but even then protests and petitions indicated that anti-Catholic suspicions ran deep: 'The evidence suggests that many ordinary Britons who signed anti-Catholic petitions saw themselves, quite consciously, as being part of a native tradition of resistance to Catholicism which stretched back for centuries and which seemed, indeed, to be timeless.'[2] The sense of Catholic alterity increased from the mid-nineteenth century onwards when the Irish emigrated in large numbers to England. Catholicism was then associated with both foreignness and poverty. One historian of nineteenth-century Judaism has suggested that in Victorian Britain anti-Catholic prejudice was stronger than antisemitism.[3] It has sometimes been said that the comparative lack of antisemitism in England was due to the fact that it was the Catholics who were regarded as the Other.

Even so, prejudice was fading by the beginning of the twentieth century. The role of Cardinal Manning in settling the Dock Strike of 1889 showed a Catholic Church growing in self-confidence and prepared to play its part in the public life of the nation. There were Catholic inhibitions to be overcome as well, however. Partly for survival, partly to preserve their own sense of distinctiveness, Catholics had tended to a measure of self-segregation. As late as 1930, a Jesuit found it necessary to write a Catholic Truth Society pamphlet emphasizing that Catholics should play a greater role in national life. Certainly, he admitted, there was 'a feeling in this country, dating from the days of Elizabeth and still widely prevalent, that sincere profession of the Catholic religion is incompatible with whole-hearted loyalty and patriotism.'[4] But, he went on to say, Catholics had allowed this to make them introverted and they now needed to overcome this unnecessary reticence and become more involved in the life of their nation.

In fact, Catholics were already doing what he wanted them to do. The interwar years were years of growth in Catholic self-confidence. The establishment of the Irish Free State in 1922 removed a source of tension within the Catholic Church in England, one that had distracted and divided it. In the 1920s and 1930s Catholics were increasingly involved in social and political affairs on a more mainstream basis. For example, in the East London borough of Stepney the Labour Party was run by a consortium of Jews and Catholics led by a Jewish politician. In areas of County Durham, leadership of the miners' union passed from Methodists to Catholics.[5] Catholics, too, were moving up the social ladder, a development seen in the growing number of students from humble backgrounds who attended the Oxford chaplaincy during Knox's time there. This process of emergence and engagement was greatly helped by the tenure in office of Cardinal Arthur Hinsley, Archbishop of Westminster 1935–1943. A spirited Yorkshireman of broad sympathies, he had been a key figure in helping Belgian refugees during the First World War and he always retained an informed interest in social issues. He was intensely patriotic and during the Second World War he used his influence for the Allied cause. At the time of Dunkirk, Winston Churchill received a letter from Hinsley encouraging him to stand firm. 'The Cardinal is vigorous and tough', minuted Churchill.[6]

Knox made his own contribution to this process of the Catholic Church slipping into the national mainstream. To begin with, there was the obvious fact of his intelligence. A man who was widely regarded as one of the brightest minds of his generation had become a Catholic. Then there was what we might call the national reach of his ministry of the word. As a writer, broadcaster and preacher he helped to give the Catholic Church a higher profile. In his panegyric at Westminster Cathedral, Fr Martin D'Arcy said that Knox would have made the perfect Public Orator of Oxford University, 'had not God instead chosen him to be the Public Orator of the Catholic Church in England.'[7] Knox wanted to convey Catholic teaching in ways that would make sense to English people. Belonging to the Catholic Church allowed him to bring together his English heritage and his faith. T. S. Eliot once said that 'It is easier for the Church of England to become Catholic, than for the Church of Rome in England to become English . . . If England is ever to be in any appreciable degree converted to Christianity, it can only be through the Church of England.'[8] By his life and ministry, Ronald Knox showed otherwise. Fr Martin D'Arcy considered him to represent the English culture, based on the Bible and the humanities, which had once been exemplified in Thomas More.[9] In his own, very English way, Knox was an apologist for the Catholic Faith, and through that, an evangelist for Christ.

His Englishness took different forms. It showed in his preaching, which was both reasoned and affective, always appealing to both mind and heart. He knew that clear, reasoned explanation would be conveyed more powerfully if it could evoke something from the experience of the reader.

Here his in-depth knowledge of English literature was crucially important. Aidan Nichols says of Knox that, 'As a former High Churchman, he was the beneficiary of an alliance going back to the Caroline divines, and their near-contemporaries the metaphysical poets of the seventeenth century. The wedding of literary culture and theological expression is celebrated throughout his writings ...'[10] There is also his typically English humour, inclined to irony, gently puncturing self-importance. Humour, he wrote, was the inseparable playmate of humanity, and was particularly at home in church 'when the spacious silences of worship and the solemn purple of prelates enjoin reverence.'[11] The English aspect of his character was shown in his sense of history, and his love of classical literature. In fact, his approach was classical in the other sense as well, in its appeal to tradition inherited and passed on, a tradition in which there was a hierarchy of values and a clear set of boundaries. Knox was a writer in the classical tradition. The past was not another world, but through tradition the past lived on in the present, in the Christian values which informed life and lifted the aspirations of people in their daily living.

His desire for certainty, for truth taught with authority, may seem surprising to present generations. But his esteem of certainty played a crucial role in the unfolding of his gifts. As an ultramontane Anglo-Catholic he felt the need to assert a particular interpretation of Anglican-style Catholicism. It was as if he had to build a spiritual home through his own efforts. Becoming Catholic meant that he no longer had to build the home: it was there already, as a gift, and all he had to do was to step through the door. Because he no longer had to assert Catholicism over and against the mainstream of the Church of England, he was, paradoxically, now more free to integrate his Englishness and his Catholicism. We can trace the arc of his journey exactly. He came into the Catholic Church, he said, Manning's disciple rather than Newman's. That is to say, he was strongly ultramontane and critical of any compromise with English culture. But twenty years later, writing to Cardinal Hinsley to decline the presidency of St Edmund's

College, he wrote that Newman was his hero rather than Manning.[12] Such a change was, he wrote, a common experience among converts when they looked back over a length of time: 'You have the curious feeling that the person who came into the Church was not you, but somebody slightly different.'[13] As a result of this process of integration he was able to bring together the different aspects of his character in a fruitful way. For example, he was the child of an evangelical family and never lost his love of scripture. The nine years he spent translating the Bible were part of that integration. So, in a different key, was the lengthy gestation of his book *Enthusiasm*. He began the book determined to refute those who appealed to special revelation from God. He ended the book appreciating that although appeal to divine inspiration had real dangers, it had often brought new fire and energy to the Church at times of torpor. The same growth into generosity can be observed in his preaching. Horton Davies, in his history of preaching and worship in England, praised Knox as one of the finest preachers of his time. But he noted that, 'The earliest sermons are often marred by the partisan spirit and by an over-indulgence in facetiousness.'[14] Becoming a Roman Catholic freed Knox from this Anglo-Catholic desire to convince others of his catholicity. He also trimmed away the facetiousness, which stemmed probably from the Anglo-Catholic mixture of earnestness and unease. In becoming one of the foremost preachers of his generation, Knox demonstrated to his fellow English men and women that the Catholic Church could be just as much at home in the word as in the sacraments.

There was a journey, however, that Knox did not make, and that was the journey beyond his social class which he never quite transcended. Through his father's episcopal labours in Birmingham and Manchester, he did have some experience of the realities of life in England's teeming cities. But he never seemed to take on board the cost of such ministry, perhaps because of a deeply-hidden need to resist his father's moulding and establish himself as his own man. The contrast with some of his Anglo-Catholic confrères is stark.

By 1900 Anglo-Catholics had an impressive record of parish service in some of the worst slums in Britain. Alongside this they had developed a strong incarnational theology that played naturally into their sacramental life and practice. This mixture of incarnational theology and life in the slums meant that many Anglo-Catholic clergy had a highly-developed social conscience. Now, Knox *was* aware of some of the social issues of the day, especially as he grew older. *Let Dons Delight* referred near its end to the 1930s' desire for a ruthlessly planned society. He had some understanding of Freudian psychology. Knox also wrote about Nazi attacks on the Catholic Church in Germany, and he wrestled with the implications for humankind of nuclear war. Yet there was a foreign land where he rarely ventured, the world of working-class Catholicism in England. Here he was barely known and of it he knew little himself. David Mathew gave an evocative word-picture of the typical Catholic homes of the interwar years. These homes were found, he wrote, in

> those short closes and places running down to the railway lines of the industrial cities where the children scrambled on the low grey pavement. In the bedrooms mild sunlight would strike the coloured oleographs of the Sacred Heart; the engines whistled and the smoke from the factory chimneys moved over slowly above the walls of sidings and the mean house fronts; the soot was flaking from the warm rose brick.[15]

This was a world that was a foreign land to Knox. But, as Mathew himself acknowledged, this segment of the Catholic community was already changing and dispersing, a process that accelerated through the 1950s and beyond. Part of Knox's success was to speak to the Catholic community as its horizons broadened and it sought a fresh understanding of the faith, new ways of appropriating ancient truths.

In his many invitations to conduct retreats and to preach, it is clear that Knox was a national treasure of the Catholic Church in England. And yet, he was an essentially private man. After his death many people commented on his shyness. Perhaps it was always so, although this is difficult to correlate with the popular Balliol student and the gifted speaker at the Oxford Union. Perhaps it would be truer to say that he had become more private, perhaps understandably so, with the death of so many of his friends in the First World War. He also shared the traditional English reserve about showing religious emotion, and his childhood bereavement seems to have left a wound that subconsciously asserted itself late in life. His writings reveal a strong faith, Christocentric, anchored in Catholic tradition, patient towards human frailty, yet they reveal his own soul only indirectly. We catch a rare glimpse of him being deeply moved in prayer in *The Mass in Slow Motion* where he writes of what a priest feels during the Eucharistic Prayer. Because it shows us how he felt, it is worth quoting in full:

> With the Consecration itself, you go off on to a quite different tack. You stop making up prayers, thinking up reverential epithets, pulling strings of participles together; you don't ask God for anything or apologize for anything or try to induce any attitude or any frame of mind in yourself; you simply stand there and record a piece of history. In recording that piece of history, it becomes necessary to recite some words our Lord used; and so, as if absent-mindedly, almost as if unintentionally, you do what you came there to do; or rather, you don't do it, you suddenly pull yourself together and realize that our Lord's words, even relaid on such lips as yours, have done it ... Christ has used you to do a miracle, and everything has become quite different. You elevate the Host, the Chalice; or are they trying to fly upwards out of your hands? You hardly know, it is all so strange.
>
> Anyhow, you start offering this precious Thing that has fallen between your hands; you connect it with this and that, the mysteries of our Lord's life, the Old Testament sacrifices, the ministry of the Angels in Heaven, the expectation of the faithful dead; another string of saints' names

occurs to you; but all this you do in a half-dazed way, still thinking about what it is that lies before you; and then, boldly, you take up Host and Chalice together and hold them up for a breathless moment. And then suddenly you are talking out loud again, and feel the ground sure under your feet as you find yourself saying the *Pater Noster*. I suppose each of us has a clause or a phase of the Mass at which, if it wasn't for the trouble and confusion it was going to cause, he would like to die. Mine is the *Pater Noster*. It is, to me, the moment in the Mass at which one is most consciously, most fearlessly, talking to God.[16]

It is his testimony of how for him the celebration of the Mass was the place where he felt that this world touched eternity.

Despite his high profile ministry, Knox remained a little on the margins. As a priest ordained under his own patrimony, he was at one remove from the ebb and flow of diocesan life. As chaplain at Oxford, he was similarly in a liminal position. He was in the diocese of Birmingham but not of it, appointed by a national committee to serve the English Catholic Church by looking after the spiritual welfare of their sons at Oxford. As priest to well-known families in country houses, he was again more free to write, to think, and even occasionally to satirize. This is a reminder of how free the preconciliar Church could be. Certainly the preconciliar Catholic Church governed itself strictly, yet within the Church there was space and air. When G. K. Chesterton was received into the Catholic Church in 1922 Maurice Baring wrote to him saying, 'Space and freedom: that was what I experienced on being received; that is what I have been most conscious of ever since. It is the exact opposite of what the ordinary Protestant conceives to be the case.'[17] The preconciliar Church is sometimes criticized as inflexible, intolerant, hierarchical. Yet this was a time and a setting in which someone like Knox could flourish. Perhaps this was possible because the Catholic Church in England during this period had a strong sense of its own identity. Nowadays the Catholic Church is part of the mainstream, but the price it has paid for that is a loss of confidence. Catholics are no longer so sure of themselves and of what they believe. The family values that were a feature of Catholicism have been eroded and often replaced by the dominant secular values of the day. Catholic children, too, seem to grow up less well informed about their own faith, and lacking the confidence to defend it when challenged. And so, strangely, a Catholic Church more widely accepted in the life of the nation is also less sure of itself.

Waugh would have us believe that Knox's talents were wasted but it is difficult to agree with this conclusion.[18] The Church was generous to Knox, just as it has been generous in more recent times to Anglicans who have made the same journey. Not for Knox high office as a bishop, or seminary rector, although given his detestation of administration such an appointment was unlikely. Possibly he could have become priest of a fashionable London parish, but this would simply have increased his pastoral ministry at the expense of his time to write. Before he was told to go to the Oratorians, Knox had considered going to live with the monks at Belmont Abbey in Herefordshire. It is surprising that he did not join one of the great Benedictine abbeys. After all, he had loved Caldey, and its Benedictine life had marked him deeply in his Anglican days. Age might have played its part in turning him away from the religious life. When he became a Roman Catholic he was already twenty-nine. In those days it was thought difficult, though not impossible, for a man who was already formed in faith and character to be conformed to the Benedictine ethos. Downside might have been particularly convivial. It combined a life of prayer with scholarship and hospitality, while building a vast abbey church that today soars above the Somerset countryside in a reminder of what medieval England must have looked like. Downside was a civilized place, suited to Knox's sense of decorum and yet with the conviviality that he enjoyed. A monk remembers that in the early 1920s, 'At the community gathering after dinner one might pass from a group, possibly including Dean Armitage Robinson of Wells, which was arguing the correct translation of a medieval Latin poem, by way of one discussing the Test Match to a description of an

encounter with the inhabitants of Afghanistan.'[19] In its combination of culture and prayer, community and ministry, an English
Benedictine community would have seemed peculiarly suited to
Knox. English Benedictinism, as the late Cardinal Hume
showed, brings together the best of English culture with an
unswerving loyalty to the Catholic faith.

Knox chose a different route of ministry and service, and
made it his own. It may explain his lack of interest in travel.
Martin D'Arcy pointed out that the 'Ecclesiastical authorities
were generous in allowing him to work out his own vocation,
and that vocation he felt confined him to this island and those
who read English ... As a Catholic he was universal, but ...
he was rooted in this island.'[20] Fifty years after the death of
Knox, Britain is a very different country. The state has taken
over the role of moral tutor. It arrogates to itself increasing
powers to achieve its own vision of what human beings need
for their flourishing. This would not have surprised Knox. In
a sermon in 1949, when the Labour administration of Clement
Atlee was bringing the welfare state into being, Knox began
by noting thankfully that the welfare state would remove much
of the fear of illness, unemployment or old age. He was glad
that the government was tackling these uncertainties which
had so blighted people's lives. But, he noted, there was a price
to be paid for this. In words which speak powerfully to our
own times, he said:

> The England in which we live is a land of diminishing
> freedom. That is inevitable; you cannot have it both ways.
> If the public purse is to underwrite for us the adventure of
> living, then our lives, at every turn must be open to the
> public scrutiny. We shall have inspectors calling at unwel-
> come hours to satisfy themselves that the law's require-
> ments are being observed; we shall have to fill in forms,
> answer elaborate questionnaires which seem to us to be of
> no importance; we shall queue up at the doors of public
> offices ... More and more we find we've got to have
> *permits* for doing this and that ... even (a very ominous
> word) that we are being 'directed' to do this and that.[21]

It was a warning that with gain there was also loss. Here, as throughout his life, Knox was mindful of an older tradition which believed in the possibility of humanity fulfilled by the integration of spirit and intellect, wisdom and knowledge, church and nation. It was this Christian balance that Knox, the Catholic, sought and which he consistently commended to his country. He believed that without faith there could be no enduring happiness for the nation. Once, in a sermon on St George, he had mused about the phrase 'Merry England' and especially about the word 'Merry' which now survived only in 'Merry Christmas' or in alluding to someone being tipsy. But the word did not come, he said, from drinking or excitable behaviour. Rather, it meant that a person was light-hearted, good-humoured and willing to share fun with others. And this in turn implied a person at peace with themselves and with God: 'A country cannot be merry while it forgets God. And a country cannot be merry for long, or with safety, if it tries to be Christian without being Catholic.'[22]

One of his longest friendships was with Hilaire Belloc. After the war Knox occasionally visited the increasingly frail Belloc at his house in Sussex, and would say Mass for him there. Belloc died in July 1953 and was buried at West Grinstead. A solemn requiem was held for him in Westminster Cathedral, at which Knox was the preacher. He said of Belloc:

> To be sure, he was a prophet rather than an apostle; he did not, as we say, 'make converts' ... But the influence of a prophet is not to be measured by its impact on a single mind here and there; it exercises a kind of hydraulic pressure on the thought of his age. And when the day of wrath comes, and that book is brought out, written once for all, which contains all the material for a world's judgment, we shall perhaps see more of what Belloc was and did; how even his most irresponsible satire acted as a solvent-force, to pierce the hard rind of self-satisfaction which, more than anything, kept Victorian England away from the Church; how the very overtones of his unostentatious piety brought back to us memories of the Faith, and of the Mass, and

of our blessed Lady, to which English ears had grown unaccustomed.[23]

Did Knox think of himself when he spoke those words? The truth is that they fit him better than the combative Belloc. Knox had brought a discreet pressure to bear on English spirituality. By his friendships, his preaching, his writing and his broadcasting, he had encouraged the English public at large to be more open to Christian faith and to Catholicism in particular. He had provided a more reflective, considered and scriptural account of Catholicism. In doing so he had given the English Catholic Church greater self-confidence. Knox's satire had brought laughter and pleasure to many and yet even as he amused his readers, he subtly challenged them to think again about truth and about history.

Notes

1 Collings, *Britons*, p. 23.
2 Collings, *Britons*, p. 330
3 David Englander, 'Anglicized not Anglican: Jews and Judaism in Victorian Britain' in Gerald Parsons (ed.), *Religion in Victorian Britain* I (Manchester: Manchester University Press, 1988), p. 239.
4 Joseph Keating, *The Things that are Caesar's* (London: CTS, 1930), p. 1.
5 Sheridan Gilley, 'The Years of Equipoise: 1892–1943' in V. A. McClelland and M. Hodgetts (eds), *From without the Flaminian Gate: 150 years of Catholicism in England and Wales* (London: Darton, Longman and Todd, 1999), p. 46
6 Quoted in John Lukacs, *Five Days in London: May 1940* (New Haven: Yale, 1999), p. 191.
7 *The Tablet* 31 August 1957, 172.
8 T. S. Eliot, *Thoughts after Lambeth*, quoted in Nichols, *The Realm*, p. 160.
9 *The Tablet* 31 August 1957, 172.
10 *Dominican Gallery*, p. 41.
11 Knox, *Essays in Satire*, p. 17.
12 *SA*, p. xiv and EW, *RK*, p. 267.
13 *SA*, pp. xiv–xv.
14 Horton Davies, *Worship and Theology in England* Volume 5: *The*

Ecumenical Century, 1900–1965 (Eerdmans: Grand Rapids, 1996), p. 247.

15 Mathew, *Catholicism in England*, p. 276.
16 Knox, *The Mass in Slow Motion*, pp. xvii–xviii.
17 Quoted in Hastings, *A History of English Christianity*, p. 151.
18 EW, *RK*, p. 292.
19 Adrian Morey, *David Knowles: A Memoir* (London: DLT, 1979), p. 49.
20 *The Tablet* 31 August 1957, 173.
21 A sermon preached in Westminster Cathedral 24 April 1949, in Knox, *Occasional Sermons*, p. 278.
22 Ronald Knox, *Captive Flames: On Selected Saints and Christian Heroes* (Ignatius Press: San Francisco, 2001), p. 21.
23 Quoted in Robert Speaight, *The Life of Hilaire Belloc* (London: Hollis & Carter, 1957), p. 537.

Bibliography

Primary Sources: Archival

BBC Written Archives Centre, Caversham
    Park, Reading   BBC/WA
Evelyn Waugh Papers, British Library
Jesuit Provincial Archives, UK Province,
    Mayfair
Knox Papers, Mells Manor, Somerset   KPM
Sir Arnold Lunn Papers and Douglas
    Woodruff Papers, Georgetown University Library
Harold Macmillan Papers, Bodleian Library,
    Oxford
Sheed and Ward Family Papers, Archives of
    the University of Notre Dame
Universities Catholic Education Board, Archives of the
    Archdiocese of Westminster   UCEB/AAW

Primary Sources: Publications by Ronald Knox
(by date of publication)
Only works cited in the text are given here

*Naboth's Vineyard in Pawn: Three Sermons on the Church of
    England* ... (London: Society of SS. Peter and Paul, 1913).
Some Loose Stones: Being a Consideration of 'Foundations',
    (London: Longmans, 1914).

A Spiritual Aeneid, rev. ed., (London: Burns and Oates, 1950; originally published 1918.)

Sanctions: A Frivolity, (London: Methuen, 1924).

The Viaduct Murder, (Merion Station, PA: Merion Press, 2001; originally published 1925).

Other Eyes Than Ours, (London: Methuen, 1926).

An Open-Air Pulpit, (London: Constable, 1926).

The Belief of Catholics, (London: Ernest Benn, 1927).

The Three Taps, (London: Methuen, 1927).

Essays in Satire, (London: Sheed & Ward, 1928).

The Best English Detective Stories of 1928, ed., with H. Harrington, introduction by Ronald Knox, (New York: Horace Liveright, 1929).

Difficulties, (London: Eyre and Spottiswoode, 1932; 3rd edition, 1958).

Let Dons Delight: Being Variations on a Theme in an Oxford Common-Room, (London: Sheed & Ward, 1939).

Captive Flames: On Selected Saints and Christian Heroes, (London: Burns Oates, 1940; new edition, San Francisco: Ignatius Press, 2001).

The World We're Fighting For, (London: SCM, 1941).

In Soft Garments: A Collection of Oxford Conferences, (London: Burns Oates, 1942).

(Translation) *The New Testament of Our Lord and Saviour Jesus Christ, Newly Translated* from the Vulgate Latin and Authorized by the Archbishops and Bishops of England and Wales, (London: Burns Oates and Washbourne, 1945).

God and the Atom, (London: Sheed and Ward, 1945).

The Mass in Slow Motion, (London: Sheed & Ward, 1948).

On Englishing the Bible, (London: Burns Oates, 1949).

Enthusiasm: A Chapter in the History of Religion, (Oxford: OUP, 1950).

Off the Record, London: Sheed and Ward, 1953).

On English Translation: The Romanes Lecture Delivered in the Sheldonian Theatre, (Oxford: OUP, 1957).

Occasional Sermons of Ronald A. Knox, Philip Caraman, ed., (London: Burns and Oates, 1960).

Secondary Sources

Anson, Peter, *The Call of the Cloister: Religious Communities and Kindred Bodies in the Anglican Communion*, rev. edn, (London: SPCK, 1964).

Anson, Peter, *Fashions in Church Furnishings 1840–1940*, (London: Studio Vista, 1965).

Arx, Jeffrey Paul von, 'Catholics and Politics', in V. Alan McClelland and Michael Hodgetts, (eds.), *From Without the Flaminian Gate: 150 Years of Roman Catholicism in England and Wales 1850–2000*, (London: DLT, 1999).

Aspden, Kester, *Fortress Church: The English Roman Catholic Bishops and Politics 1903–63*, (Leominster: Gracewing, 2002).

Barnard, L. W., *C. B. Moss: Defender of the faith*, (London: Mowbray, 1967).

Barnes, A. S., *The Catholic Schools of England*, (London: Williams and Norgate, 1926).

Begbie, Harold, *Painted Windows: A Study in Religious Personality*, (London: Mills & Boon, 1922).

Belloc, Hilaire, *Letters from Hilaire Belloc*, selected and edited by Robert Speaight, (London: Hollis and Carter, 1958).

Benson, Robert Hugh, *The Light Invisible*, (London: Burns Oates & Washbourne, n.d. [1903]).

Bowra, C. M., *Memories 1988–1939*, (London: Weidenfeld and Nicolson, 1966).

Briggs, Asa, *History of Birmingham*, Vol. 2: *Borough and City 1865–1938*, (London: OUP, 1952.)

Buchanan, Tom, *Britain and the Spanish Civil War*, (Cambridge: CUP, 1997).

Burns, Tom, *The Use of Memory: Publishing and Further Pursuits*, (London: Sheed & Ward, 1993).

Byrne, L. S. R., *Changing Eton*, (London: Cape, 1937).

Campbell, Patrick, *Siegfried Sassoon: A Study of the War Poetry*, (Jefferson, NC: McFarland, 1999).

Card, Tim, *Eton Renewed: A History from 1860 to the Present Day*, (London: John Murray, 1994).

Carpenter, Humphrey, *The Brideshead Generation: Evelyn Waugh and His Friends,* (Boston: Houghton Mifflin, 1990).

Chadwick, Owen, *Hensley Henson: A Study in the Friction between Church and State,* (Norwich: Canterbury Press, 1994).

Chadwick, Owen, *The Victorian Church* Part 1, 3rd edn, (London: Adam and Charles Black, 1971).

Chadwick, Owen, *The Victorian Church* Part 2, (London: Adam and Charles Black, 1970).

Chambers, F. W., *Ronald Knox and the Converts' Aid Society,* (London: CAS, 1960).

Clements, Keith, *Lovers of Discord: Twentieth-Century Theological Controversies in England,* (London: SCM, 1988).

Colley, Linda, *Britons: The Forging of a Nation 1707–1837,* (London: Yale, 1992).

Corrigan, Felicitas, OSB, (ed.), *Siegfried Sassoon: Poet's Pilgrimage,* (London: Gollancz, 1973).

Couve de Murville, Maurice and Jenkins, Philip, *Catholic Cambridge,* (London: Catholic Truth Society, 1983).

Dataller, Roger, *A Pitman Looks at Oxford,* (London: Dent, 1933).

Davage, William and Orford, Barry, (eds.), *Piety and Learning: The Principals of Pusey House* 1884–1902, (Oxford: Pusey House, 2002).

Drumm, Walter, *The Old Palace: The Catholic Chaplaincy at Oxford,* (Dublin: Veritas Publications, 1991).

Duffy, Eamon, *Saints and Sinners: A History of the Popes,* (London: Yale, 2006).

Fergusson, Bernard, *Eton Portrait,* (London: John Miles, 1938).

Fitzgerald, Penelope, *The Knox Brothers,* (London: Macmillan, 1977).

Flint, James, '"Must God Go Fascist?" English Catholic Opinion and the Spanish Civil War', *Church History* 56.3 (1987) 364–74.

Gilley, Sheridan, 'A Tradition and Culture Lost, to be Regained', in Michael Hornsby-Smith, (ed.), *Catholics in England 1950–2000: Historical and Sociological Perspectives,* (London: Cassell, 1999).

Gilley, Sheridan, 'The Years of Equipoise, 1892–1943', in V. A. McClelland and M. Hodgetts, (eds.), *From Without the Flaminian Gate: 150 Years of Catholicism in England and Wales, 1850–2000,* (London: DLT, 1999).

Green, V. H. H., *A History of Oxford University,* (London: Batsford, 1974).

Gribbin, W. T., (ed.), *St Edmund's College Bicentenary Book,* (Old Hall Green, Herts: Old Hall Green Press, 1993).

Hastings, Adrian, *A History of English Christianity 1920–1985,* (London: Collins, 1987).

Hastings, Adrian, 'Some Reflexions on the English Catholicism of the late 1930s', in Adrian Hastings, ed., *Bishops and Writers: Aspects of the Evolution of Modern English Catholicism,* (Wheathampstead, Herts: Anthony Clarke, 1977).

Hill, Rosemary, *God's Architect: Pugin and the Building of Romantic Britain,* (London: Allen Lane, 2007).

Hollings, Michael, *Living Priesthood,* (Great Wakering, Essex: McCrimmon, 1977).

Hollis, Christopher, *Along the Road to Frome,* (London: Harrap, 1958).

Hollis, Christopher, *The Oxford Union,* (London: Evans Brothers, 1965).

Horne, Alistair, *Macmillan,* Vol. 1: *1894–1956,* (London: Macmillan, 1988).

Houselander, Caryll, *The Reed of God,* (London: Sheed and Ward, 1944).

Hunt, Tristram, *Building Jerusalem: The Rise and Fall of the Victorian City,* (London: Weidenfeld and Nicolson, 2004).

Huxley, Julian, *Memories,* (London: Allen and Unwin, 1970).

Hynes, Samuel, *The Auden Generation: Literature and Politics in England in the 1930s,* (London: Bodley Head, 1976).

Hynes, Samuel, *A War Imagined: The First World War and English Culture* (London: Bodley Head, 1990).

Iremonger, F. A., *William Temple, Archbishop of Canterbury: His Life and Letters,* (London: OUP, 1949).

Jelland, Pat, *Death in the Victorian Family,* (Oxford: OUP, 1996).

Johnson, Niall, *Britain and the 1918–19 Influenza Epidemic: A Dark Epilogue*, (London: Routledge, 2006).

Jones, L. E., *An Edwardian Youth*, (London: Macmillan, 1956).

Keating, Joseph, *The Things That are Caesar's*, (London: Catholic Truth Society, 1930).

Keegan, John, *The Second World War*, (London: Arrow/Random Century, 1990).

Kemp, Eric, *N. P. Williams*, (London: SPCK, 1954).

Knight, Stephen, 'The Golden Age', in Martin Priestman, (ed.), *The Cambridge Companion to Crime Fiction*, (Cambridge: CUP, 2003).

Knox, Edmund, *Reminiscences of an Octogenarian 1847–1934*, (London: Hutchinson, 1935).

Kollar, Rene, 'Anglo-Catholicism in the Church of England, 1895–1913: Abbot Aelred Carlyle and the Monks of Caldey Island', *Harvard Theological Review* 76.2 (1983) 205–24.

Kynaston, David, *Austerity Britain 1945–1951*, (London: Bloomsbury, 2007).

Lambert, Angela, *Unquiet Souls: The Indian Summer of the British Aristocracy 1880–1918*, (London: Macmillan, 1984).

Lees-Milne, James, *Harold Nicolson: A Biography*, Vol. 1: *1886–1929*, (London: Chatto and Windus, 1980).

Lister, Charles, *Charles Lister: Letters and Recollections, with a memoir by his father, Lord Ribblesdale*, (London: Fisher Unwin, 1917).

Lloyd, Roger, *The Church of England 1900–1965*, (London: SCM, 1966).

Lubbock, Percy, *Shades of Eton*, (London: Cape, 1929).

Lunn, Arnold, *And Yet So New*, (London: Sheed and Ward, 1958).

Mack, Edward, *Public Schools and British Public Opinion 1780–1860*, (London: Methuen, 1938).

Mack, Edward, *Public Schools and British Public Opinion since 1860*, (New York: Columbia University Press, 1941).

Macmillan, Harold, *Winds of Change: 1914–1939*, (London: Macmillan, 1966).

MacNeice, Louis, *The Strings are False,* (London: Faber, 1965).

Malden, Charles, *Recollections of an Eton Colleger,* (Eton: Eyre and Spottiswoode, 1905).

Manwaring, Randle, *From Controversy to Co-Existence: Evangelicals in the Church of England, 1914–1980,* (Cambridge: CUP, 1985).

Marcus, Laura, 'Detection and Literary Fiction', in Martin Priestman, (ed.), *The Cambridge Companion to Crime Fiction,* (Cambridge: CUP, 2003).

Mathew, David, *Catholicism in England – The Portrait of a Minority: Its Culture and Tradition,* 2nd edn, (London: Eyre and Spottiswoode, 1948).

Mathew, David, 'Old Catholics and Converts', in George Beck, (ed.), *The English Catholics 1850–1950,* (London: Burns and Oates, 1950).

Micklem, Nathaniel, *The Box and the Puppets,* (London: Bles, 1957).

Mitchell, Leslie, *Maurice Bowra: A Life,* (Oxford: OUP, 2009).

Morse-Boycott, Desmond, *They Shine Like Stars,* (London: Skeffington, 1947).

Mosley, Nicholas, *Julian Grenfell: His Life and the Times of his Death 1888–1915,* (London: Weidenfeld and Nicolson, 1976).

Muggeridge, Malcolm, *The Thirties: Great Britain 1930–1940,* (London: Hamish Hamilton, 1940).

Neill, Stephen, *The Interpretation of the New Testament 1861–1986,* 2nd ed., revised by N. T. Wright, (Oxford: OUP, 1988).

Newsome, David, *Godliness and Good Learning: Four Studies on a Victorian Ideal,* (London: John Murray, 1961).

Nichols, Aidan, *Dominican Gallery,* (Leominster: Gracewing, 1997).

Nichols, Aidan, *The Realm: An Unfashionable Essay on the Conversion of England,* (Oxford: Family Publications, 2008).

Norman, Edward, *Roman Catholicism in England: From the*

Elizabethan Settlement to the Second Vatican Council, (Oxford: OUP, 1986).

O'Donovan, Patrick, *A Journalist's Odyssey*, with a personal recollection by Robert Kee, (London: Esmonde Publishing, 1985).

Ousby, Ian, *The Cambridge Guide to Literature in English*, (Cambridge: CUP, 1993).

Page, Norman, *An Evelyn Waugh Chronology*, (London: Macmillan, 1997).

Pakenham, Frank, *Born to Believe: An Autobiography*, (London: Cape, 1953).

Parsons, Gerald, 'Victorian Catholicism', in G. Parsons, (ed.), *Religion in Victorian Britain*, Vol. 1: *Traditions*, (Manchester: Manchester University Press/Open University, 1988).

Pearce, Joseph, *Old Thunder: A Life of Hilaire Belloc*, (London: HarperCollins 2002).

Pearce, Joseph, *Wisdom and Innocence: A Life of G. K. Chesterton*, (London: Hodder and Stoughton, 1996).

Peck, Winifred, *Home for the Holidays*, (London: Faber, 1955).

Peck, Winifred, *A Little Learning*, or *A Victorian Childhood*, (London: Faber, 1952).

Pevsner, Nikolaus, *Hertfordshire* (The Buildings of England Series), rev. edn by Bridget Cherry, (London: Penguin, 1978).

Pinnington, Judith, 'Rubric and Spirit: A Diagnostic Reading of Tractarian Worship', in Kenneth Leech and Rowan Williams, (eds.), *Essays Catholic and Radical*, (London: Bowerdean Press, 1983).

Pope, Hugh, OP, *A Brief History of the English Version of the New Testament First Published at Rheims in 1582, Continued Down to the Present Day*, (London: Bibliographical Society, 1940).

Roberts, John Stuart, *Siegfried Sassoon*, (London: Richard Cohen Books, 1999).

Rowell, Geoffrey, *The Vision Glorious: Themes and Personalities of the Catholic Revival in Anglicanism*, new edition, (Oxford: Clarendon Press, 1991).

Rumbold, Richard, *A Message in Code: The Diary of Richard Rumbold, 1932–60,* with an introduction by William Plomer, (ed.), (London: Weidenfeld and Nicolson, 1964).

Rumbold, Richard, *My Father's Son,* (London: Cape, 1949).

Sassoon, Siegfried, *Collected Poems 1908–1956,* (London: Faber, 1961).

Sassoon, Siegfried, *Diaries 1915–1918,* edited and introduced by Rupert Hart-Davis, (London: Faber, 1983).

Sassoon, Siegfried, *Sequences,* (London: Faber, 1956).

Scott, Drusilla, *A. D. Lindsay: A Biography,* (Oxford: Blackwell, 1971).

Sewell, Desmond, *Catholics: Britain's Largest Minority,* (London: Penguin, 2002).

Smith, F. B., 'The Russian Influenza in the United Kingdom, 1889–1894', *Social History of Medicine* 8.1 (1995) 55–73.

Speaight, Robert, *The Life of Hilaire Belloc,* (London: Hollis & Cater, 1957).

Speaight, Robert, *Ronald Knox the Writer,* (London: Sheed and Ward, 1966).

Stannard, Martin, *Evelyn Waugh: No Abiding City, 1939–1966,* (London: Dent, 1992).

Stansky, Peter, *Sassoon: The Worlds of Philip and Sybil,* (New Haven: Yale University Press, 2003).

Streeter, B. F., (ed.), *Foundations: A Statement of Christian Belief in Terms of Modern Thought,* (London: Macmillan, 1912).

Sykes, Christopher, *Evelyn Waugh: A Biography,* (London: Collins, 1975).

Tavard, George, *The Quest for Catholicity: A Study in Anglicanism,* (London: Burns and Oates, 1963).

Taylor, A. J. P., *English History 1914–1945* (The Oxford History of England, Vol. 15), rev. edn, (Oxford: OUP/Clarendon Press, 1986).

Thompson, E. S., *Influenza, or Epidemic Catarrhal Fever: A Historical Survey of Past Epidemics in Great Britain from 1519 to 1890,* (London: Percival and Co, 1890).

Usborne, Richard, (ed.), *A Century of Summer Fields,* (London: Methuen, 1964).

Tillich, Paul, *A History of Christian Thought: From its Judaic and Hellenistic Origins to Existentialism*, edited by Carl Braaten, (New York: Simon and Schuster, 1968).

Walsh, Milton, *Ronald Knox as Apologist: Wit, Laughter and the Popish Creed,* (San Francisco: Ignatius Press, 2007).

Ward, Maisie, *Gilbert Keith Chesterton,* (London: Sheed and Ward, 1944).

Warrener, Rodney and Yelton, Michael, *Martin Travers 1886–1948: An Appreciation,* (London: Unicorn Press, 2003).

Waugh, Alexander, *Fathers and Sons: The Autobiography of a Family,* (London: Headline, 2004).

Waugh, Evelyn, *Brideshead Revisited,* (London: Penguin, 2000; first published by Chapman and Hall, 1945).

Waugh, Evelyn, *The Diaries of Evelyn Waugh,* edited by Michael Davie, (London: Penguin, 1979).

Waugh, Evelyn, *The Essays, Articles and Reviews of Evelyn Waugh,* edited by Donat Gallagher, (London: Methuen, 1983).

Waugh, Evelyn, *The Letters of Evelyn Waugh,* edited by Mark Amory, (London: Weidenfeld and Nicolson, 1981).

Waugh, Evelyn, *The Life of Ronald Knox,* (London: Chapman and Hall, 1959).

Waugh, Evelyn, *Mr Wu and Mrs Stitch: The Letters of Evelyn Waugh and Diana Cooper,* edited by Artemis Cooper, (London: Hodder and Stoughton, 1991).

White, James, *Roman Catholic Worship: Trent to Today,* (New York: Paulist, 1995).

Williams, Charles, *Harold Macmillan,* (London: Weidenfeld and Nicolson, 2009).

Wilson, Jean Moorcroft, *Siegfried Sassoon: The Journey from the Trenches,* (London: Duckworth, 2003).

Winter, Jay, *Sites of Memory, Sites of Mourning: The Great War in European Cultural History,* (Cambridge: CUP, 1995; Canto edition, reprinted 2000).

Wolfe, Kenneth, *The Churches and the British Broadcasting Corporation 1922–1956: The Politics of Broadcast Religion,* (London: SCM, 1984).

Yates, Nigel, *Anglican Ritualism in Victorian Britain,* (Oxford: OUP, 1999).

Yelton, Michael, *Anglican Papalism: A History 1900–1960,* (Norwich: Canterbury Press, in association with The Society of the Faith, 2005).

Index

Lightning Source UK Ltd.
Milton Keynes UK
12 January 2010
148438UK00001B/93/P